For Roy & Colin

Best wishes

MY GOLDEN FLYING YEARS

Norman Franks

Simon Muggleton

January 2011

This book is dedicated to all those involved with the Schneider Trophy races that helped so much in the development of the Spitfire in later years.

MY GOLDEN FLYING YEARS

From 1918 over France through Iraq in the 1920s
to the Schneider Trophy Race of 1929

AIR COMMODORE D'ARCY GREIG DFC AFC
Edited and Annotated by Norman Franks
with Simon Muggleton

GRUB STREET • LONDON

Published by
Grub Street
4 Rainham Close
London
SW11 6SS

Copyright © Grub Street 2010
Copyright text © D'Arcy Greig DFC AFC, Norman Franks and Simon
  Muggleton

British Library Cataloguing in Publication Data

  Greig, D'Arcy.
  My golden flying years : from 1918 over France, through
  Iraq in the 1920s, to the Schneider Trophy race of 1927.
  1. Greig, D'Arcy. 2. Great Britain. Royal Air Force--
  History--20th century.
  I. Title II. Franks, Norman L. R. III. Muggleton, Simon.
  358.4'0092-dc22

ISBN-13: 9781906502805

Cover design and typesetting by Sarah Driver

Printed and bound by MPG Ltd, Bodmin, Cornwall

Grub Street Publishing only uses
FSC (Forest Stewardship Council) paper for its books.

CONTENTS

ACKNOWLEDGMENTS

We'd like to give special thanks to the following people: Jamie D'Arcy Greig, Judy and Douglas Burchett, Janet Trythall of the Elgin Museum, fellow Grub Street author Ralph Barker, Mr. Michael Kent of Bexhill and the Science Museum London.

ORIGINAL FOREWORD

by
Marshal of the Royal Air Force,
Sir Dermot Boyle GCB KCVO KBE AFC

The author of this book is a pilot of distinction and great courage, whose flying days covered an exciting period in aviation history.

This is a true account of the author's personal experiences and is not distorted by attempts to prove a point or by exaggerations or by a desire to justify what occurred. It is a true, fascinating and lively narrative of things as they were.

The reader may well be surprised that the author survived to tell this tale, because he certainly lived dangerously, not only in the air but also in the midst of his original and virtually continuous practical jokes and pyrotechnical innovations.

This book will evoke many a chuckle from those who have experience of the activities it covers and must fascinate and doubtless startle readers to whom the life it describes is as remote as it is unrepeatable.

Dermot Boyle

INTRODUCTION

During the early seventies, my wife and I decided to move away from London in order to bring up our young family in the countryside. I joined Sussex Police as a constable, and having completed my initial training was posted to Bexhill-on-Sea in East Sussex. This small town on the Sussex coast, to the west of Hastings, had about 28,000 inhabitants at that time. It was soon evident that a large majority of the residents had been in the services, and had also taken part in one, or both of the world wars. Bexhill-on-Sea appeared to be an ideal retirement area with excellent facilities, and the bonus of sunny Eastbourne just along the coast.

I knew little about the area when we arrived there. However, my keen interest in aviation history, led me to the local museum and it wasn't long before I discovered that the De La Warr Pavilion on the seafront in Bexhill had been adopted by the Luftwaffe as a marker by their bombers en route to London, during the Second World War. The two adjacent towns to the east, Hastings and St Leonards, were both locations that had been used by the RFC and RAF for initial training. This looked like a promising start for pursuing my hobby.

Being young in the police service, and keen to work in the CID, I would be among the first to volunteer to respond to calls from victims of burglaries or thefts. My training on police motor cycles meant that I could often be at a scene of crime before the CID had arrived. It was as a result of responding to a report of a theft that I first met up with Air Commodore D'Arcy Greig DFC AFC in the mid 70s.

Bexhill was (and probably still is) a prime target for the criminal activities of the 'antique knocker' whose tactics are to take advantage of the elderly and infirm. This breed of criminal usually work in pairs and specialise in obtaining valuable items by persuading the home owner to let them in for a free valuation, or a straight offer to purchase. Once inside, their skill lies in distracting the unsuspecting resident (for example by wrongly informing them that their furniture has woodworm) or offering generous amounts to purchase a particular antique on display. Meanwhile, the unobserved accomplice would be free to locate and pocket any cash or small valuable items on display, with both of them leaving pretty quickly after that.

Unfortunately this is an all too common crime, and D'Arcy Greig had become one more victim. It transpired that he had initially sold a desk for cash to these callers, probably after some heavy persuasion. After they left his home, he realised that a silver cigarette box and case and other small items were missing, which he duly reported to the police.

Arriving at the address in Birchington Close, Cooden, the door was answered to me by a spritely and fit elderly gentleman with a prominent hooked nose and pencil moustache. I asked if he was the Mr Greig who had reported a theft of silver items. He corrected me, saying that his name was in fact D'Arcy Greig, and invited me in. As soon as I entered, my attention was drawn to a couple of very large black-and-white framed photographs hanging in the hallway, one of which I instantly recognised as a Supermarine seaplane. The second frame held a photograph of two gentlemen, one with a blackened oily face, (and obviously him), whilst the other person was in RAF uniform, both of them displaying beaming smiles. Being distracted by these photographs, I was curious about the occasion captured in this image. D'Arcy Greig just smiled and explained that he had been one of the pilots in the Schneider Trophy race, and the photo had been taken at the conclusion of one of the 'runs'. He identified the person in RAF uniform as another pilot, Flt Lt 'Dick' Waghorn. D'Arcy Greig went on to tell me that he had eventually ended up third in the 1929 race.

Although I was by this time fascinated at the prospect of knowing more about the Schneider Trophy, I was there to investigate a crime. D'Arcy Greig told me that two unknown men had knocked at his door and had talked their way uninvited into the house, asking to purchase antiques. Spotting a desk, they had persuaded D'Arcy Greig to part with it for an agreed sum. After their departure he discovered they had also taken the other items without him knowing. Both the silver cigarette case and the box meant a lot to him, as they were associated with the Schneider Trophy contest. Facsimile signatures were engraved within, and they were therefore unique and identifiable.

We eventually moved into the living room where I noticed something on the dining table which the offenders had fortunately missed. It was a solid silver replica scale model of the Supermarine S6 aircraft on a wooden base, which I later learned from D'Arcy Greig had been presented to all the participating British pilots. So much fascinating information unravelling from this chance meeting, but I had to complete my enquiries. I took descriptions of the two offenders, along with the property taken, and assured him that the stolen items would be difficult to dispose of because of their rarity. He escorted me to the front door, and as I left, invited me to visit again whenever I had the time as it showed I was obviously interested in aviation. On the basis of that open invitation I visited D'Arcy Greig and his wife Eve on many occasions to discover more about the trophy and his flying career.

The theft of the silver items was obviously upsetting for him and I desperately wanted to find whoever had committed this theft and recover his property as quickly as I could. I later made enquiries with all the local antique dealers and auction rooms giving them a description of the stolen items. It wasn't long before one in Sussex informed me that the silver case and box had turned up in their auction rooms for sale, giving me the name of the vendor. When I finally tracked down the 'knockers' who had visited him they produced a receipt of sale with D'Arcy Greig's signature on it, making a prosecution virtually impossible. (All part of the well tried and tested scam, where a bill of sale is given to the 'seller' which they are asked to sign. Later, the 'knockers' add other details such as 'sold as seen'.)

Fortunately, in this case the tale did have a happy ending. D'Arcy Greig's son, Jamie managed to buy the case and box back from the auction room and both items are still in Jamie's possession today.

D'Arcy Greig was initially rather reluctant and hesitant to share his recollections of his part in the Schneider Trophy during my visits, but would always answer my (often ignorant) questions with a twinkle in his eye. He eventually gave me his personal copy of Wing Commander A H Orlebar's book titled *Schneider Trophy* in order that I could read about it first hand. He didn't mention at that time that he had written his own autobiography, and felt it would be of no interest to anyone. I tried to convince him otherwise mentioning the crowds who attended the many air-shows and numbers of books published on aviation. Eventually he gave me the large manuscript that his wife Eve had typed for him which I found to be humorous as well as informative, although rather long. After showing the manuscript to my co-editor Norman Franks he agreed and suggested that it should be concentrated around 'The Golden Flying Years' of D'Arcy Greig with annotations and information on his early life, and it now forms the basis of this book.

D'Arcy Greig never seemed to glory in the past, but was obviously proud to have been in the RAF, and especially 'The High Speed Flight'. He rarely 'dropped' names, but if you mentioned a famous name of the day, he would casually respond that he had made their acquaintance at some stage (for example the Prince of Wales, Malcolm Campbell and R J Mitchell to name just three).

He would recount his service days between the wars, taking great delight in explaining all the practical jokes he later became famous for. Just one example he mentioned to me concerned his time in the desert with 6 Squadron when he would drive his motor bike up the steps and into the officer's mess and park it there while he ate his meal. Other examples of his sense of fun and fascination for explosives can be found within the book.

D'Arcy Greig was also famous in the 1920s for flying low over his local pub, The Bell in the Old Town of Bexhill. This signalled an early warning to the landlord to have a pint ready on the bar for D'Arcy who would have landed in a nearby field.

He would often play practical jokes on many of the residents of Bexhill; a lot of these would be tried out on his old friend, Mrs Dunn who lived in the Old Town. She drove an Alvis motor car and would often offer lifts to fellow customers from The Bell, only to find a dreadful smell en route home because D'Arcy had tied a kipper to the exhaust! Mrs Dunn would often reciprocate by playing similar tricks back on him. His visits to Bexhill would not be complete until he had seen his mother, who lived at a house called Draycot in Buckhurst Road, before flying off back to base.

During one of my visits to his house, D'Arcy Greig recounted his experience of having to use his parachute over Kenley airfield in 1927. He gave me his copy of the *London Evening News* 'billboard flyer' for that day which reported the incident. (He modestly forgot to mention to me that he had been decorated with the Air Force Cross for this feat!) You can see by the entry in his logbook for that incident that he took it all in his stride.

Over the years that I was fortunate enough to know him he gave me several souvenirs. The most treasured by far is his flying helmet and the goggles used for the Schneider Trophy race. These and his personal copy of the Schneider Trophy programme, along with his car mascot of the S6, and a photograph of him were lent to the Science Museum in London during August 2005 when they held an exhibition on Supermarine and the Spitfire. I'm confident that D'Arcy Greig would have been amused to think that he was in the public eye once again. I feel very honoured to have known him, and glad that his memoirs can now be read by all.

NB: The reader will find our annotations at the end of each chapter.

Simon Muggleton
August 2010

PROLOGUE

Born at the family home at Spynie House, in New Spynie, north of
Elgin, in Morayshire, Scotland on 1st February 1900, David D'Arcy
Alexander Greig was the youngest of eleven children. His father was
Henry Greig of Demerara and Elgin, who had worked in British Guiana
as a sugar planter. Ever since the emancipation of the country in 1834,
there had been social and political unrest, especially within the sugar
trade. This came to a head when labour was shipped in from India,
bringing trouble for the European plantation managers and owners.
Henry Greig had only one arm, (as the result of an accident whilst playing on the railway as a child), and it was during one of these periods
of unrest that the labourers threatened to cut his remaining right arm
off. Henry Greig took this threat seriously, and returned to live in Scotland with his family just before the turn of the century.

David D'Arcy Greig was given a private education, firstly at Weston
House School, Hay Street, Elgin and then at Elgin Academy, Morriston
Road, Elgin. After his father died on 24th November 1913, his family
moved to the south in the following year, settling to live at Kingston-
upon-Thames, and later in Bexhill-on-Sea in East Sussex. Having left
school whilst the First World War was still being fought, D'Arcy Greig
decided to do 'his bit' for king and country and went to work at a local
munitions factory where most of the work-force were women. He was
soon given the post of floor manager, despite his tender years.

Greig had always been interested in engineering and anything associated with aircraft, always hoping to fly. Now the family were living

close to Brooklands, this must have inspired him to enlist as an officer in the Royal Flying Corps (RFC) on his eighteenth birthday. No doubt hoping to see some action before the end of the Great War, he was however, told by the enlisting sergeant to get fitter. The aspiring young officer took him at his word and started training by running every day, and then went to work on a farm located between Bexhill and Hastings in order to build up his strength.

On 6th February 1918, having been accepted into the RFC, Greig was given the lowly rank of cadet, and sent to begin his training at the No.1 Officer Cadet Wing at St Leonards-on-Sea, East Sussex. He was then sent to No.1 School of Aeronautics HQ at Wantage Hall, Upper Redlands Road, Reading on 12th March 1918.

Less than a month later, on 1st April 1918, the British government decreed that the Royal Flying Corps and Royal Naval Air Service should merge into a new independent service, to be known as the Royal Air Force. Like many other officers, Greig had eventually to change his uniform from a 'maternity' style jacket to that of an army officer's field service jacket.

The School of Aeronautics consisted of about thirty buildings where ninety-five officers, 1250 cadets and 700 warrant officers and NCOs were trained to be pilots or observers. Those chosen to be pilots undertook eight weeks of training in engine-running, rigging, aerial navigation and photography. Greig did in fact also become an excellent photographer using an expensive Leica camera he had purchased some years earlier. This expertise would bring him financial rewards from magazines during his later service in Iraq.

Greig then attended the No.1 Technical Training Squadron on June 15th, which was located on the RAF Halton Estate in Buckinghamshire. Here the pupils would get further intensive training in engineering within the workshops that had been built by German POWs. On July 6th he was transferred to 190 and 192 (night training squadron) at Upwood, Cambridgeshire. This was a newly established airfield (previously Ramsey) with just five hangars and a number of huts. It was here that he would be trained to fly the BE2 bi-plane, the De Havilland 6 (Skyhook) and the FE2b pusher bi-plane. On August 20th 1918 Greig was appointed 2nd lieutenant in the RAF Aeroplane & Seaplane Branch (old army ranks were still being used until the end of the war).

Eight days later, the newly promoted D'Arcy Greig was posted to 83 Squadron, flying out of Franqueville, in France on night reconnaissance and bombing operations in a FE2b as part of the British Expeditionary Force. This squadron had a long-standing association with Scotland; it was formed originally in Montrose. His roots in the Highlands may well have influenced his posting to this squadron.

By mid-September 1918, 2nd Lt D'Arcy Greig found himself in the thick of the attacks along a seven-mile front which were being launched by the allies on the outlying fortifications of the Hindenburg Line. These attacks, in addition to those from the tank and artillery regiments, were given air cover by the RFC. During this period, intelligence had been obtained that the Germans were intending to bomb Paris at night with a large number of incendiary bombs. Therefore 58, 83 and 207 Squadrons were detailed to bomb the aerodromes from which this attack might originate.

On 20th September 1918 at 2045 hrs, Greig was the pilot of a FE2b (F5853) in company with Observer 2nd Lt W A Armstrong on a night-bombing sortie when they came under anti-aircraft fire over Cambrai. The aircraft sustained considerable damage but Greig managed to make a landing, albeit in enemy territory. Although both pilot and observer were pretty shaken up by this episode, they managed to trudge back the thirteen miles to the safety of their own lines. Whether as a punishment for losing the aircraft or as a form of recuperation, Greig was then sent back to the UK for further training at 191 and 192 Night Training Squadrons. By this time the war had ended, and he stayed with these squadrons until 15th March 1919.

In May 1919, Greig was sent back to RAF Halton to join No.3 Boys Training Centre, and then went onto RAF Eastchurch on 1st October 1919, where he stayed until 25th January 1920. Then on 13th February 1921, he was again posted abroad, this time to Iraq, with 6 Squadron (part of the Mesopotamian Wing), where he stayed for the next three years.

6 Squadron was originally used as a tactical reconnaissance and artillery spotting unit in the First World War, but its commanding officer, Captain Hawker VC soon changed it to an air-to-air combat squadron in the summer months of 1915. In 1920 the squadron was sent to the Middle East with RE8s and Bristol Fighters, to operate against the Turk-

ish army and dissident sheiks in Mesopotamia and Kurdistan. Greig,
like other members of the squadron, would see plenty of action in this
theatre. His fearless flying in action culminated on 28th October 1921
when he was decorated with the Distinguished Flying Cross for service
in the field whilst flying in Mesopotamia. The *London Gazette* published a citation stating:

> *'For gallantry and devotion to duty. All through the pe-*
> *riod of hostilities this officer has proved himself to be a*
> *very keen and daring pilot, and has on every possible*
> *occasion engaged the enemy from very low altitudes*
> *with excellent results.'*

On 14th January 1923, Greig returned to the RAF depot in the UK and
went on to complete a pilotage course at RAF Calshot from 25th May
to 27th July 1923. He was posted to 24 (Communication) Squadron at
Kenley on the 1st October where he stayed until 14th March 1924, providing air transportation for the government and heads of the three
services. He was known for his practical jokes throughout this time
with the squadron, often leading 'raids' on other aerodromes by dropping toilet rolls and old boots out of the various types of aircraft allocated to them. This became well known in the squadron as 'The
Northolt-Kenley War'. By the end of the year his ability as a pilot had
obviously shone through and he was sent on an instructor's course at
the Central Flying School (CFS) on 17th March 1924. This was followed
on the 15th June by a permanent posting to the CFS as a qualified flying
instructor and test pilot. Some of his flying antics terrified the students
at the nearby No.1 Flying Training School at Netheravon, and many of
his escapades were retold several years later to other student pilots.

During this posting he linked up with Flt Lt John Boothman, who
would also later join the High Speed Flight and be part of the winning
Schneider Trophy team. The two of them would put on several flying
displays. Their 'party piece' was to fly as a mirrored 'falling leaf' with
Boothman's aircraft being inverted. It was during one of these displays
in 1926 that Greig misjudged the manoeuvre and hit the ground. Amazingly he walked away from the wreckage uninjured.

On 1st January 1927 Greig was promoted to flight lieutenant and by

11th April of that year he was on the staff of HQ fighting area, where he stayed until 1st May 1928. On Friday the 22nd April 1927, he was flying a Gamecock aircraft over London in order to test spinning problems when the aircraft got out of control, forcing him to use his parachute at 6,000ft, and giving him membership of the Caterpillar Club. He landed safely onto Kenley Aerodrome, whilst his aircraft crashed in flames some two miles away, narrowly missing some houses. The story made front page banner headlines in the *London Evening News*:

'Leap for Life from Falling Aeroplane'

His entry in his logbook however simply records: 'aircraft spinning!' The death-defying escapade was rewarded in May 1928 when Greig was decorated with the Air Force Cross by the king at Buckingham Palace. The citation as shown in the *London Gazette* stated:-

> *'This officer served as a flying instructor at the Central Flying School for over three years, and by his extreme thoroughness, untiring energy and keenness, set a high standard to all. Flight Lieutenant Greig has since been employed as area examining officer in the fighting area and has performed excellent work in that capacity. On one occasion, he displayed remarkable courage and skill in carrying out a test in connection with the investigation of the report that a particular type of aeroplane had a tendency not to come out of right hand spins. On the instructions of the air officer commanding, he took an aeroplane in which this tendency was very marked, put it into a spin, and found that he was unable to check the spin after about twelve turns. He spun from 12,000 to 6,000 feet, and then, realising that the aeroplane was completely out of control, managed with difficulty to leave the machine and descend by parachute, the machine being completely wrecked after spinning into the ground. It was, moreover, only by direct orders that Flight Lieutenant Greig was stopped from carrying out further similar tests.'*

Greig went on to take part in the RAF displays at Hendon each year eventually leading the Central Flying School aerobatic team of five Genet Moths in 1927. On 1st May 1928, he was posted on to the staff of the Maritime Aircraft Experimental Establishment (MAEE) at Felixstowe (where TE Lawrence was subsequently posted in April 1933). And on 5th November, whilst still with the MAEE, D'Arcy Greig raised the World Air Speed Record to 319.57 mph (in four consecutive flights) in his 'Flying Bullet'. This feat however, was not officially recognised as there was less than a 5 mph advantage from an earlier record held by the Italians.

Flight Lieutenant S Kinkead, a member of the RAF High Speed Flight, had been killed in a S5 seaplane whilst attempting to raise this same world speed record in March 1928. Greig now became an official member at Calshot in February 1929 as a direct result of Kinkhead's death. The new team had to be ready for the Schneider Trophy race due to be held on 7th September the following year.

R J Mitchell had already started to design the Supermarine S6 in 1927 for the race, and decided it needed a more powerful engine than the Napier Lion used previously in the 1927 races. He approached Sir Henry Royce to use the new engine developed by Rolls-Royce known then as the 'R' Type, which could supply at least 1500 hp and up to 1900 hp if needed. The floats on the aircraft were moved forward to carry the extra weight of the engine and these were also used as fuel tanks, whilst the wings acted as radiators.

As 1927 holders of the trophy, Britain elected to hold the 1929 race at Cowes. On 7th September the race course started and finished at Ryde Pier, and was thirty-one miles long on each lap, consisting of a four-sided 'kite' pattern with yellow and black pylons mounted on destroyers in the Solent to be used as markers. The British team consisted of Squadron Leader A H Orlebar as its flight commander, with Flight Lieutenant Stainforth, Flight Lieutenant D'Arcy Greig, and Flying Officers R L R Atcherley and H R D Waghorn as competing pilots. The aircraft consisted of two Supermarine S6 seaplanes, N247 and N248 which would be flown in the race by Flying Officer 'Dick' Waghorn and Flying Officer 'Batchy' Atcherley respectively, whilst Flight Lieutenant D'Arcy Greig was allocated a Supermarine S5 N219.

Only Italy had sent a team of competitors for this particular race, providing the challenging pilots with two Macchi M67 aircraft and an older Macchi M52R. France had made preparations to compete after a six-year absence, but their designs never got off the drawing board and they withdrew. The Americans had intended to use the Kirkham-Williams Mercury aircraft but its chosen engine was incapable of sustained flight and they also withdrew. The Germans also hoped to compete using a Dornier aircraft, but had to withdraw as the designers failed to produce a competitive aircraft.

The weather was perfect on the day of the race, and F/O Waghorn had drawn the first attempt, with Greig going third and Atcherley fifth. Waghorn flew cautiously, not wanting to miss a turn, but his engine started to misfire on the last lap and he eventually landed short of the finish line. He thought he would be disqualified but had in fact miscounted his laps and flown one extra, all in record time. F/O Atcherley on his first run lost his goggles in the slipstream, and was immediately disqualified by misjudging a turn, and flying inside one of the pylons. Greig reached 282.11 mph in the S5 but this was no match for Waghorn (who despite having a misfiring engine) reached an average speed of 328.63 mph, and won the race. Sadly, Flt Lt Richard Waghorn AFC lost his life on 5th May 1931 whilst using a parachute at 500 feet after jumping from an aircraft he was flight testing.

Neither was he fast enough to beat the older M52R, flown by the only remaining Italian pilot Dal Molin who reached 284.2 mph, thus coming second in the race. The two other Italian M67 aircraft were forced to retire due to overheating on their second laps, one aircraft suffering a broken coolant pipe which scalded the pilot severely.

It is estimated that over 1.5 million people watched the race from both shore sides of the Solent and also on a flotilla of ships along the course. The British team were feted much the same as footballers are today with their photos appearing in all the newspapers and journals of the day, accompanied with many stories of 'derring-do' by the team. These results meant that the team had a good chance of winning the race for a third time, and thereby within the rules, keep the trophy outright. Prime Minister Ramsay MacDonald was also caught up in the celebrations, announcing: "We are going to do our level best to win again." Even the *New York Times* of 25th September 1929 reported in its social pages that D'Arcy Greig was the only member of the victorious High

Speed Flight not married, but that he intended to do so the following year.

Greig's time with the High Speed Flight had come to an end, and he was posted away on 9th September 1929. On 28th October, he was posted to 9 (Bomber) Squadron at RAF Manston in Kent (flying Vickers Virginia aircraft). On 14th March 1930, he was transferred to 216 (Bomber Transport) Squadron at Heliopolis, Egypt (flying Vickers Victoria aircraft). By 12th January 1931, he was the lead pilot of three of these Vickers Victoria aircraft that carried troops of the King's African Rifles on an epic flight from Heliopolis (close to Cairo) onward to Cape Town, South Africa. Returning without the troops on March 11th this made a total journey of 11,237 miles, quite a feat in those days.

During January 1932 Greig was posted on to the staff at the RAF depot, Middle East until 5th October 1933 when he became the adjutant at RAF Amman. On 19th August 1935, D'Arcy Greig was posted back to the UK and onto the Royal Aircraft Establishment, then promoted to squadron leader on 1st December that same year.

On 2nd March 1936, Greig was made the commander of No.9 Flying Training School at the Central Flying School, Cranwell, until 4th May 1937, when he became the chief flying instructor until 18th November 1938. He was promoted to wing commander on 1st November 1938. The commandant of the Central Flying School at that time, Group Captain J M Robb (later to become an AVM) performed an assessment of Greig's flying ability in June 1938, naming it 'exceptional' and wrote in his logbook, 'a brilliant pilot and without equal as a chief flying instructor'.

From the Central Flying School Greig was posted to be the officer commanding 75 (New Zealand) Squadron at RAF Honington in Suffolk, flying Vickers Wellington aircraft, part of No.6 (Training) Group, until being posted yet again on 14th January 1940. This time his posting would take him out of the UK to Canada attached to the No.1 Air Training Course at RCAF Trenton and Camp Borden, under the Commonwealth Training Programme. Both of these bases were situated midway between Ottawa and Toronto and had the opportunity of using Lake Ontario for seaplane testing. It was during this period that he was involved with The Banting and Best Institute in Toronto, working with Wilbur Franks testing the anti-g suit. This involved wearing the experimental suit for forty to fifty minutes each time whilst flying Spitfire

L1090 in early June 1940. Greig refers to these tests in his manuscript, but also includes a reference in his flying logbook.

> *'I carried out a number of flights in the Spitfire when my suit was ready, and tried without success to "black myself out". On one trip I dived the aircraft until the airspeed went "off the clock" (over 450mph). I then pulled the stick back with considerable violence. The needle of the Kollsman Visual Accelerometer went to the limit of its scale at 9g! No black-out.*
>
> *I considered this to be quite remarkable as I was forty years of age and obviously could not possess the physical tone and stamina of a young fighter boy half my age.'*

D'Arcy Greig stayed here until 25th February 1941, and four days later was promoted to temporary group captain and posted to No.4 Training Course at RCAF Regina and Calgary. Here he flew Tiger Moths, Dragonfly and Beechcraft aeroplanes, until 16th April 1942. The next day he was posted to No.31 Service Flying Training School at Kingston Ontario, flying Harvard and Crane aircraft. It was during this period that he met up with Group Captain Bonham-Carter, another test pilot who would become a good friend. This posting finally finished on 15th November 1942, when Greig returned to the UK.

On 22nd December 1942, he was again posted to the Marine Aircraft Experimental Establishment at RAF Helensburgh, Dunbartonshire, This had been a top secret base during the 'phoney war' situated at Folkestone in Kent, and now relocated, hopefully far enough away from any German spy planes or bombers. Many experiments were undertaken here on various methods of sinking U Boats using Sunderland aircraft. The operation to sink the *Tirpitz* was also planned here. Sunderland aircraft were adapted to carry torpedoes on some of these experiments, as well as using parachute-type dive brakes. It's interesting to see that Greig's logbook shows he flew Sunderland K7774 with Wing Commander Paddon on 13th January 1943, and Sunderland DD832 on 24th with Squadron Leader Percy Hatfield DFC AFC. Hatfield was an exceptional Coastal Command pilot who had been the first to spot the *Bis-*

marck in May 1941, and went on to become a U boat 'destroyer' and test pilot on all types of flying boats. Greig also flew a Walrus (W 2782) on a few occasions in the same month with a full crew.

By 22nd February 1943 Greig had been moved again, this time to the Aeroplane and Armament Experimental Establishment (AAEE) at RAF Boscombe Down, Wiltshire. It was here that many trials of experimental aircraft were undertaken; the School of Aviation Medicine also had its base here. He stayed here for over a year flying twenty-six different types of single and multi-engine aircraft. One entry in his logbook made on 24th February, and which he underlined is very significant.

'First Flight in Jet Propelled Aircraft'

This jet propelled aircraft was in fact the Gloster Jet Serial No.DG/205/G, a precursor of the Gloster Meteor. The Gloster chief designer, George Carter, had designed a fighter aircraft powered by two jet engines in August 1940. Twelve of these were ordered, but only eight were ever built. This became the model for the Meteor jet fighter.

On 25th February 1943 Greig was made acting air commodore, and a few days later he met up with his old friend Bonham-Carter when they flew together in a Mentor aircraft from RAF Boscombe Down to RAF Farnborough. Greig was given the rank of group captain (war substantive) on 25th August and flew a Spitfire XIV F318 (Griffon engine) for twenty-five minutes the next day. The next month he flew Air Chief Marshal Sir Wilfred R Freeman KCB DSO MC from RAF Boscombe Down to RAF Hendon in a Stinson (Gullwing) Reliant FK 818.

This posting at Boscombe Down was concluded on 5th July 1944 and three days later he arrived at his new station at RAF Newmarket, Suffolk where 1688 (Bomber) Defence Training Flight was based within 3 Group. This was only a short posting, as he was sent to 15 Base at Scampton, Lincoln on 25th October 1944 to continue with the Bomber Defence Training Flight. Again this was to be another short posting, because on 10th November 1944 Greig was posted to RAF Feltwell, Norfolk, which was still associated with the Bomber Defence Training Flight (BDTF).

At the start of December he was promoted to group captain and stayed at RAF Feltwell until 23rd January 1946, when he was posted to RAF Station Wing. It's difficult to know exactly what duties he performed here, his logbook records flights in an Anson between RAF Wing and RAF Feltwell, as well as flying a Spitfire to RAF Boscombe Down.

On 18th July 1946 he was posted to HQ 91 Group (OTU) Abingdon, Oxfordshire, retiring as an air commodore on 23rd November 1946. His last flight as a pilot with the RAF was in a Proctor aircraft LZ 564 from RAF Marham to RAF Abingdon on 21st August 1946.

In all, D'Arcy Greig clocked up 4,547 hours and fifty-five minutes flying fighter, bomber and transport aircraft as well as being a test pilot through two world wars. He flew 140 different types of single and multi-engine aircraft as well as jets.

Darcy Greig died on 7th July 1986, his ashes were scattered by his son Jamie from an aircraft that flew over the area of the Solent where the Schneider Trophy races had taken place over fifty years earlier.

1

HARVEST MOON

For me, the evening of Friday, 20th September 1918, had started very
badly. We were due to take off from our airfield at Franqueville at 7.45
pm to bomb a German aerodrome near Basual, a village a short distance beyond Le Cateau, but at the last moment James, my observer,
had gone sick.

Now James was a very special chap, and senior to me by six or seven
years (I was eighteen), quiet of manner and possessing the gift of being
able to inspire the new and inexperienced pilot with confidence. In
fact, these qualities combined with months of practical experience, had
gained for him the unenviable task of shepherding most of the raw pilots through their first sorties. He had accompanied me on my first
mission four days previously, and this evening was to be my third. The
experienced RAF observer of those far off days was a very stout fellow.

James's place was taken by Armstrong, who like me was a second
lieutenant, but some months older and almost at the end of his first
tour in France. The RAF at that time was five months old, and we still
used the Royal Flying Corps army ranks.

The aircraft of No.83 Squadron were FE2b, commonly referred to as 'Fees'. They had started life in France as fighters, or scouts as they were then called, more than two years previously. The Fee was a two-seater 'pusher' biplane of about fifty foot wingspan and powered by a 160 hp Beardmore engine that sat behind the pilot. As the pilot and observer were located in front of the engine, and with a perfectly un-obstructed view, it readily became adaptable for tactical night bombing and reconnaissance, when obsolescence ended its life as a day fighter.

Our airfield at Franqueville was roughly fifty-eight miles from the front lines, so, to give some idea of the Fee's performance as a bomber, carrying three 112 lb bombs, a Lewis gun and a few pans of .303 am-munition, from take-off to reaching the front lines in a full throttle climb all the way took, as a rule, just one hour, by which time the ma-chine had reached an altitude of 4,000 feet and generally would go no higher until the bomb load had been released. This may seem rather quaint to the reader, particularly when one considers the performance of modern aircraft.

Well, Armstrong and I took off at 7.45 as planned and had barely set course for Bapaume when the fuel system air pressure pump failed, and we were forced to return to base. I had been feeling vaguely ap-prehensive all day, and for three successive nights previously, I had been plagued by an identical dream of being taken prisoner. The change of observer, plus the abortive mission, increased this state of disquiet. Tactical night bombing was generally regarded as being a 'cushy' job as there were practically no enemy night fighters to worry us, and apart from the frightful aspect of enemy anti-aircraft fire, which was pretty inaccurate anyway, I had little to worry about, apart from flying over France in the dark, with no aids and only one's skill to locate one's airfield upon return.

As a matter of interest, at the time of this event, my total flying ex-perience amounted to just fifty-one hours, of which nineteen had been night flying. My training had been very rudimentary, so my ability was limited to the most elementary manoeuvres, apart from being able to get off the ground and back down again without breaking the aero-plane. In those days a little natural aptitude plus a lot of luck were great assets, and a chap with over 100 hours in his flying logbook was regarded as a veteran flyer.

To cut short this digression, we took to the air once more in a reserve aircraft, at around 8.45 pm [serial no. F5853]. In those pre-radar days, one navigated at night as far as the front lines by reference to a system of lighthouses which were placed at fairly regular intervals throughout the Western Front. Each lighthouse flashed its own characteristic identification in Morse Code at, as far as I can recollect, intervals of about one to two minutes, the position and code of each being clearly marked on our maps. To eliminate the risk of the enemy becoming too familiar with the location of these lights, the code letters were changed periodically. After reaching the front lines, navigation to the target entailed following well defined landmarks or recourse to dead reckoning, depending on the visibility. After bombing the target all one had to do was to steer due west until the lines were once more crossed, then follow the lighthouses home.

It was a really lovely night, a full moon, a cloudless sky and a calm atmosphere, acting like a tonic in restoring my confidence and dissipating my recent attack of the 'willies'. Our plan was to follow the lights to Bapaume where we could pick out one of those marvellous dead straight roads to follow to Cambrai. Another straight road from there would lead to Le Cateau, followed by a few minutes by compass to the target.

We crossed the front line just over half way between Bapaume and Cambrai but from 4,000 feet one could see nothing of the trenches, and were it not for the stabbing flashes of artillery fire, it would have been difficult to imagine that down below, thousands of men of two great armies were engaged in mortal combat. This evening there seemed to be considerable activity and as we passed over Bapaume a German ammunition dump some distance ahead, blew up. It was an awe-inspiring spectacle which rather baffles description. Not a sudden explosion but rather a progressive upsurge of vivid and concentrated flame, a giant mushroom of fire, or a gigantic rising sun which, after reaching its zenith, seemed gradually to subside into the ground again.

Some miles ahead, searchlights were active, with red tracer and strings of 'flaming onions' indicating that one of our chaps was having a thin time. Before crossing over the enemy side, all navigation and instrument lights were switched off, the only light emanating from the aircraft being the red glow and sparks from the engine's exhaust. As we approached Cambrai all the searchlights, which hitherto had been very active, were, one by one, extinguished. Like a stupid ass I thought that perhaps they could not hear us coming. I was soon to be sadly disillusioned.

Over the middle of Cambrai no lights were visible and everything seemed really quite peaceful. Suddenly, I became aware that the underside of my top plane seemed to be glowing brightly. One searchlight immediately below had got us. Within a further moment dozens more opened up and the machine was beautifully coned in the intersection of many beams of dazzling light. My reaction to this situation was one of unadulterated terror; and the following events took place with lightning rapidity. As a crude attempt at evasive action was made, I felt the shock of two shell bursts, almost simultaneously. The engine ceased firing and from the blinding glare of searchlights the Fee seemed to plunge into inky blackness to the accompaniment of a sickening sensation in my stomach.

When I next saw the searchlights, they appeared to be shining on me from the sky and rotating madly around the nose of the machine. In my panic I pulled the control column hard back with both hands to try and check what I now realised was a spin towards the ground. The impression of the lights being in the sky had been due to loss of orientation under stress of the moment. There appeared to be no response to any of my control movements and I was convinced that we had only seconds more in which to live. I was, of course, taking every known incorrect action to right the aircraft and my thoughts might well have been crystallised in one short sentence: "Hell, what lousy luck; think of all the fun I shall be missing."

Suddenly the stable old Fee decided she had spun enough and we found ourselves in a shallow dive. On levelling out, a glance at the compass showed us to be on a north-westerly heading and the altimeter registered one thousand feet. I set the machine in a steady glide at around 60 mph, fully determined that, come what may, I would not deviate a fraction either to right or left, in case we went out of control again. Our heading was fortunate as we had the moon at our back, which meant that our forward view could not have been better. The engine was dead, but as there seemed to be some kind of mechanical noise to the rear, I turned on the gravity fuel tank and wound the impulse magneto to try and restart the motor, but not a sign of splutter resulted. From somewhere below, a machine gunner sent a burst of fire uncomfortably close.

I yelled to Armstrong, "Shall I set off the flares?" The answer, an emphatic negative! Holt magnesium flares fitted below the wing tips and fired electrically by the pilot, were provided for emergency use in the event of a forced landing at night. They were effective but liable to be too much so, were the aircraft to crash on touching the ground. The sudden anti-climax on regaining control gave me a feeling of confidence amounting almost to exhilaration. We were still alive and I did not give a damn what happened next, as the prospect of hitting the ground just passed me by. A canal slipped by below, the ground now being only a hundred or two feet away.

Directly in our path and at right angles to our track, I dimly saw a road, and almost at the last moment, telegraph wires loomed ahead. I yelled a warning to Armstrong. Fortunately, the Lewis gun was stowed vertically in its clamp immediately in front of his face. The gun struck and parted the wires as I pulled the control column back. The Fee sank somewhat heavily to the ground, ran a short distance and came to a halt all in one piece. We had touched down in a field of thick clover and on a slight upward gradient – an astonishing piece of luck.

Before jumping to the ground I found that the flare igniter used for destroying the aircraft was missing, and whilst I fumbled for a match the unmistakeable sound of a car approaching at speed along a nearby road made us both bolt up the slope till a clump of nettles provided a spot of welcome cover. We left the aircraft, complete with bombs and gun, as well as our maps, showing the positions of our lighthouses, etc, as a nice gift to the enemy.

The car stopped and four men got out and rushed to the aircraft. As they were obviously looking for its late occupants it dawned on us that it might be as well to increase our distance from them without further delay. A careful crawl to the far side of our nettle clump revealed that the crest of the rise was but a short distance away. On reaching the top we found that the opposite slope was more pronounced, so an attempt at rolling rather than crawling was made, our Sidcot flying suits absorbing most of the lumps and bumps in the ground. However, we quickly became giddy, so decided to change to walking.

No conversation took place until we were at least half a mile from the Fee with no one in sight. I informed Armstrong that it was quite stupid to think that we might evade being taken, for I was recalling my recent vivid dreams of capture. Armstrong's response was unprintable, or in polite language: "To hell with that for a yarn, I'm due for home leave next week, so we'll something-well have a shot at getting back!"

Neither of us had any experience of soldiering, and knew nothing about trench lines, barbed wire, etc, which, as it transpired later, perhaps worked out to our advantage. We estimated that we were about twelve to fourteen miles inside enemy territory, so for the moment out of sight and hearing of the front lines. The time was getting on for about 10 pm.

I had a cheap wrist compass which had been purchased some months previously, solely because I liked collecting gadgets, but I now regarded this as a godsend. Three decisions were made: (1) We would continue wearing our Sidcot suits, for September nights could be chilly and we had no idea for what length of time we would be fugitives. (2) We would walk on a westerly bearing until it was obvious that the front line was near, then be guided by existing circumstances. (3) We would not behave like fugitives, but conduct ourselves generally in as nonchalant a manner as possible. However, it was not long before the first decision had to go by the board and the cumbersome flying suits hampered our progress so much they were discarded. So our dress was identical, RFC double-breasted tunics, breeches, knee high flying boots and no caps. In all, quite a comfortable rig for a long walk.

A further mile or so brought us to the Cambrai-Douai road, which had to be crossed. However, a large party of men was approaching, carrying picks and shovels, presumably German engineers returning to camp. We decided to keep on the road and pass them in the opposite direction and with our hands thrust into our pockets, we strolled by. Not a soul took any notice until that last file had passed by, when someone shouted to us in German. Our pretence at not hearing succeeded and nothing further happened, but an uncomfortable moment or so was experienced. After a short lapse of time we left the road and took to the fields once more.

We trudged along uneventfully for about another fifteen minutes and were approaching a small spinney slightly to the left of our track, when there came a blinding flash from the trees and a thunderous explosion, followed by the roar of what must have been a large shell being fired. It made a noise like an express train and as the sound faded in the distance it seemed to produce an occasional 'creak' like a dry axle on a farm cart. The target must have been some great distance away as no resulting explosion occurred. The spinney was then given a wide berth and twenty minutes later the gun went off once again. After a third round it remained silent.

Rapid progress was now made for about an hour; we then encountered our first patch of barbed wire. It was in no great depth but nevertheless hampered our progress and was responsible for the production of quite an amount of noise. When in the clear once more, we sat down among what appeared to be an area of mounds and held a brief con-flab. At the start of the walk I had been keen on finding a hideout for the rest of the night, with the object of being able to reconnoitre the countryside by daylight the following morning. Armstrong had stamped out this suggestion very firmly.

However, having now covered at least five or six miles and run into our first serious obstruction, he seemed inclined to retract his decision. Pointing towards a wood, visible in the dim distance to our left, he hinted that it might afford excellent cover. He did not realise that my ideas on this subject had also undergone a change, for the hard exercise had made me both hungry and thirsty, so I insisted on pressing on regardless. This friendly chat had just finished when a faint click and shuffle was heard and the upper part of a man with a shovel over one shoulder, popped above the ground only two or three paces away. We made a pretence of sitting back and loading a pipe with tobacco, when to our intense relief, the intruding mole returned to his burrow.

This experience sharpened our senses and we became acutely aware of even the proximity of other human beings. The faintest smell of burning tobacco, the slightest noise or the vaguest sign of movement, put us on the qui-vive immediately. This was all well and good as desultory gunfire was now within earshot and the occasional star shell illuminated the horizon ahead of us. A few aircraft passed overhead flying to the west, and we envied them intensely.

Around 2 am the going became increasingly difficult, as the ground was broken by numerous shell holes, clumps of wire, etc, and caution had to be exercised in giving the odd German battery a wide berth. At one or two places we stumbled across un-manned gun positions and fortified shell-holes. The personnel were not far away for we could hear snatches of conversation. If anyone saw us they apparently took no notice as our nonchalant mien was paying dividends. My thirst was now worrying me considerably and I was tempted to drink from one of the many flooded shell holes. Only the possibility of a rotting corpse at the bottom deterred me.

As 3 am approached it became obvious that the crucial stage of our journey had been reached. Activity was at a low ebb, nevertheless, there were quite enough odd bangs and bursts of machine-gun fire to make us fully alive to the close proximity of the firing line. Presently, after skirting to the east of a shattered village, we reached the bank of a canal. It did not seem to be very wide and the water was at a low level, although the banks were fairly steep. Keeping to the top, we trod wearily away from the vicinity of the village till we arrived at a lock, well covered with barbed wire. We were about to tackle this obstruction when a machine gun opened up only a few feet away, the gun being situated about the middle of the lock.

It was then that we noticed the remains of an improvised footbridge at the bottom of the masonry. There were no handrails but a wooden strip about two feet wide connected the two sides of the canal. Having retraced our steps to avoid the wire and managing to clamber along the edge of the canal to the bridge, which looked a very rickety affair, do or die we started to cross.

After crawling over on hands and knees, I paused a few paces along the opposite bank to watch Armstrong's progress. He was about halfway over, crawling on his tummy, when the machine gun above him opened fire again but almost immediately jammed. A volley of German, that I took to be violent abuse, to the accompaniment of much hammering of metal, then took place. The situation suddenly struck me as extremely funny – the discomfort of Armstrong crawling across the plank not more than about twenty to thirty feet from the blaspheming German. However, I refrained from laughing.

It was not more than a few minutes before Armstrong was with me, and after walking along the edge of the canal till clear of the lock, we climbed the bank and headed west once more, still as if not caring, hands thrust deeply into our pockets. Our general attitude struck me as odd in the extreme, if not downright stupid, to be strolling along in 'no-man's-land' in such a casual manner. Had we carried things a bit too far in following this course of action?

An answer to these thoughts was shortly to be forthcoming. Suddenly Armstrong, who was about two paces behind me, threw himself flat on the ground. I was a bit slow in realising this, so decided to stand perfectly still and endeavour to discern the cause of his alarm. After a moment or two of complete silence, to my astonishment I heard an English voice to our rear say in a very subdued interrogative tone, "Who the hell's that?" I slowly turned my head. At a distance of about twenty yards to our left and in what seemed to be a clump of tree stumps, two hemispherical objects were just sticking above ground level. Were they German or British tin hats? I picked up a further whisper in English, then walked towards them, followed by Armstrong, and came face to face with two Canadian 'Tommies', with their mouths wide open and rifles at the ready.

We quickly disclosed our identities and jumped into their trench. The Tommies seemed quite overwhelmed with astonishment, stuck their hands into their pockets and produced cigarettes and chocolate biscuits, being under the impression that we had probably been on the loose for several days, instead of little over five hours. They were part of an outpost in 'no-man's-land', but quickly escorted us to their company commander, who received us in a more matter of fact manner.

During a brief chat the Tommies explained that they had been completely foxed by the curious sight of two hatless men taking what to them seemed to be a casual stroll in between the British and German lines and apparently unharmed. They could not size it up at all and consequently had not followed the normal procedure of shooting first and challenging afterwards. In fact they did not challenge at all, but merely looked threatening and flabbergasted.

The company commander then arranged for us to be escorted without further delay to their battalion commander. There followed a long and winding walk through a labyrinth of communication trenches, ending eventually with a steep descent into a very deep concrete dugout, recently captured from the Germans. It must have been of remarkably solid construction for just as we descended, field guns almost overhead commenced firing. The sound did not penetrate to the compartment below, we were just conscious of a succession of dull thumps which in no way impeded normal conversation.

The colonel was a burly, jolly chap, of about middle age, who explained that his sector of the line was held by the 1st Canadian Division which had recently advanced to its present position on the Hindenburg Line. The water we had crossed was the Canal du Nord, British forces being on one side, Germans on the other.

I suddenly remembered my frantic thirst and asked for a drink. The colonel pushed an ordinary army issue water bottle across the table. I removed the stopper and began to take a deep draught but choked in the process. It contained practically neat whisky. When I recovered my composure, a more cautious approach was made to the bottle and I was greatly comforted.

A map was now produced and I handed over the field to Armstrong who explained in careful and accurate detail all that we had observed during our trek. I was much amused on finding out that the wood Armstrong had spotted as a possible hiding place for the night, was Bourlon Wood, which, according to the most recent intelligence reports, was teeming with German troops. Thank goodness for my thirst.

Just as dawn was breaking we said farewell to the colonel and were escorted to the nearest casualty clearing station, where we were given breakfast and issued with tin helmets. Then on to brigade HQ for a quick interrogation. The staff here were busy dealing with a number of German prisoners, so we got off lightly, were packed into a Vauxhall car and despatched on a very bumpy drive to divisional HQ in Arras, where we had a thorough going over by the intelligence staff.

Immediately after lunch a Crossley tender from our squadron arrived and we were soon on our way along the Doullens Road en-route for Franqueville. The drive through the country over which the soldiery had been fighting the war was an eye-opener to us. It seemed unbelievable that humanity could exist under such conditions. The ruin, desolation and torn-up ground gave one the impression of an army of drunkards, running amok with hundreds of giant bull-dozers. Among the chaos of shattered trees, ruined buildings, wrecked transport, abandoned guns and tanks, was the occasional crashed aeroplane that pointed its tail forlornly at the sky.

Franqueville was reached by tea-time and after a quick 'cuppa' we made a full report to Jack Young, our recording officer. Apparently our escapade had caused a certain amount of confusion, as we had first been reported to wing as 'missing', then we'd been reported at the CCS, with the impression we'd crashed in the forward area and were either wounded or injured. Then within the hour a further signal arrived requesting transport to pick us up in Arras.

That evening we had a bit of a 'do' in the mess and woke up on Sunday morning with a hangover, to find we were required at wing. A quick breakfast, then sent on our way by road. The interview did not take very long and we were about to return when a 'phone message requested our presence at brigade, which was reached in time for lunch. A slightly more elaborate interrogation followed and we eventually arrived back at base for tea, feeling very 'brassed off' and rather tired. We had barely sat down however, when a further 'phone call requested our presence at HQ, 1st Army, without delay, so once more we dashed to the Crossley tender.

It was a long drive and the staff of 1st Army had just sat down to dinner, when two weary RAF second lieutenants reported to the château (or at any rate, a fairly large country house). When ushered into the dining hall, we felt completely overawed by the galaxy of red tabs, medal ribbons and grey heads. However, our welcome was so informal and friendly that we quickly felt at home and tucked in with great gusto. They dined and wined us with the utmost hospitality and I regret to say that when the time came to rise from the table, I felt utterly unsteady on my pins and rather tipsy. Armstrong seemed to be in good form and appeared to be shooting a good line. I became a little apprehensive on his behalf in case there were discrepancies in what we had reported to all the various authorities concerned in this apparently unending series of interviews.

On entering the ante-room, I was casting a bleary eye in search of a comfortable armchair in which to pass out, when a very charming Lt-colonel, ushered us along a passage, then into a large room with the walls covered with maps. This, thank goodness, was to be our final interview. We had not appreciated the fact that the war was rapidly drawing to a close and that the soldiery were committed to their final push. Consequently, what information we had regarding enemy terrain we had traversed was naturally of great interest to the HQ staff. I felt incapable of coherent speech and sat on a swivel chair whilst Armstrong held forth with great éclat. I managed to concentrate on his statement and answers, although here and there, he might have made the odd embellishment. Yet all the salient features tallied with what had passed previously, so all was well. The colonel, when winding up the interrogation, gave us a few items of personal interest.

The big gun we had spotted had been confirmed as a long-range weapon that had been bombarding Arras sporadically from a distance of nearly twenty miles. He ended by saying: "Really you lads are very lucky, for two nights before you came down, we plastered that area with three hundred gas containers. If you had been there then, and without respirators, you'd have been right out of luck."

So our little adventure was at last over and during the days that followed I had ample time in which to reflect upon all that had happened. There were three questions to which I wanted answers. First, why did the engine of my Fee stop functioning when we were coned in the searchlights over Cambrai? I suppose the obvious answer was that the fuel line or some other vital part was put out of commission by a shell fragment. However, during a brief cursory glance I had of the Fee before making our getaway after landing, my impression was that it appeared undamaged. Had this spare aircraft been adequately fuelled before we took off?

Problem two. Why had the Fee spun out of control from 4,000 feet to about 1,500 feet? The answer to this is simple. Without delving too far into technicalities, a spin is a state of auto-rotation following a stall or loss of flying speed and will not stop until full flying speed has been regained. When the engine failed I was engaged in a very heavy handed attempt at evasive action, a perfect state for starting a spin. Had I pushed the stick forward immediately the spin most likely would have stopped. That the Fee recovered normal flight was sheer luck, though possibly the extra weight and position of the bomb load might have had some bearing on the matter.

The fact that I had acted according to instinct and not reason was due entirely to lack of proper flying instruction during my training. Oddly enough, at ground school, No.1 School of Military Aeronautics, Reading, the lecturer on rigging and theory of flight was a man approaching middle age, Captain Fleming Williams. Although apparently not a pilot (he wore no wings on his tunic), he was a teacher par excellence. A soul of wit and a master of analogy as well as a first-rate artist, he never had the slightest difficulty in claiming the full attention of his class. In one lecture he told us in accurate detail all that was then known about spinning and stalling. Good though this lecture was, it lacked the power of practical application. It has since been recognised that the essence of sound instruction lies in practical demonstration in the air. In my time of crisis I had completely forgotten the existence of our worthy lecturer and his wise council. I never met him again after the war but saw his signature on a number of paintings, and I recall him saying that one day aircraft will need to have wheels that retract, just as birds pull up their legs once airborne.

Third, and finally, concerned my successive dreams about being a prisoner. I later came to the conclusion that it was brought on by stress or anxiety. Odd that they did not feature aircraft but I assume now that they did. Perhaps becoming a prisoner symbolised a state of physical security.

Well, what of the future? Many and diverse are the paths taken in the relentless march of destiny. For myself I eventually made a career of the Royal Air Force and completed my time on the active list.

What of Armstrong, my companion on this very early and quite exciting experience? He went on leave soon after our adventure and we did not meet again until a squadron re-union party at the Savoy Hotel in early 1919. Not long after this he was posted to Egypt for training as a pilot. One Saturday afternoon two aircraft took off at about the same time, to fly a cross-country flight, in one aircraft was Armstrong. Although I cannot say for certain, it is quite possible that they might have been the only two aircraft in the air over Egypt at that time. One took off from Heliopolis, bound for Ismailia, the other from Ismailia, bound for Heliopolis. They met half way to their respective destinations – head on!

2

NO. 6 SQUADRON, 1920

On the radio and sometimes in conversation, one hears of such and such a tune referred to as nostalgic. It can safely be said that most people, provided they have an ear for music, can readily connect certain tunes with incidents, places or periods in their lives, right back to early childhood. Looking back over the years I can call to mind one batch of popular melodies that always remind me very forcibly of the time I spent in No.6 Squadron, particularly the years 1920-1921.

The tunes are Avalon; Everybody's Blowing Bubbles; Whispering; Dardanella; The Japanese Sandman, and a few others. If I live to be a hundred I shall always have the most pleasant recollections of my service in this unit. It was, in fact, an important landmark in my career, as it was in No.6 that I was granted a permanent commission in the RAF. I could never have wished to serve with a finer bunch of chaps.

We were a merry lot and a bit wild at times. Our discipline was not of the orthodox barrack square variety, but was based entirely on good comradeship and éspirit de corps. I think we had the minimum of pa-rades; in 1920 and 1921 I can distinctly remember one being held on the king's birthday. Which reminds me of a funny story, alleged to be true, about an elderly and absent-minded station commander in the early 1920s, who, on the occasion of the monarch's birthday, formed up his parade on three sides of a square and facing the flagstaff, then gave the order to remove head-dress. He then called for three hearty cheers for His Majesty the King, Edward VII. Before the first 'hip, hip' passed his lips, a very audible cockney voice from the rear called: 'Wot abaht Queen Anne?' What followed is best left to the imagination. Any-way, apart from some tragic moments, I spent three very happy years with No.6.

Well, to connect up with the previous chapter, I finished a month's leave on 11th November 1918, and far too dutifully reported to No.192 (NT) Squadron at Newmarket to which unit I had been posted as an instructor. As it happened, I had learnt to fly at Newmarket only a few months previously. On my arrival at the airfield not a soul was to be found. The war had ended that morning, so everyone had vanished on a spree. I spent the rest of the day very miserably entirely on my own. What a clot!

I remained with this unit until March 1919, at which time the 6th (Home Defence) Brigade was disbanded and with it my squadron. I flew one of the last remaining FE2s over to Bury aerodrome, near Ram-sey, towards the end of the previous month. As it turned out it was to be my last flight that year. I then went on indefinite leave, which was fun to start with, but began to pall after three months, by which time I was broke and bored. I visited the Air Ministry, at the Hotel Cecil, and urgently requested employment of some kind. I was forthwith posted to Kidbrooke to learn all about storekeeping – hardly my cup of tea.

The year 1919 was a most unsatisfactory year, the service being full of disgruntled people awaiting demobilisation. My future was uncer-tain, as I had applied without success for a permanent commission. I was desperately keen on continuing flying and the RAF seemed to afford the best opportunity in this direction at that time. During the summer the new ranks were published and I found myself with the title of pilot officer. I was thoroughly disgusted as I thought this had neither the dignity nor prestige of second lieutenant. However, in September I was granted a three-year short service commission plus promotion to flying officer, so life took on a rosier hue.

October found me at Eastchurch, on the Island of Sheppey, just filling in time doing odd station duties, but no flying and I became bored again for most of the time. However, towards the end of the year I received preliminary warning of a posting to Mesopotamia early in the new year. The outlook brightened considerably at this prospect and I conjured up visions of this historical land, with Baghdad – the City of Caliphs – the glories of Nineveh, the Hanging Gardens of Babylon, Uncle Tom Cobley and all. I regret to say that my first impression on eventually arriving in this country did not come up to my expectations. I found a land of sweaty heat, dust, mud, boils, blains, bed bugs and bad odours – not one little bit of glamour.

Nevertheless, things did improve on further acquaintance. Stationed at RAF Eastchurch with me had been a very nice chap by the name of Winfield-Smith. Originally a regular soldier [East Surrey Regt, Ed.], he had learnt to fly before the war [1912] and had seen active service in Mesopotamia and been taken prisoner by the Turks at the fall of Kut el Amara in April 1916.[1] As a source of information on this country he was a godsend. On his advice I purchased a good shotgun, a Mauser Sporting rifle [2] and a 'chop box' from Fortnum & Mason; the last named being a plywood contraption containing a vast amount of tinned and bottled food to supplement service rations. He also provided a very fine portable bath, rather like an old fashioned hip bath with a lid which locked. It contained a detachable wickerwork lining in which one could pack a large quantity of clothing. All was now set for the great adventure.

On Friday 13th February 1920, a very mixed gathering assembled on the dock at Tilbury, awaiting transportation by tender, out to H.M. Transport *Macedonia*, which was a rather elderly P & O liner which had seen service as an armed merchantman during the war. The passenger list included troops of the Manchester Regiment, a mixture of officers and other ranks from various army units and the RAF, and a few nurses. The dying influence of the RFC and RNAS was still very evident in the variety of uniforms which presented quite a spectacle. Some officers were in their original 1918 khaki, some in pale blue with gold braid, a few others in the latest dark blue with dark braid, and finally the odd one or two who seemed to be wearing a mixture of old and new.

There was one superlative sartorial specimen, Flying Officer Ralph Sorley [3], who was clad in an extremely well cut tunic and slacks of lightish grey, with a cloth peaked hat to match – black patent leather peaks were regulation at that time. Although irregular, this uniform which was obviously for tropical use, bore a marked resemblance to the present day garb of the RAF except in colour.

I eventually got aboard, found my cabin which had two berths and deposited on the floor a cabin trunk, suitcase, gun and rifle cases and my chop box. I was pondering on whether to select the upper or lower berth, when the door opened to reveal a rugged figure of an elderly man of ruddy, bulldog countenance, flying officer's rank braid and a great array of campaign ribbons, but no flying insignia. He glanced at my various cases with an expression of astonishment, and muttered, "Blimey, what's all this junk?" Taken somewhat aback, I replied apologetically, "Sorry old boy, that's my cabin baggage." This brought forth the immediate response, "All right chum, here's the whole bloody lot of mine." With that he heaved one naval pattern kit bag into the cabin. Such was my introduction to Charlie Knowlson, my cabin companion as far as Bombay.

Charlie was fifty-five years old and certainly a character. An ex-chief petty officer, Royal Navy, now technical officer, Armament, RAF, I enquired his destination. "The silly B's at the Bolo (slang for Air Ministry) have posted me to Mespot and I'm due for pension in April," he replied. "Why didn't you point out their mistake?" I asked. "Me? Not bloody likely, I've never been to Baghdad and these Arab bints are the only pieces of skirt I've never given the once-over."

Sure enough, old Charlie got to Baghdad, and was there a month by the time the authorities discovered their error and had him returned poste-haste to England and retirement. He proved to be an amusing and interesting companion on the journey, and I learnt a lot about his varied wartime experiences. These began with the bombardment of

Alexandria in 1882, including the Boxer Rising in China.

The voyage to Bombay apparently followed the usual pattern of eating, drinking, deck games, circuits of the promenade deck and listening to the band of the Manchester Regiment each afternoon. The occupant of the next cabin to mine was Bill Sowrey [4], the commanding officer of the squadron in which I had learnt to fly and one of three well known brothers, all of whom were in the RAF. When I first made his acquaintance two years previously, he had been a major, but with the post-war general reduction in ranks he was now a flight lieutenant. I remembered having a great admiration for his prowess as a pilot and for his exuberance in the mess. He now seemed somewhat subdued and spent a great part of his time practising on the ukulele, an instrument on which he was obviously a novice.

On disembarkation at Bombay, a number of us, including myself, found our way to the best hotel in the city – the Taj Mahal. The following day, however, on discovering that no arrangements had been made for our onward conveyance to Basra or for the provision of funds, we moved smartly out and eventually found much more modest accommodation. It was just as well we did, as three weeks passed before we embarked on the SS *Varsova*. The day of our departure was most embarrassing, and I had just enough money with which to settle my hotel bill and had to leave the premises ignoring in the most brazen fashion the line of hotel staff which had formed up in the entrance in the hope of receiving a tip. I was flat broke!

Aboard the *Varsova* we were joined by a number of officers who had not been with us in the *Macedonia*, including Jimmy Lawson, a 'ray of sunshine' who had a wonderful natural aptitude for cheering the despondent and promoting an atmosphere of bonhomie and joie de vivre. As a pilot Jimmy was probably rated below average but as an asset to the community and a morale booster he was unquestionably 'exceptional'. His cheery disposition combined with his artistry at the piano more than offset what he might have lacked in flying ability.

At last the sea voyage was over, and at the end of March we found ourselves in a transit camp at Makina, on the outskirts of Basra. As I have mentioned previously, my first impressions of the country were not good. The fact that the rains were not yet done with did not improve matters. Neither did the several days delay in this scruffy camp, waiting for posting instructions to come through from Baghdad. Eventually, however, they did arrive and we started the slowest railway journey I had ever experienced – 350 miles to Baghdad took about three days. Frequently it was possible to get out and walk alongside our compartment by way of getting a spot of exercise and relieving boredom.

Baghdad West station was reached at breakfast time, the station being an open expanse of sand, lacking platforms, booking office, buffet or any other amenities. It did possess, however, a sign board and an engine shed. The front end of what was apparently an unserviceable locomotive protruded from the latter. This poor engine must have been suffering from an incurable malady for it remained in this position throughout the three years that I spent in the country.

At the station to meet us were two RAF officers, smartly attired in bush shirts and jodpurs, and mounted on horseback. One was Wing Commander O T Boyd OBE MC AFC [5], the senior RAF officer in the country, the other, Flight Lieutenant George Pirie MC CdG [6], the CO of No.6 Squadron, who had recently suffered the same fate as Bill Sowrey, in having to drop a rank. In no time at all we found ourselves at last in our respective units, but what of our job in this country?

With the end of the war and the final ousting of the Turk, Britain became responsible for administration under a mandate granted by the League of Nations. The end of hostilities left the mass of semi-civilised tribesmen in a state of turmoil and unrest. Troubles kept continually erupting and had to be suppressed. The Bolshevik menace too threatened in north-west Persia, in the vicinity of the Caspian Sea. In June 1920, a full scale insurrection started, so there was never a dull moment for us.

At the time of our arrival the civil commissioner was Sir Arnold T Wilson, but he was shortly to be replaced at the end of his term of office, by Sir Percy Cox. The commander-in-chief of the armed forces was General Sir Aylmer Haldane. The strength of the military forces amounted to 120,000 men, the bulk of which were Indian troops. In addition, in north-west Persia, a force of 13,000 men was employed in containing the Bolsheviks. Concurrently, the air forces available for co-operation with the army were:

At Baghdad.
No.31 Wing HQ (directly responsible to GHQ) Aircraft Park.
HQ and one flight of No.6 Squadron.
HQ and one flight of No.30 Squadron.

On Detachment.
No.6 Squadron. One flight at Albu Kemel, in Syria, 230 miles away.
One flight at Bushire, on the Persian Gulf, 500 miles away.
No.30 Squadron. One flight at Mosul, 230 miles north of Baghdad.
One flight at Kasvin, north-west Persia, 450 miles away.

As the cruising speed of the RE8 aeroplanes that we were using was
well below 100 mph, these detachments constituted quite a wide measure of dispersal. The RE8 was a two-seater biplane with a 140 hp air-
cooled engine, which was chiefly used for artillery observation during
the First World War.

Owing to the critical situation which developed later that summer
it became necessary to reinforce both military and air forces considerably. When we first arrived at Baghdad, No.30 Squadron was in the
process of being re-equipped with the DH9a aircraft, of superior performance to the old RE8, while No.6 Squadron were awaiting the arrival
of Bristol Fighters, the first of which took to the air in June. Another
veteran of WW1, the 'Brisfit', eventually replaced our 'Harry Tates' later
that summer.

Aircraft re-equipment coincided with the almost complete replacement of flying personnel. Most of the chaps in the two squadrons at
that time had been out there since the end of the war, some earlier,
and were due for home, and left. Our base airfield at Baghdad West
was shared with No.30 Squadron and the Aircraft Park. Our first few
weeks were spent under canvas but the building of a mess and quarters
was under way and we eventually moved into these mud-built structures, in early May.

These mud walls were immensely thick, so they were fairly cool in
summer and warm in winter. The general finish was austere in the extreme, with no baths or running water, latrines being of the bucket or
petrol tin variety. In summer, bath water in empty oil drums was heated
very adequately by exposure to the sun.

On 6th April, after a lapse of nearly fourteen months, I once more became airborne. The RE8 was an unfamiliar aeroplane to me and as the Aircraft Park possessed an old BE2e, supposedly in serviceable condition, I decided with the concurrence of my B Flight commander – Ralph Sorley – to borrow this machine. I had flown BEs during my training. My first take-off was rather erratic but I soon felt at home again. However, I was not up for more than fifteen minutes, as the engine had started to vibrate badly. The following day I again took to the sky in the same machine, being assured the engine fault had been rectified. This time I had to take off towards a bund (high bank to control flood water) which formed the southern boundary of the airfield.

Over the other side of the bund was a tented camp of Indian troops. I had just become airborne and was about to cross the bund when, with a warning splutter, the engine completely failed. The golden rule in such circumstances, is always to glide straight ahead, never turn back. In this instance I had insufficient height in which to turn in any event, so had no alternative but to try and land between two rows of tents. Fortunately the troops had quickly appreciated the situation and were scattering willy-nilly in all directions ahead of me. The poor old BE responded valiantly to some very ham-fisted control movements, weaved her way successfully onto the ground and came to a halt with one bell tent completely enveloping the port wing tip. I decided – wisely I think – against any further BE flying.

Two days later I made my first and quite uneventful flight in an RE8. These aircraft were commonly referred to as 'Harry Tates', phonetically named after the well-known comedian on the London stage. Firstly they were reputed to be prone to uncontrollable spinning, and secondly, owing to the fact that the upper wing was considerably wider than the lower, the extended portions were supposed to be rather frail and liable to failure in a dive. From personal experience I found them to be quite amenable and rather gentlemanly aeroplanes. In the early days of flying, vicious qualities were sometimes attributed to certain aircraft, often without justification. More often than not the fault lay with the pilot, not the machine. Inefficient training methods, lack of knowledge and practical experience were at the root of the trouble.

Early in 1920 the French were given the mandate for Syria, and in consequence, the military detachment and flight of No.6 Squadron were withdrawn from Albu Kemel and moved some sixty miles eastward to Anah, on the right bank of the Euphrates. I believe I am right in saying that Anah was reputed to be the longest village in the world, as in those days it straggled in a thin line for about six miles. An interesting feature of the Euphrates from this locality westward is the irrigation system, used in watering the cultivated land along the river banks. Gigantic and very spindly wooden water wheels, at least twenty feet in diameter, pick up the water in earthenware jars tied to the rim of the wheel, and empty into elevated aqueducts which lead to the various irrigation trenches. The system is very efficient and had probably been used since biblical times. The wooden spindles and bearings produced a mournful groaning sound which could at times be irritating, especially at night.

I spent May and June 1920 almost entirely with the Anah detachment. The highlights of the period, from my point of view were, a forced landing, a dust storm which wrecked all our aircraft and an exciting interlude on the ground with a bold rebel. The RAF had no camp of their own, but lived with the 2nd Battalion, 6th Jats, an Indian regiment. The other components of the force were the 10th Indian Lancers, a detachment of field and mountain artillery, a section of armoured cars. plus the usual services. The Jats had their camp right on the river bank, a mile or two from our airfield.

Our RE8s were picketed out in the open, and one evening towards the end of May a terrific dust storm blew in from the west and continued throughout the night, wreaking havoc among our tents. The following dawn revealed a sorry state at the aerodrome. All our aircraft had been torn from their screw-pickets and were strewn about in fantastic disarray all over the place, one having been blown a distance of three-quarters of a mile. I cannot remember how many were repairable but the flight was out of action for some days whilst repairs and replacements were made. That storm taught us an expensive but nevertheless valuable lesson on the correct way in which to picket the old-fashioned, fixed undercarriage type of aircraft, out in the open.

From then on pits for the wheels were dug, with an inclined approach on the reverse side from the prevailing wind, so that the aircraft could with ease be run in. The tail was then jacked up in such a way to ensure that when secured to the screw-pickets the aircraft would be in flying attitude with the wings at the minimum angle of attack. As an added precaution a low semi-circular sandbag wall was erected on the windward side of each pit. This device proved effective against the severest sand storm.

Our main duties at Anah were co-operation with ground forces, reconnaissance and bombing. Recalcitrant tribes abounded in the area, including a very bold fellow named Nidgeris, who only had a very small but nevertheless active and resourceful following. He considered that he should have been paramount sheik of a certain tribe, an opinion to which the British administration did not subscribe. One day to our intense surprise and amusement, he sent Colonel Hardie, the detachment commander, an ultimatum to the effect that if we did not break camp and start marching back to Baghdad by 8.30 pm the following evening, he would come and drive us out.

To the best of our knowledge he had only fifty to sixty followers, so for sheer unadulterated cheek this took the proverbial biscuit. We all laughed heartily and metaphorically threw the ultimatum in the waste paper basket. After dark the following day, having finished our supper, we were relaxing on the river bank, telling stories and drinking whiskey, sitting in the cool breeze in an atmosphere of calm and good humour.

Although zero hour was rapidly approaching, nobody mentioned the ultimatum or even thought for one moment that anything would happen. The battalion adjutant, Pepperell, had just started to recite a rather bawdy monologue called 'The Happy Family' and had completed the second line, when our blissful calm was shattered by the ping and whine of bullets, the fusillade coming from the opposite bank. We all threw ourselves flat on our faces and all camp lights were immediately doused. The Jats had a small outpost in a blockhouse on the opposite bank and were quick off the mark in replying to the hostile fire, and in no time at all quite a 'Brocks Benefit' was taking place. Verey lights, star shells and an occasional bursting of a grenade, adding variety to the fun.

As all action now seemed to be concentrated on the opposite bank we got to our feet. Our camp was now in total darkness, all fires having been put out. Colonel Hardie, ostensibly to boost morale in true Francis

Drake style, cracked a joke or two, then produced a large cigar which he proceeded to light. The first flicker of his match resulted in an immediate and intense volley of fire from the opposite bank. Never have I seen a bunch of chaps quicker off the mark in taking evasive action!

Very shortly after this ill-advised show of bravado, the raid ended and we took stock of the damage. There were one or two casualties in the outpost, some of our pack animals had been hit and one of the cooks killed. Many tents had been riddled, but as all floors were dug well below ground level, any occupants had escaped injury. The following afternoon, one of the armoured car officers invited me to accompany him on a reconnaissance, cum foraging, expedition westwards along the river, the main object being to shoot a sand grouse or two for the larder. As we still had no aircraft I gladly accepted his invitation.

In the light armoured motor batteries or Lamb cars, as they were known, the operational vehicles employed were from two extremities of automobile social scale, 40-50 hp Rolls-Royce and the T-model Ford. We took a Rolls and as a very necessary precaution, two belts of ammunition for the mounted Vickers gun, in addition to our shotguns. We cut inland for a few miles and then headed back towards the river. Emerging on the bank from behind a line of low sand-hills, we were immediately aware of a small party of men, half a dozen or so, on the opposite bank about 600 yards away, who at once started to run away. Aha, we thought, guilty conscience, suspicious characters, probably some of the Nidgeris gang. In a trice we trained the Vickers and gave them a very long burst of fire. What followed had some of the characteristics of a comic film. We were uncertain about the range of the targets, and instead of them running for the nearest cover, they ran like stags along the line of the river, spurts of dust from our bullets overtaking and passing them. Eventually they were either knocked over or deliberately threw themselves flat. Ceasing fire, we turned for home, bagging a few grouse on the way.

The next day brought news that the men we had shot up were of the hostile gang but at the time of the action were harmlessly engaged in tilling the soil. Ah well, honour had been vindicated, after all, they had caught us with our pants down the previous evening.

On 10th June I was pilot of one of three aircraft detailed to co-operate with a punitive expedition which had set out some days previously, to attack the village of Husaibah, about fifty miles distant, and close to the Syrian border. Attack by aircraft was to precede bombardment by field artillery, following which the other forces were to enter and destroy the village. On completion of the operation the whole force was to return to Anah. Our aircraft carried twelve 20 lb Cooper bombs each, plus Lewis gun and ammunition.

As this show was on a relatively big scale, the Jat officers at Anah, who had not gone with the column, were falling over each other in their efforts to fly with us as rear gunners. I took Captain Heaton, an enthusiastic infantryman, who knew all about Lewis guns but had never before been up in an aeroplane. Not long after setting course, the leading 'Harry Tate' developed engine trouble and turned for home, followed a little later by the other machine, similarly affected.

All seemed well with my machine and soon afterwards we sighted the column about six miles from the target village. Diving down slightly I dropped my bombs from a height of 3,000 feet, then decided to come down low and let Heaton have a go with the Lewis, so throttled back. At 1,800 feet when over the middle of the village, I opened up again but got no response from the engine, other than some intermittent banging in the exhaust pipes which belched forth flame and black smoke.

It didn't take a genius to realise that my second landing in enemy territory was imminent, so I turned in the direction of the column and managed to get well over a mile from the village before being compelled to turn into wind at a very low altitude to make some sort of landing. The machine touched down among sand dunes and ran a few yards before the wheels dug into the soft ground, causing her to tip vertically onto her nose. I kept my fingers firmly crossed in the hope that our landing had been seen from the column and that help would arrive before any unwelcome attention from irate Bedouin.

Despite our somewhat uncertain situation, Heaton was as pleased as a dog with two tails on a street full of lamp posts. Not only had he survived his first flight but had crashed into the bargain, thus, in his opinion qualifying for the title VEA – Very Experienced Aviator. Our luck was in, for a Rolls armoured car arrived in a matter of minutes, picked us up after we had set fire to the wrecked RE8, and drove us back to the column, which had halted whilst the field guns carried out their bombardment.

By the afternoon the village was in flames, the operation completed and the return march under way. The driver of the armoured car was a well known character of that period, Charles Goring, a man whose exploits in armoured cars had won him a DSO and the MC, in addition to the enmity of Arab and Turk. It was rumoured that the Arabs had a price on his head. Charles, a very delightful 'rough diamond' who had obviously been born within earshot of Bow Bells, and whom I had only met for the first time a few days previously, now took me in hand. His job with the expedition was to lead the advance guard and reconnoitre all wadis and other points where ambush was possible.

As I was now at a loose end, he invited me to keep him company in Harvester, his armoured car, for the three or four days that the withdrawal to Anah would take. Apart from a desultory shoot up, without casualties, on our first night bivouac, the journey proved to be fairly uneventful but rather hot and stuffy, especially when driving with the steel radiator guard doors closed, when nosing our way through tricky terrain. A week after our return, the flight was withdrawn to Baghdad, as the mounting pressure of the insurrection necessitated the deployment of the bulk of our forces to the south of the city.

[1] Captain S C Winfield-Smith and his observer, Captain S C P Munday, of 30 Squadron, were both captured at Kut, while the RFC were attempting to supply the besieged town from the air in April 1916.

[2] Some years after WW2, Greig sold his Mauser to Mike Payne of Bexhill, a policeman who often spoke to Greig about his flying days. Greig told him he had used it to shoot mountain lions in Iraq.

[3] Later Air Marshal Sir Ralph S Sorley KCB OBE DSC DFC. His DFC was awarded for operations with 6 Squadron in Mesopotamia in 1921 and his DSC with the RNAS in WW1. Post-WW2, he retired in September 1948 and became deputy chairman and MD of de Havilland Propellers. Died in November 1974.

[4] Later Air Commodore W Sowrey CBE DFC AFC. RFC/RAF, WW1. His DFC was awarded for services in Iraq during the 1920s. Retired in September 1942 and died in February 1968.

[5] Owen Tudor Boyd won his MC with the RFC in 1916. His AFC and OBE came in 1919 following commands in the RAF in both UK and Mesopotamia. Later rose to air marshal CB but was taken prisoner in 1940 yet successfully escaped in early 1944. Died in August 1944 whilst commanding 93 Group of Bomber Command.

[6] George Clark Pirie won his MC in 1917 with the RFC in France and he later served in Italy where he was awarded the Medaglia al Valore Militare, and the French Croix de Guerre. In 1918 he received the DFC too. Later became KBE 1946, then KCB in 1951. Died January 1980.

3

LIFE IN MESPOT

From early July until the end of October 1920 constituted a very hectic period for us all, then operations became desultory and eventually petered out by the end of the year. The insurrection involved the whole country, but the vital line of communication, the railway joining Baghdad to Basra, was undoubtedly the greatest headache of all.

The causes of the general conflagration are somewhat obscure, but it was thought to be due chiefly to the application of Indian methods of administration, which might have been too rigid for the somewhat primitive tribesmen. Taxation might also have some bearing on the matter. One particular tribe in the rebellion, were upset because their sheik had been arrested for the non-payment of an outstanding agricultural loan amounting to less than 1,000 rupees.

During this period the RAF lost eleven aircraft in hostile territory, plus fifty-seven put temporarily out of action by rifle fire from the ground. Six officers and two other ranks were wounded. The casualties among ground troops totalled 2,269 killed, missing or wounded. Arab casualties were estimated in the region of 8,500 killed and wounded. In terms of hard cash the insurrection was estimated to have cost the British government 32 million pounds.

As an enemy the Arab was an unpleasant customer, particularly if one had the misfortune to be taken prisoner. For this reason all flying personnel carried with them what were commonly referred to as 'meal tickets' [or even goolie chits. Ed.]. Briefly, they offered substantial financial rewards for the safe return of the captive, and also provided they were returned 'intact'. Prisoners were frequently slaughtered but as the final coup de grâce, they invariably had to suffer mutilation which generally included emasculation and the gauging out of eyes. Teeth were also removed, especially if they happened to have any gold crowns or fillings. The reason for mutilation had, I believe, some religious significance. Although I can lay no claim to detailed knowledge of the Islamic faith, I believe I am right in saying that the incomplete human body is very seriously handicapped on entering paradise. This practice also explains why, on the North-West Frontier of India in the not too distant past, capital punishment was carried out by tying the condemned man, if a Mahommedan tribesman, to the muzzle of a field gun and blowing him to pieces.

I can recall four instances of RAF personnel being captured during this period, but only one ending in death of the pilot and observer. The first pair, Flying Officers Gardiner and Herbert of 6 Squadron, had an extremely lucky escape. Their Bristol Fighter had been disabled by rifle fire and forced to land between Hillah and Diwaniyah. They were immediately captured and taken to a village at some distance from their machine, where they were tied to stakes around which women of the village danced whilst brandishing knives and making uncomfortably suggestive gestures.

However, a man arrived on the scene and berated the villagers for having failed to loot the aeroplane, which he had been told was taking a large sum in gold from Baghdad to Basra, when brought down. The effect was electric. There was a general stampede from the village, leaving the captives unguarded. As soon as the coast was clear, the man who had caused the exodus and who was apparently a friendly Arab, cut their bonds and led them to a couple of saddled horses. In no time they were in a frenzied gallop in the direction of the nearest British outpost which they eventually reached without further incident.

Two other officers, Flying Officers Dipple and Sewell, the wing photographic officer, in a Bristol Fighter of 6 Squadron, force-landed while on a photo-reconnaissance mission between Baghdad and Ramadi. Both were captured but fortunately Sewell, who had some medical training, managed to convince their captors that he was a doctor. European doctors were held in very high esteem by the Arabs and by a lucky coincidence the sheik's small son happened to be ill. To the best of my recollection the boy was suffering from a painful eye infection. Sewell was conducted to the small invalid and was successful in extracting a foreign body from the eye thereby alleviating his suffering. In a day or two the eye was as good as new. The sheik showed his appreciation by returning both airmen, unharmed, to the squadron. After the end of the insurrection, this sheik and members of his family became frequent visitors to Baghdad West and their one-time captives.

Two officers of 30 Squadron, Flying Officers 'Fiery' Lock and Gowler, force-landed their 'Ninac' (DH9a) a few miles to the south west of Hillah. They presented their meal tickets to the leader of the party that had captured them, but this individual regarded the documents with the utmost contempt and tore them up, so not very encouraging. From then on the two men had to endure very rough treatment, including a march of about eight miles tethered behind a donkey. Their shoes were removed beforehand and as the trek was over terrain amply covered with camel thorn bushes, their feet were soon in an appalling condition. They were eventually incarcerated in the Holy City of Najaf, from whence their ultimate release was obtained. It was weeks before the last thorn was removed from their feet, during which time Lock truly lived up to his explosive nickname.

The final instance involved two officers of the newly arrived 84 Squadron. During August, the river gunboat *Greenfly* ran aground on the left bank of the Euphrates about five miles north of the village of Khidr, which is situated well down the river towards Basra and about midway between the towns of Samawa and Nasiriyah. The crew of this craft put up a heroic resistance for more than fifty-four days before they were eventually overcome. During this time they were sustained entirely by supplies dropped from low flying aircraft. The natives of this area were almost entirely Marsh Arabs, a much more unpleasant type than the comparatively gentlemanly Bedouin.

The two officers concerned were actually dropping food on the gun-boat when their machine was brought down by rifle fire. They were unhurt in the crash-landing but were at once captured and marched off in the direction of Khidr. En-route the observer managed to break away from his captors and made a dash for the river, only to be shot down and killed. The unfortunate pilot was taken to the village where he was dismembered alive, starting with the finger and toe joints, relics later being distributed in the local bazaar. However, it was not long before nemesis overtook Khidr, which, in biblical language, 'was put to the sword'. A Ghurkha regiment made a very thorough job of killing every living being in the village and burning the place to the ground. In the latter part of the insurrection this treatment was meted out to a number of places in this locality, a line of action which produced results and earned the respect of the inhabitants of the area. The primitive or semi-civilised foe has nothing but contempt for kindly treatment – the fellow who wields the mailed fist with the utmost ruthlessness is the chap to be looked up to.

Looking at the more domestic side of things, important changes occurred during this summer of 1920. Wing Commander Boyd, OC of 31 Wing left for home, his place being taken by Wing Commander C S Burnett, a veteran of the South African War [1]. The new 'head man' came to us with a reputation for being a 'fire eater' and with 'Screaming Lizzie' as a nickname. He was certainly a man of martial bearing and a rather abrupt manner. He shook us all to the back teeth when he first inspected the squadron. However, he mellowed considerably on further acquaintance and in the years to come I was destined to serve under him again in his capacity as commandant of the Central Flying School, and finally as commander-in-chief, Flying Training Command. He was a man to compel both respect and affection.

Squadron Leader E A B Rice [2] arrived from England to take over 6 Squadron from George Pirie, who moved to wing HQ for the remainder of his overseas tour. Pirie was a remarkable man. We all had the impression he was a 'one man band' who required no adjutant or other subordinate to assist in the running of the squadron. It was even suggested that he carried all the squadron records, files, etc, in his pocket. He ultimately became Inspector General of the RAF and retired in 1951 as Air Chief Marshal, Sir George. Having reached such eminence, one would imagine he might now have been content to rest on his laurels and spend the rest of his days in quiet retirement. Not a bit of it. George Pirie, at the age of fifty-five, decided to launch forth on a new career, and became a barrister at law.

Before handing over the squadron he tackled me in the mess one morning in early July and said, "Greig, I want you to take over the job of mess secretary." He forthwith produced a book of sorts in which were kept the mess accounts and proceeded to go through the details with me. In those days there was no accountant or secretarial branch of the RAF, consequently things were at times inclined to be somewhat haphazard in what might be termed the quartermaster's department. Personally I had no knowledge of accounts, could barely add two and two together and knew nothing about catering. In other words – clueless. George explained the functions of the job to me in considerable detail and ended by saying: "You will see that the account is a little in the red, to the extent of about 300 rupees. Pull in your horns a bit and you should soon be on the credit side again." To this, 'Clueless' replied: "Very good, Sir. After all the debit only amounts to the equivalent of about £20, so it shouldn't take very long to square up such a trifling sum."

At the time of this general change over, C Flight was withdrawn from Bushire, so the strength of the mess was increased by a few bright characters: Reggie Smart [3], the only flight lieutenant in the squadron apart from Pirie; my old sailing companion, Jimmy Lawson, complete with piano, Rex Beach, Eric Wormell; and one or two others. Our tented camp was now a thing of the past and the new mess was in process of settling down. No attempt was made at creating a garden but we managed to get works services to provide a good mud-surfaced tennis court in front of the building.

For interior decoration, 'Ma' Briggs, who was a bit of an artist, painted an ornamental frieze, with an Eastern motif, around the walls of the ante-room. Not only was the mess building itself austere, but the furniture also. We had no easy chairs or chesterfields, every item being essentially 'hard-arsed'. This was probably just as well, because rough parties were almost the rule, seldom the exception, our Maltese carpenters gaining ample experience in furniture repair. Eventually, about a year later, a portion of the mess-room was partitioned off and fitted with heavy deal tables and benches, screwed to the floor and became known as the 'Drunk Hole' – a rather slanderous appellation.

Although the contrary might be the impression, I must emphasise that we were never what might be termed a bunch of inebriates and although some of the things we did might have been considered rather unwise, notably what Jimmy Lawson referred to as 'Gin-sling parties', held at mid-day during August when the thermometer was registering about 120 $^{\circ}$ in the shade, not one of us was ever unfit for duty as a result of over indulgence in alcoholic liquors. I mentioned earlier in this chapter that we were a wild bunch, well, it was a type of wildness which attracted all and sundry, so the mess soon became well known as a good place to visit.

This uproarious atmosphere might well have had some effect on the performance of my duties as mess secretary. Anyway, appreciating the sterling equivalent of my companions, I set about the task with a view to making mess life in this grim country as pleasant as possible, with the result that the urgent need for economy passed me completely by. When necessary I used to go shopping in Baghdad, taking our chef with me to make the purchase of fruit and vegetables, etc, from the native bazaars. He seemed to enjoy these expeditions and it did not occur to me that he might be making substantial rake-offs in true Eastern fashion, on every item purchased. I had a Service P & M motor cycle and sidecar, and took a delight in charging down the narrow alleys in the bazaar, scattering the natives in all directions.

Although Baghdad is a city of some million inhabitants, in those days it really only had one main thoroughfare, New Street (later Raschid St), that joined the north and south gates and ran parallel with the River Tigris. There were two pontoon bridges across the river, with access roads meeting New Street at right angles. One was named after General Maude [4], the captor of Baghdad in the 1914-18 war, the other was known at Kotah Bridge. Traffic from the south and west entered the city via Maude Bridge and left by the other, the pontoon bridge being only wide enough for single line traffic. Apart from New Street and the approach roads from the two bridges, the city was a maze of narrow alley-ways in which one could easily get lost. In wet weather Baghdad became a morass and motor transport frequently got bogged down to the axles in New Street.

In the course of my mess secretarial peregrinations I discovered quite a large general store off the bazaar to the south of New Street, that belonged to a French firm called Orosdi-Back. In the grocery section of this emporium were some delicious delicacies such as tinned ham and large tins of thick, juicy asparagus. Goody-goody, I thought, just what the doctor ordered, and forthwith laid in a large stock regardless of cost. These items were received with considerable acclaim and were made available for sale from the bar in addition to gracing the dining table on special occasions.

This blissful state of affairs went on through the summer. Whenever I went away on detachment I generally handed over some cash to any chap willing to undertake the shopping in my absence. I can't remember exactly when it was that it eventually dawned on me that I was really getting deeper into the financial mire, but by the time I went on a short period of detachment with A Flight, to Hillah, I was sufficiently het up to take the keys of the mess bar with me. This ridiculous subterfuge was to no avail, for Stuart Culley, to whom I had entrusted the mess, arrived in high dudgeon and almost within the hour, demanding the keys which I meekly relinquished.[5]

By sometime in October I had made the shattering discovery that far from liquidating the 300 rupee debt in the accounts, I had allowed it to increase to the overwhelming total of 3,000! Something drastic had to be done. I quickly owned up to the CO who called a general mess meeting. I made a clean breast of the whole affair and the assembled company received my distressing financial report with remarkable equanimity. I seem to remember that Jimmy Lawson made the first utterance with, "I say, this is a bit of a do isn't it? We'd better sell the old Joe-anna." The idea of the mess piano being sold struck horror into the hearts of the assembled company and was promptly quashed. In the discussion which followed I was very surprised at not receiving even a note of censure, let alone some other and deservedly merited penalty. In the end, the following decisions were arrived at:

– No action would be taken which would lower the standard of mess-
ing. To this end the daily charge would be raised.

– Each member of the mess would contribute the sum of £10 towards
the liquidation of the debt.

– Any new arrivals in the squadron would also, if it were still necessary,
contribute the sum of £10 on becoming a member of the mess. No ob-
jections to this contribution would, in any circumstances, be tolerated.
So that was that, and in due course someone else took on this onerous
task. I did say at the outset that they were a jolly good bunch of chaps
in No.6, and this illustrates the point.

I have also mentioned the addition of a few bright characters in the
mess, following the withdrawal of C Flight from Bushire. I regret to
say that I nearly forgot to include a most important member, a four-
legged one at that – 'Jane' our squadron mascot.

Jane, a dog of doubtful ancestry who might well be described as a
'Dachsealyham', was a truly wonderful character. She was short in the
leg, long in the body, colour white with one brown patch, and a smooth
coat. A dreadful snob, the only building she would patronise being the
officer's mess and quarters. I am sure she knew everyone individually
and regularly studied routine orders. If anyone had been away on detachment, Jane seemed to know about it and was quick to run forward
with a wagging tail to welcome their return. She lorded it over other
mess dogs, so 'Spider', 'Bruno' and 'Lion' took rank and precedence
far below that of the undisputed queen.

However, Jane had one serious fault, the production of pups with
monotonous regularity and with the minimum lapse of time between
successive litters. These events invariably took place in Jimmy Lawson's
bath-tub, Jimmy being her immediate boss. In an attempt to induce a
pause in operations, Jimmy had some calico drawers made and fitted
at the proper time. It made not the slightest difference and to quote
Jimmy, 'drawers and all' was the appropriate term.

Fifteen years after these events, when I was once more serving in
the Middle East, I received an invitation to attend the 'coming of age'

celebration of 6 Squadron, which at the time, was stationed at Ismailia, on the Suez Canal. When we entered the mess dining room that evening, I casually cast my eye over the various trophies on the table. At the very centre was a highly polished 20 lb Cooper bomb mounted on a plinth. Thinking this was probably an inter-flight or squadron bombing trophy, I wandered over to read the inscription on the silver plaque on the plinth. It read:

> *THIS BOMB CONTAINS THE ASHES OF*
> *JANEY*
> *No. 6 (AC) SQUADRON DOG*
> *JOINED THE SQUADRON IN FRANCE 1918*
> *REMAINED WITH THE SQUADRON IN BELGIUM*
> *AND IRAQ UNTIL JULY 16th 1926*
> *DIED JULY 16th 1926*
> *PRODUCED 96 PUPS*
> *ATTENDED ALL FUNCTIONS WITH 'AERO SIX'*

Ed Rice, the new CO, was not a 'new broom', and took his time settling down and did not throw his weight about. Although he did little flying, he was a good mixer and quickly became popular. He was, moreover, able technically and clever with his hands, a fact which had some influence on an off duty activity which emerged in the Squadron at this time – the re-building of derelict cars and motor cycles. I stress this point as I cannot recall any similar activity among the members of 30 Squadron, our close neighbour.

This interest originated in the discovery of an enormous dump of surplus material left over from the Great War, a veritable mountain of rusting metal just off the Bund Road, north of Baghdad and close to the tomb of the Prophet Omar. I remember spending man hours, rather like a rag and bone man, sorting over frames, wheels, engines and other accessories, until I had accumulated sufficient parts to assemble one Douglas motor cycle. This process was repeated and in time two Triumph machines joined the Douglas. The average cost of such a machine worked out at about 150 rupees – roughly £10 at the then rate of exchange.

Work benches and tools were taken on loan from unit workshops and erected under the verandah of our quarters. It was not long before we could muster between us four or five good machines and about three Model-T Ford cars. Great pride in workmanship prevailed all round, and Reggie Smart's Triumph become a masterpiece of scraping and buffing in the brilliance of crank case, gear box and cylinder. The best however was a rebuilt Ford and put together with modifications by Ed Rice.

Early in this summer of 1920 we made the acquaintance of two chaps from other services who were destined to have some influence on our future activities. Kendall, a gunner subaltern who had served in the RFC, and Captain Barton, an engineer of the Indian Army who was also an official on our local railway. Kendall was a very fine trap drummer and was largely instrumental in the formation of the 6 Squadron Officer's Dance Band. Other members were Lawson (piano), Smart (saxophone) and Briggs (banjo). When Kendall eventually left the locality, his place in the band was taken by Ralph Sorley. This band became very popular and performed at nearly all the dances held in the cantonment, when such functions were possible.

Barton was a cheerful and hospitable chap whose Indian chef produced curries which removed the lining of one's throat. He flew with us a great deal and soon became known as our 'unofficial observer'.

Towards the end of June the scale of Arab attacks was stepped up vigorously. The railway between Baghdad and Basra was severed in many places and bridges destroyed. Then the city of Rumaitha, a small place on the Euphrates, with a garrison of about 500 men, was besieged. At one railway station further to the south, it was found that the insurgents had, with a macabre sense of humour, laid out the station staff in line on the down platform and in strict order of seniority, with all their throats cut.

The Rumaitha garrison occupied a serai (square fort) near the centre of the town. Early in July aircraft observed distress signals by popham panels (a system of white ground strips laid out in accordance with a specified code), that indicated that they urgently needed food and ammunition. Supplies were dropped from the air, a tricky operation entailing very low flying. Low slow flying aircraft provided an excellent target for the 5,000 or so Arabs investing the serai. Some packages missed their target and were recovered later, one being found to have struck a sepoy on the head, killing him instantly.

A few days later food became desperately short, so a raid on the bazaar by the garrison was organised, with a covering force of aircraft carrying out diversionary bombing and machine gunning of the town, except for the immediate area of the bazaar. This operation proved highly successful, the garrison obtaining enough food to last them out for the remainder of the siege. Had it failed they would have been compelled to surrender, with a probable massacre as a consequence. The actual garrison casualties during the siege amounted to about 150 killed, missing and wounded. Ground to air communication throughout this effort was by panel code and message-dropping by aircraft.

At the time of this event, 6 Squadron was not fully equipped with the new Bristols, so consequently I found myself as a very junior officer, compelled to fly as an observer/gunner to one of the more senior chaps. We were operating from Diwaniya, a town a few miles upstream from Rumaitha, and my pilot was Flying Officer Ffoulkes-Jones [6], a real 'indeed to goodness' Welshman from Llangollen. Ffoulkes was a delightful chap, but I regret to say he scared the daylights out of me in the six sorties we made during the foraging action. Flying at an unnecessarily low altitude – just missing the roof tops – I could practically identify the types of firearms levelled at us, a mixture of modern rifles and the old fashioned Jeszail, a thing with a rather small yet fancy butt. It had a very long barrel similar to a length of gas piping, which discharged anything from lead slugs to rusty nails in our direction. Judging by some of the jagged holes we collected in various parts of our aircraft, the latter type of projectile seemed to have found favour for anti-aircraft work.

Many months later, I plucked up the courage to take Ffoulkes to task for his low flying stunts at Rumaitha. "It might have been good fun for you," I said, "and a bit foolhardy, but I thought you were obviously very courageous so did not dare to ask you to fly higher, in case you thought me windy." "Good Lord," he replied, "I was scared stiff too, but because I was carrying another pilot as my observer, I thought I had better put up a good show, so as not to give you a bad impression!" We enjoyed a good laugh over this revelation.

In August the trouble spread to the north of Baghdad and the railway to the Persian frontier at Khanikin was put out of action. This meant the cessation of all normal means of surface communication with our forces in north-west Persia, including a very large hill station and rest camp at Karind. This was a delightful spot situated at an altitude of about 4,500 feet above sea level, at which all the service's families were spending the summer. We were well and truly cut off by the Arab rebels to the south and the Bolsheviks to the north. However, there was no danger of attack, ample supplies were held and in any event the garrison was more than adequate for almost any contingency which might arise.

Karind had no airfield but it was decided to establish a temporary air link with Baghdad, using the garrison's polo field as a landing ground. That old warhorse the RE8 was considered the most suitable machine for landing on this restricted area and it fell to my lot to do the first trip. In addition to mail, I carried spares for one of our Crossley tenders which had taken two of our officers, Culley and Glaisher [7], up to Karind to recuperate from wounds received in action some time previously.

The news of this air mail service travelled swiftly through the Bagdad cantonment, with the result that, in addition to official mail, I found myself landed with many letters for private delivery. I duly took off on the morning of 31st August and arrived at Karind two and a half hours later. I remember distinctly my engine seemed to be running very rough for the duration of the flight over hostile territory. However, as soon as I entered the Pip Tak Pass, running through the Persian mountains, and had left those horrid Arabs with their long knives far behind, the engine ran as sweetly as a sewing machine. It is remarkable what tricks one's imagination can get up to.

On arrival I handed over the official mail to John Glaisher who had established himself as local RAF commandant, then set off on a private delivery round to the families' rest camp. I found myself to be very welcome at each tent and had to partake of hospitality in the form of a bottle of Bass or a nice cool John Collins. What with the mountain air and scenery, and these drinks inside me, I thought Karind a simply wonderful place. But I had been briefed to return to Baghdad the following day, and to carry out a reconnaissance on the way.

On 7th September I did my only other trip to Karind. On this occasion, in addition to mail I had to convey a sack containing three lakhs of rupees (300,000) in paper money for the Imperial Bank of Persia. On arrival I dumped the sack at John Glaisher's feet, asked him to deliver it to the local bank manager or whoever it was, then set out on another Bass and John Collins round. On my return to Baghdad the next day, the bank authorities were quite put out because I hadn't bothered to obtain a receipt for their precious sack – as if anyone would want to bother about such a trifling amount of £20,000.

When rail and road communications were eventually re-established, all service families were brought down from Karind and repatriated, either to India or England. Thenceforth, service families in Mespot were barred, as the political situation, plus the climate, was considered both unsuitable and an unnecessary risk.

Operations continued fairly uneventfully and on 17th September most of us had a day off. After a pleasant lunchtime session we retired to our room for a siesta. This, however, was rudely disturbed by the sound of a fire tender arriving with a great clanging of bells and hooting of klaxons. My flight commander, Ralph Sorley, burst into my room exclaiming: "Turn out the fire brigade, Carpenter has just landed from a recce and has reported that Sheik Dhari has been spotted in the desert a few miles north of Akkar Kuf and heading out into the blue. All available aircraft will be bombed-up by the time we get to the hangars."

A few days earlier, Colonel Leachman, a man renowned in the world of Arab affairs and a close collaborator with the famous Gertrude Bell, had been murdered at Khan Nucta, a serai situated roughly midway between Baghdad and Fellujah. The details of the murder were somewhat obscure, but Leachman was parleying with Dhari when someone must have spoken out of turn and the story goes that he was shot in the back by one of Dhari's sons. Leachman was, in fact, accepting Dhari's hospitality at the time, so, quite apart from any other aspect, the affair was deplorable, as a flagrant infringement of the Arab code of hospitality. Dhari and his followers had immediately gone into hiding.

The squadron was soon on its way to the reported pinpoint and it was not long before we spotted the column of about a hundred camels, heading north west. They were in flat desert without a vestige of cover. The first bomb caused a stampede which rendered the riders virtually powerless and we flew back and forth at nought feet dealing out havoc and destruction with the utmost impunity. I felt desperately sorry for the unfortunate camels, but that was the last we heard of Sheik Dhari.

I had known Colonel Leachman slightly, as he had been my passenger on a flight to Anah three months previously and found him a charming chap. The mention of Arab affairs reminds me that there was a young officer named Glubb in Mespot at that time, who was destined ultimately to make a great name for himself in this field [8].

At the time of the foregoing events we had acquired a new neighbour in addition to 30 Squadron, in the form of 84 Squadron. Reformed a little over a month earlier, they shared the camp site but were, owing to lack of other accommodation, living under canvas. Bill Sowrey of 30 Squadron eventually became its commanding officer. They were equipped with DH9a aircraft. At the end of September, 55 Squadron arrived at Baghdad from Constantinople, so further tentage mushroomed into existence. All this meant an increase in 'get together' parties when opportunity so favoured.

This oddly enough brings me to the subject of fireworks. It was found that the bomb and pyrotechnic store at the airfield contained an immense number of things of interest to those keen on Guy Fawkes displays. There seemed to be an inexhaustible supply of two ounce bags of black gunpowder for operating puff targets, a synthetic device used for training in artillery observation, miles of Bickford fuse, Verey lights, rockets and finally, a type of star shell fired from a compressed cardboard or papier mâché mortar. These shells were propelled aloft by a small charge of gunpowder and then burst into a cluster of three or more coloured lights which descended earthwards attached to a small paper parachute.

As if to add to our mischief-making potentialities, some misguided person in authority presented 6 Squadron and the Aircraft Park with trophies of the late war, in the form of two pairs of Turkish field guns of about the same calibre as the British 25-pounder, possibly a bit smaller. One of the four still had a breech-block, but minus its firing pin. This gun, luckily, found its way to our mess. During the ensuing two years much fun and some ill-feeling resulted from the possession of these hostile weapons.

Shortly after 55 had got themselves settled in, and their aircraft unpacked and assembled, news got around that they were going to hold a 'Dining In' night in the officer's mess, which consisted of two adjoining marquees. Such functions are parades involving compulsory attendance of all mess members, with much attention to ceremonial etc – really upstage. This was to be quite a family affair, no outsiders invited. We, in 6 Squadron, took a poor view of this and decided on a little 'surprise' visit to 55's mess shortly after their dinner had got underway. Each member of our squadron raiding party was armed with a mortar star shell outfit with the exception of Jimmy Lawson, who carried a trombone. The plan involved a stealthy approach to the mess, which would then be surrounded by mortars and at a given signal trombone blast from Jimmy, all fuses were to be touched off. Following this salvo we were to enter the mess and pay our respects to their CO.

Everything went off splendidly. A series of shattering explosions and the sky filled with descending coloured lights. By some remarkable fluke not a single tent was set alight. We then entered the marquee and as none of us knew the CO, a bow was made to the most distinguished-looking officer present, an apparently elderly, bald headed and somewhat astonished chap at the end of the table. This turned out to be none other than a 'squadron character', Flying Officer 'Daddy' Lochner. I'm afraid that all ceremony attending that dinner went by the board and the evening ended with 55 back in our mess, one of their flight commanders – R S Maxwell – seated at Jimmy's piano singing the most remarkable series of rude songs that I had ever heard [9].

A few days later Maxwell's Ninac was shot down. Another pilot, Flying Officer Lloyd Evans, followed him down, landed alongside the crippled bomber and literally snatched Maxwell and his observer from under the noses of the enemy. Maxwell rode back on the bottom plane of the Ninac, his observer sharing the rear cockpit with his opposite number [10].

By now considerable progress had been made against the insurgents and rail communication with Basra re-established. The repair train through from the south had had a hectic journey, the crew having to replace dislodged track, repair bridges, etc. For some distance between

Diwaniya and Hillah the track, in addition to having been dislodged had been removed altogether. To get the train through, the repair team had to pick up sections behind the train and relay them in front, repeating this procedure until clear of the damaged area.

To ensure no further interference with the railroad, a continuous series of sandbag block-houses were erected at regular intervals of about a mile, each being occupied by a small detachment of Indian troops. The pilots of 6 Squadron thenceforth made a regular practice when flying between the landing ground at Hillah and Baghdad, a distance of about sixty-five miles, of contour chasing just clear of the track. The sentries on patrol duty at the block-houses regarded our aircraft as 'armed parties', a very reasonable deduction and presented arms to each aeroplane as it flew by. We, in turn, solemnly acknowledged the compliment by saluting in conventional manner from our open cockpits! The whole procedure was quite amusing. As we passed one sentry with rifle at the 'present', the sentry at the next block-house could be seen going through the preliminary movements. I am quite sure that the sepoys enjoyed these unusual formalities just as much as we did.

[1] Later Air Chief Marshal Sir Charles Stuart Burnett KCB CBE DSO. South African War 1900-02, West Africa 1904-07, RFC 1914, WW1 then Iraq 1920. Became AOC British Forces in Iraq. Seconded to RAAF as chief of staff until retirement in 1943. Died in 1945 aged sixty-three.

[2] Later Air Vice-Marshal Sir Edward Arthur Beckton Rice KBE MC. Soldier and airman in WW1, he won the MC in 1917. A career officer he served in Iraq and Egypt post-war, and in WW2 was with Bomber Command. Retired in 1946 but sadly died at the early age of fifty-four in April 1948.

[3] Actually Harry George Smart DFC. REs and RFC in WW1. He was awarded his DFC after twenty-seven low bombing raids against Arab insurgents in 1921. Commanded CFS in 1935. By 1939 he was an Air Commodore OBE AFC, and SASO on the staff of 12 Group, Fighter Command. Retired in September 1945; died in June 1963.

[4] General Sir Frederick S Maude who took command in August 1916.

[5] Flying Officer S D Culley DSO had shot down the Zeppelin L53 on 11 Au-

gust 1918, flying a Sopwith Camel. This Camel survives today and can be seen hanging in the Imperial War Museum, Lambeth, London.

[6] By 1936, Edwin Jocelyn Ffoulkes-Jones had risen to squadron leader, retiring at the end of WW2 as a wing commander.

[7] Became Wing Commander John Malcolm Glaisher DFC in 1938. He had been decorated in 1918 during a bombing mission and a battle with German fighters.

[8] Later Lt-General Sir John B Glubb KCB, CMG, DSO, OBE, MC. Wounded three times in WW1 with the REs. Eventually became Chief of the General Staff of the Arab Legion, 1939-56.

[9] Reginald Stuart Maxwell MC DFC had been a fighter pilot in WW1, in 1918 commanding 54 Squadron in France. In 1921 he received a Bar to his DFC while serving in Iraq. In 1929 he received the AFC and in 1936 was a group captain. During WW2 he served with the Royal Navy as a Lt-commander. Died in 1960.

[10] Dudley Lloyd Evans MC DFC had also served as a fighter pilot in WW1. This rescue took place on 1 November 1920, for which Evans received a Bar to his DFC.

4

NOT ALL WORK, BUT SOME PLAY

On 18th October 1920, our flight, with Ralph Sorley in command, went on detachment, to take part in operations following the relief of Kufa, which had taken place the previous day. Kufa was a small town on the Hindiyah branch of the Euphrates and not far from the Holy City of Najaf. It had withstood a siege that lasted for eighty-nine days in extremely hot weather. The garrison was in a serai on the right bank of the river, and as with the siege of Rumaitha, inter-communication ground to air had been by panel and message dropping. Throughout the whole period of the siege, aircraft had been employed in dropping food, ammunition, medical requirements, newspapers, private mail, cigarettes, etc., to the hard-pressed soldiers, thus giving a much needed boost to their morale.

An earlier attempt to relieve Kufa had misfired rather badly. Troops of the Manchester Regiment, plus details from other units, had set out from Hillah, but were ambushed during a dust storm near Birs Numrud, the site of the legendary Tower of Babel. Nearly 200 men were killed,

170 taken prisoner to Najaf and a great deal of equipment lost. At the end of the rebellion I witnessed the return of these captives and am glad to say they had been reasonably well cared for.

Some enterprising Arabs hauled a captured 25-pounder field gun to the left bank of the Euphrates at Kufa, and aimed it at the beleaguered garrison in the serai. Moored alongside this serai was the gunboat *Gadfly*. The Arabs had only a rudimentary knowledge of the working of the gun, but took aim at the boat by looking down the barrel before inserting the round. They were successful in firing two or three shells before something happened that gummed-up the works. One of the shells hit *Gadfly*, setting her on fire, and she immediately became a serious menace to the garrison, owing to the risk of fire exploding the vessel's magazine. It therefore became necessary to scuttle the boat with all speed. The crew had not been on board, but this urgent problem was solved by aiming a machine gun at a point just below the water line and pumping thousands of rounds of precious .303 ammunition through the steel plating. The garrison, meantime, kept their fingers firmly crossed. Fortunately this expedient was successful and the gunboat eventually settled onto the bottom, her deck and superstructure still above the water, but she had taken on enough water to douse the fire.

The Kufa incident afforded a fine example of the use of aircraft in the support of ground forces and also the maintenance of communications between the CinC and the garrison, as well as bombing and machine-gunning points in front of the advancing relief force. Our flight detachment operated from Hillah for nine days, harassing the enemy by frequent bombing and strafing attacks until his nerve centre was eventually concentrated at Abu Sukhair and Jaarah, about sixty miles south of Hillah. We returned to Baghdad on 26th October to prepare for the knockout blow.

One thing I shall never forget about the camp at Hillah was the mosquitoes, real man-eaters, which attacked with such ferocity at sundown that we were compelled to burn paper and wood shavings in our tents before turning in for the night. From a personal point of view the period was noteworthy for the fact that I had for the first time my own Bristol Fighter – D7888 – and did not have to share it with another pilot. It was an outstanding machine. When I took her on a test after being assembled, on 6th September, she simply roared up to over 17,000 feet.

One very unusual incident happened a day or two before our return to Baghdad, concerning Sorley who had had some minor trouble with his Bristol. After rectification he prepared to take off on a short test flight, with ballast in the rear seat in lieu of a passenger. The engine had already been run-up, so Ralph climbed aboard, and Corporal Viggars, his rigger, thinking that Ralph would once more check the running of the engine, stretched himself, as was usual procedure, across the fuselage in front of the tail fin, to help keep the tail section firmly on the ground. Instead, Ralph merely waved away the chocks and as there was a clear run into the wind straight ahead, opened the throttle and took off. On becoming airborne, he began to wonder if Viggers had put too much ballast in the rear seat area, for the Bristol was amazingly tail-heavy. He needed both hands on the stick to keep the machine in a normal flying attitude. Upon reaching 1,000 feet, he peered round and to his utter astonishment, he spotted his rigger, astride the tail, with both feet on the leading edge of the elevators and hanging on grimly to the fin bracing wires. Ralph gingerly completed a circuit and landed successfully, with Viggers none the worse for his trying experience.

On our return to Baghdad we were informed that an attempt at a final onslaught upon the insurgent's cracking morale, was to be made by bombing his HQ at Abu Sukhair and Jaarah by night. In those days night flying was still regarded as a rather specialist job, so three pilots of the squadron, who had some previous night flying experience, Reggie Smart, Ralph and myself, were selected for the job. On the day following our return from Hillah, 27th October, I flew down to the target accompanied by the wing photographic officer, who took vertical photographs of the two practically adjoining towns and their approaches, from a height of 12,000 feet.

On the evening of the 28th, we got in some night flying practice – just circuits and bumps – with Jimmy Lawson taking on the job of organising the paraffin flares, a quite superfluous quantity of pyrotechnics and a refreshment bar located adjacent to No.1 flare. There was an air of novelty about the whole procedure which became quite a social occasion except for those vitally concerned.

The night raids were carried out, one on each night of the 20th and 31st, bombs being released over the towns. In order to avoid any risk of running out of fuel, we flew down to Hillah by day, filled right up with petrol and took off after dark at the appropriate time. The two raids took two and a half and two and three quarters hours respectively. Barton, the 'unofficial observer' flew with Reggie on the first raid and with me on the second. The weather was perfect on each occasion and the target visible for miles, the extent of the camp fires indicating that the men at the receiving end of the raid were in no way expecting trouble.

As we approached Baghdad after each raid, it was clearly evident that Jimmy was determined that we should not miss the airfield through lack of illumination. From a distance of at least thirty miles, one could see his 'Brock's Benefit' – rockets, coloured lights, flares – the lot. Well, these modest night excursions had the desired effect and the insurgents very shortly afterwards threw in their hand. Apart from one or two demonstration flights and the odd mopping up, peace was once more restored. Between the end of October and New Year's Eve, I only took part in two bombing raids, one demonstration flight and one long distance reconnaissance.

Throughout the rebellion we experienced no serious trouble in the immediate vicinity of Baghdad. The wrecking of the rail line came to within about fifteen miles of the city, certainly no nearer that I can recollect. During a dust storm one night a small raiding party broke through the wire near our quarters, looted a room or two and got swiftly away again. Their booty included 'Ma' Briggs' white pony which, luckily was recovered the next day. Although nobody was hurt, we were all extremely angry. For about a week following this incident, I slept on the roof of my hut, complete with Aldis lamp, a ground Lewis gun and my Mauser rifle, in the hope of bagging a Bedouin, but I was out of luck. It was a case of shutting the stable door after the horse had bolted.

One afternoon in early November John Glaisher came into the mess after a return flight from Basra and informed us that while he was re-fuelling at Kut el Amara, two odd specimens had come up to offer a hand, saying that they were just out from England and on their way to 6 Squadron. Our mess, by this time, was a very close-knit and happy family, and our reaction to this news was one of resentment. What the hell did we want a couple of new boys for? We'd show 'em. The following day, Flying Officers V C Cordingley and A E Beilby reported in. Apart from a slightly frigid welcome, the newcomers were flabbergasted by an immediate demand for a contribution of £10 towards the liquidation fund of the mess debt incurred by me a short time earlier. Their protests were of no avail and they just had to fork out. A few days later we all decided that perhaps they weren't such bad chaps after all and accepted them wholeheartedly into our family.

Arthur Edward Beilby, a very tall and thin streak of a man became one of our characters and was known as either 'String' or 'Long John'. He eventually became a very close friend of mine until his untimely death from chronic leukaemia, in May 1937 [1].

Earlier I referred to my personal, outstanding, Bristol Fighter. I now held that it was by far the best machine in the squadron. This assertion aroused the ire of Stuart Culley, a very dashing pilot in B Flight, who maintained that his machine was far the better of the two. We put each other on trust not to cheat and carried out test climbs and flat-out runs at ground level. On the climbs my machine beat Culley's by 1,000 feet, reaching 20,500 against his 19,500. Our level speeds were about the same, roughly 110 mph. There was not much to choose between them, both were exceptional.

Until the end of the year we enjoyed a period of relaxation, with mess parties galore. Somehow or other I acquired a reputation for being an expert on pyrotechnics and I was quite hard pressed to live up to this. However, with the exercise of a little ingenuity in the use of the materials available, I got by quite well, once I got over the problem of getting the old Turkish field gun up and running. The mechanism was well and truly rusted but yielded eventually after many applications of penetrating oil. Owing to the lack of a firing pin and blank ammunition the gun could only be operated in the manner of an old fashioned cannon, the charge being rammed down the barrel and fired by the insertion of a length of Bickford fuse through the breech-block. It invariably had to be fired on guest nights, birthday parties and so forth. The preparation of suitable charges frequently took the best part of a day, and the contents of star shells, Verey cartridges, etc, having to be rendered down in order to produce just the right colour for flash and so on.

My early attempts at making roman candles frequently became near disasters. The first and not very ambitious effort was loaded in an empty mortar case which was placed on one of our dining table chairs. It failed to function and simply detonated instead, mortar and chair both disappearing! I made a further one out of an aeroplane exhaust pipe, and fortunately, especially after the first showing, everyone took cover before firing. Stage one fired quite well but stage two could not quite make it and the pipe blew up. My researches in this field were well before their time, for I am sure today I would have been well qualified for a job at Cape Kennedy.

One of my other outstanding efforts, owing to its simplicity, concerned one of the chaps who used a very strong, circular, galvanised iron tub as a hip bath. It was about two feet deep, three feet across the open end and tapered slightly towards the base. Moreover, the rim was reinforced by a fairly wide flange. With the tub inverted, this flange made a flush fit on level ground – just the job for a ballistic missile. After further research, I found the ideal propellant to be a two ounce bag of black gunpowder fired by fuse. Bickford fuse had the outstanding merit of a constant burning speed of about four seconds to the inch, so one could therefore time a 'launching' to a nicety, to coincide with the arrival of a distinguished visitor, or some other solemn event. The launching of the tub was really quite impressive, as well as startling. The noise made on take-off was the kind of very loud 'zump'. The tub then sailed vertically into the air on a column of smoke, to a height of about thirty feet before losing impetus and crashing back to earth. To the unsuspecting passer-by, this amazing phenomenon could be a shattering experience, but giving great joy to those in on the act.

It must be pointed out that none of us at this time was completely au fait with normal peacetime service routine, consequently the CO decided that at guest nights, due observance must be made to correct ceremonial, with grace before being seated down to dine, the loyal toast, and so on. For the following guest night, therefore, the CO decided that on this occasion, for instructional purposes, he would occupy the mess president's chair, the vice president being chum Culley.

Ed Rice gave us a thorough briefing on procedure for the loyal toast, he striking the table, rising to his feet with glass in hand, to announce in a loud voice, "Mr Vice – the King." The vice would then rise and respond with, "Gentlemen – the King."

The dinner went according to plan until the loyal toast part. Ed Rice dutifully rose at the appropriate time, his voice ringing loud and clear, "Mr Vice – the King." Friend Culley, presumably caught unawares, looked startled but leapt to his feet and called, "Mr Rice – the King." I cannot quite recall what happened in the resulting uproar, but it was probably the usual penalty for such miscreant deeds, being crowned with half a very ripe water-melon, pushed firmly down over the recipient's ears, presenting a most inspiring spectacle.

A further means of recreation now lay in the open desert, and we ranged far and wide with our 'pack' of Ford motor cars and motor bikes. Between Baghdad and Baquba to the north, also to the east beyond Ctsiphon, the desert was hard and flat with the exception of the odd outcrop of sand-hills. On Saturday afternoons or Sunday, now that the hot weather had gone, these outings combined with picnic parties were really very enjoyable. A popular sport was hunting jackal and gazelle, the hunters being mounted on motor bikes and armed with revolvers. I regret to say that I was a leading spirit in this ruthless pastime. Today, the very thought of ever having done such a thing fills me with revulsion. Our prey, owing to the flatness of the terrain, was usually first sighted at some considerable distance, resulting in a long chase. On overtaking we would take a 'no deflection pot shot' from alongside the unfortunate animals. On sunny days a curious mirage effect was often discernible on first sighting a herd of gazelle, as they would appear to have enormously long legs and to be running in the middle of a shimmering lake. The only redeeming feature of this so-called sport lay in the fact that, in modern RAF parlance, it was a 'dicey' form of amusement, particularly in the case of gazelle which could run at a steady 40-45 mph and swerve and double back in the most amazing fashion in their endeavour at evasive action. On one of these outings I was in the act of shooting, when out of the corner of my eye I spotted a trench line, a relic of the late war, directly in my path. The fact that my bike was going flat-out saved the situation, as a very slight ramp at the edge of the trench shot the machine sufficiently into the air to clear the open gash in the ground. The gazelle is such a graceful and harmless creature, I can only blame our beastly persecution on to the hunting instincts inherited from primitive times, or merely a desire to show what clever chaps we were.

On 9th December, Narry Essel [2], one of the 'old brigade' due for a posting home, was detailed to fly a government official, I believe his name was Garbett, up to Kirkuk. Early that afternoon a signal came in from a levy outpost at a place called Tauk, a few miles south of Kirkuk, that an aeroplane had crashed there and that medical assistance was urgently required. It fell to me to fly Doc. Canton up there, the intention being to land at Kirkuk and get the political officer there to drive us to Tauk. By the time I took off I realised that we would be very hard pressed in getting to Kirkuk, a town in a region completely unfamiliar to me, before dark. A little over two hours later, and in gathering dusk, I spotted the crashed Bristol, so decided to land in the immediate vicinity, rather than risk landing in near darkness on a strange landing ground devoid of night flying facilities. We were in foothill country, much different from the flat desert to the south and west. Moreover, the land seemed to be fairly well cultivated.

In the half light I selected a field which seemed all right, but I fluffed the approach and overshot. I opened the throttle to clear the far boundary, but the ground at the other side of the hedge seemed passable. I made a snap decision, closed the throttle again and landed somewhat roughly on a field which had obviously been under the plough about a year previously. All was well, so we picketed the machine down head to wind and walked to the outpost. Narry was dead. For some reason unknown he had attempted a landing on a good stretch of ground but unfortunately his wheels had struck a small eminence, turning the machine very sharply over into its back, breaking his neck. The passenger had got away with a broken arm and had been taken to Kirkuk.

Doc. Canton and I dossed in a small tent, our slumbers being rudely disturbed by a pack of jackals which broke into song just outside – a weird sound very similar to the howling of the North American coyote. The following morning we flew on to Kirkuk where Narry was buried that afternoon. We stayed the night and flew back to Baghdad next day. Narry's death cast a gloom over the squadron. He had been a very vital person, good looking and always bubbling over with fun. Perhaps the 'Director of Celestial Postings' had need of his services elsewhere.

Before saying farewell to 1920, I might devote a little time to describing my first Christmas overseas. In the RAF the very nature of our work fosters a great spirit of comradeship between the men who actually fly the aircraft and those responsible for their maintenance, from the chief of the air staff down to the humblest aircraft hand, all are cogs in a machine. To give a detailed account of every NCO and man in the unit would more than fill a chapter as well as taxing one's memory. Taking our Flights A, B and C, in sequence, our flight sergeants, Wilson, Tuckey and Williams, were splendid fellows. Wilson had a beautiful voice and was consequently much in demand for concert parties. I did not have much personal contact with the other two, but Tuckey eventually retired as a wing commander (engineering) [3]. A junior NCO I remember well was Corporal Burfield, one of our riggers, who was also an artist of no mean ability. All our individual whims regarding flight identification marks and other designs, were met by Burfield. He designed a squadron crest consisting of the number six with an Albatros flying through it, also our Christmas card. On the fin of my Bristol he painted an excellent copy of my family crest.

The set routine for Christmas Day invariably follows this sequence. The officers call on the senior NCOs who do their utmost to ensure that their guests are at least a little unsteady on their feet before departure. The officers and senior NCOs then go on to the airmen's mess to serve the dinner. Those officers who survive the total ordeal then have to face their own repast, generally fairly late in the afternoon.

On this particular occasion the officers thought that, as a gesture of good will to the airmen, a gift of fruit would not be out of place. We therefore armed ourselves with baskets of oranges and apples and off we went to the cookhouse. After entering the dining hall and upon reaching a fairly central position, we proceeded to lob the fruit to the men seated at the tables. They all obviously thought, 'By George, this is a cracking good game,' retrieved the fruit and began throwing it back at us as hard as they could. Although taken aback by this turn of events, the spirit of the 'game' quickly caught on and a 'free-for-all' followed. In a few minutes the dining hall was reduced to a shambles, with broken windows and crockery galore, and everyone slipping and sliding about on the squashed fruit – all very wasteful but oh so enjoyable.

In the course of time, what time I haven't the foggiest notion, we arrived back at our own mess and in no fit state to face turkey and plum pudding. I can recollect arriving at the mess on my motor bike, with my rigger on the carrier, and riding straight into the building, did a couple of circuits round the table, much to the detriment of chairs and furniture. I suppose I must eventually have reached a glorious state of complete exhaustion, for I can remember no further incident.

Boxing Day – Oh dear, Oh dear, what a schemozzle! We were battered and worn, with the village blacksmith hard at work on each individual forehead. The senior NCOs were due to call on our mess at noon and after lunch we were to play them at football in fancy dress. It was raining in torrents and had been the whole previous night. The world suddenly seemed a very grim place. However, such is the resilience of youth, the 'hair of the dog' at about 11 am put us all in fine fettle and we welcomed our guests with considerable gusto. A very convivial morning was followed by an enormous lunch, followed by immediate adjournment to the football field, arrayed in a fantastic variety of garments.

The field was virtually a morass, much of the surface being inundated. Despite the appalling weather, we had a fine turn out of spectators. It was understood that the game was to be strictly in accordance with the 'Marquis of Queensbury's Rules', with no holds barred. Both teams were allowed unlimited reserves. Barton, our unofficial observer, turned up to play for our side. The game while it lasted was indescribably funny, the ground being so slippery it was almost impossible to remain upright. We had a referee who, poor chap, was set upon by both sides whenever he attempted to blow his whistle. Owing to the unusual exercise immediately following a heavy and hearty lunch, members of both teams retired with monotonous regularity to the touch line, to be sick. Others were carried off, hors de combat, their places being taken by anyone willing to chance their arm. At the end of about half an hour, the result was declared a draw, honour all round having been fully satisfied.

So ended the Christmas festivities. I think I must have been suffering from delayed concussion for the next few days, as I have simply no recollection of Hogmanay, a dreadful admission for a Scot. The year 1920 was at last over, the end of my third year in the service, a period which started in the RFC and witnessed the birth of the RAF. Three down, twenty-six to go.

[1] Arthur Beilby was D'Arcy Greig's best man at his wedding in 1930.

[2] Flying Officer Robert Narcissus Essel, was twenty-one years old. He was the son of Colonel F K Essel CMG of Bevere Knoll, Worcs. He was later interred in Baghdad (North Wall) Cemetery.

[3] Wing Commander J H Tuckey, commissioned in 1935, S/Ldr 1942, retired in 1946.

5

A YEAR OF CONTRASTS

The year 1921 started with an unwelcome assignment. An air display had been planned for Friday, 7th January, with all sorts of contests, races, and landing competitions. I had high hopes myself of pulling off an event or two with my redoubtable Bristol Fighter.

The display was really quite an ambitious affair which even included a 'beauty competition' for aircraft. However, the day before this event was to be held, orders came through for a special bombing mission to be undertaken by 55 Squadron on the 7th and moreover, a specific instruction from the wing commander that I was to fly as a guide and observer in the leading aircraft, the target being the fort at Rawa.

Rawa is a town on the Euphrates facing the village of Anah, where I had spent my first period of detachment the previous year. The fort was on a lofty promontory jutting out into the river which, at this point, was very wide. The town had for a long time been suspect as a place of refuge for rebels and other undesirable characters and information had now come through that the fort had indeed been taken over by a

gang long overdue for elimination. Wing HQ made it clear that it was
especially important that the bombing be confined to the fort alone.
The fact that I knew the locality really well was probably the reason for
my selection for this job, although I'm sure that 55 would have done
just as well without me, as the target was a really prominent feature,
easily discernible from a considerable distance.

The mission was to be non-stop from Baghdad and would take over
four hours. I therefore arranged for Brewerton to fly my Bristol in the
display, in case I was not back in time. Owing to early fog, the formation of twelve Ninacs did not take off until 11.30, and the trip out was
uneventful. We made the attack from a very low level with 112 lb
bombs, saw a number of direct hits although a greater number of
bombs fell into the river, sending up great plumes of water to the height
of the attacking aircraft. We were heavily fired at from the fort and I
noticed that white flags were being flown at Anah.

It was all over very quickly and we set course for home, the whole
trip taking, as it turned out, just under five hours. My pilot was the
squadron commander, Squadron Leader Nicholas, although the entry
in my logbook reads 'Major' Nicholas [1]. It was curious the way in
which this particular army rank still clung to the service, almost three
years after the formation of the RAF. The reason was probably a deeply
rooted desire among former COs of the RFC to retain some identification with this now defunct branch of the army.

Our flying display had just finished when we landed at Baghdad
West, and my Bristol had let the side down by failing to start, and Ralph
Sorley's machine had won the 'beauty contest', doubtless owing to the
ministrations of our Corporal Burfield.

On 30th January, Flight Lieutenant E R Tempest MC DFC [2] arrived
having been posted in from 216 Squadron in Egypt, so we now had
two officers of this rank. Sorley, long overdue for promotion, went to
A Flight after Tempest's arrival. He was later promoted, thus bringing
the squadron up to establishment in flight lieutenants.

Tempest had had a distinguished career thus far, and prior to serving
in 216, had been a test pilot at the experimental establishment at
Martlesham Heath. He therefore came to us with the reputation of
being a pilot of exceptional ability. He was not at all pleased at being
posted to us, having been very happy in 216, which was equipped with

DH10, twin-engined high performance (for those days) bombers.

February 1st was my twenty-first birthday. A few days previously I had consultations with Long John Beilby and Eric Brewerton, who were both due for their coming of age celebrations. It was settled that I would entertain the mess to dinner at the Officer's Club in Baghdad, on the 1st, and they would combine and give a 'super' party during the following month. There were other alternatives to the club, the Maude Hotel, or the recently opened Beau Monde and Zia Hotels, the latter being famed for the quality of its steaks.

Seventeen guests turned up at my dinner party, at the end of which I was called upon to make a speech. On rising with some difficulty, I was immediately bombarded with asparagus tips by the entire assembly and the party ended in a rough house with minor damage to the premises. My bill for the evening's entertainment left no change out of a month's pay. To the eternal shame of Beilby and Brewerton, their twenty-first birthdays passed by without comment and no party. They were really very wise!

A week after Tempest's arrival he took over my precious D7888 and made me share another machine with Cordingley. I was extremely fed-up and Tempest's name was mud as far as I was concerned. However, it was not long before I realised that he was really a decent chap and a good flight commander, so I duly forgave him. My loss was one of the penalties for being a very junior 'bog-rat'.

From time to time during my service, I came across aircraft which seemed to have a better performance and to be nicer to handle than others of similar type and mark numbers. One could check general conditions, rigging, loading and so on, and still be at a loss to account for the superiority of a particular machine. With old fashioned 'stick' and 'string' aircraft, slack fabric could cause loss of performance and sluggish handling, but what gave an aeroplane just that little extra 'zip' I had no idea.

Very many years later I happened to be talking to a worker in an aircraft factory and I asked for his opinion on this tantalising question. Without hesitation he gave me the following answer. "Whenever you fly a kite which seems better than the others, you can bet your bottom dollar that is was made by a team of men who took great pride in their work and put themselves into the machine."

Early in the year 55 Squadron left for Mosul, some 150 miles to the north west, and 8 Squadron, which also had DH9a machines, arrived at Baghdad West from Egypt. A few months later 1 Squadron, equipped with Sopwith Snipe fighters arrived from Bangalore, India. A new airfield was now under construction at Hinaidi, on the left bank of the Tigris and about seven miles south east of Baghdad. No.1 and 8 Squadrons were the first to move in, as soon as work on the aerodrome and building had sufficiently advanced. The ultimate plan was to move all units over from Baghdad West, as Hinaidi was a much larger airfield with much better technical and domestic accommodation.

In mid-February I had a very welcome break from normal squadron routine, in accompanying Ralph, Culley, Ffoulkes-Jones and a political officer named Lees, on a trip by rail trolley to Khanikin, near the Persian frontier. The object of this exercise was to select and mark out landing grounds at Mirjanah and Baquba. We were away for a week and managed to get in some excellent shooting at the various halts. The jheels (marshes) at Abut Djisera and Shahraban simply teemed with wildfowl of almost every variety.

Shortly after our return we attended a farewell party to our wing commander, who was returning to England, his place having been taken by Group Captain A E 'Biffy' Borton. By squadron standards it was a fairly solemn occasion – we were sad at having to say farewell to 'Screaming Lizzie' [3].

A further innovation in 1921 was the introduction of a new means of ground to air communication – the picking up of messages with a grapnel, slung from under the aircraft. The message to be collected was enclosed in a standard message bag, with coloured streamer as used for dropping and the bag then attached to a length of cord slung between the tops of two poles. To pick up the message, the observer had to lower the grapnel, the pilot flying the aircraft so that it would pass just above the poles and engage the cord, dragging it and the message from its suspended spot.

On 4th April, our old friend Charles Goring, without malice aforethought, had a good attempt at killing four members of the squadron, including the CO. He arrived at the mess at teatime, driving a brand new Rolls-Royce chassis replacement in blue anti-corrosion paint. The chassis was of 1912 vintage, magnificent cars they were too. I was told that, during the withdrawal from north-west Persia, one armoured car section mislaid its supply of lubricating oil. However, the journey to Baghdad was successfully accomplished with the engine sumps filled with ghee, the cooking oil used by Indian troops. Charles was extremely excited. "Come for a trip across the airfield and see what she'll do," he cried.

The chassis was fitted with a wooden seat and a crude type of framework, aptly known as a 'soap box body'. Ed Rice took the spare place on the bench, Reggie Smart sat on the side, with his feet on the steel running board, and Eric Wormell and myself climbed on the back of the contraption. Off we went in great style but with little comfort, as the suspension was well reinforced to take the weight of a steel armoured body. On reaching the airfield Charles put his foot hard on the accelerator and off we shot like a rocket. The speed of the vehicle must have passed the 50 mph mark, when we struck a couple of sharp ridges. I had a faint recollection of the wooden framework parting from the chassis and of me sailing through the air, a blinding flash of light, then oblivion.

When I recovered consciousness I was vaguely aware of being supported by two people and being led to an ambulance. My left arm was useless, the shoulder joint seemed to be at the back of my neck, my face felt a frightful mess and my mouth and nostrils were full of sand. At sick quarters I was given a shot of morphia, had the dislocated shoulder re-set and was then driven to hospital, where I remained for the following two weeks recovering from concussion, extensive bruising and abrasions. The concussion had had an odd effect on me, as on the ambulance drive to Baghdad North, I was firmly convinced that I was being driven through London.

Of the other participants in this disastrous drive, Ed Rice and Wormell were also thrown off, the former having an arm broken and the latter being quite unhurt apart from a bad shake-up. Charles stopped the car whilst standing on the chassis members and gear box and Reggie managed to retain his seat on the running board. On coming to a halt, Charles saw three prostrate bodies on the ground and feared the worst. According to an eye-witness, a bouncing spare wheel smashed Ed's arm, while Wormell picked himself up after a few seconds, walked directly to his quarters and went to bed in a complete 'dizzy'. With regard to myself, the back of my head took the initial impact, this being followed by a number of somersaults, ending finally in a long slide on my face, hence all the muck in my nose and mouth. Altogether a very shaky do!

Our more serious activities this year tended to rather drift away from the flat desert and palm grove terrain of central and southern Iraq, the trouble spots now being located in the mountainous country of Kurdistan. Without going into elaborate detail, the chief trouble makers up north were infiltrating Turks and a sheik named Kerim Fatah Beg, the latter being generally known as KFB for short. The situation did not develop seriously until August and built up gradually to a climax the following year.

There could be no greater contrast, topographically and climatically, between the central plain of Iraq and the mountainous valley system which runs roughly from west to south and through Kurdistan and Persia, to Afghanistan and India. The mean maximum average height of the ranges was from 4,500 to 9,000 feet, with occasional peaks up to 12,000 and over. Apart from the distinct possibility of getting one's throat cut, the country was pleasant to live in and delightful for a holiday. Although warm in summer, the air was crisp and one abounded in energy. The scenery was in most respects similar to that in other mountainous countries at that latitude, but with a complete lack of big timber. There was plenty of scrub, oak and walnut, and the grapes and other fruit thrived at the lower altitudes. Further north, out of our sphere of influence, there were considerable forests.

During the spring and early summer we made a number of flights to Kirkuk, to give the brigade stationed in that area experience in ground to air inter-communication, using Aldis lamp, popham panels and the new message picking-up technique. Most of the exercises went according to plan, but we had some trouble finding cord strong enough to withstand the snatch of the message bags.

Kirkuk is a fair sized town on the northern fringes of the plain between the Gebel Hamrin, a range of foothills rising to about 500-1,000 feet, and the main mountain ranges of Kurdistan. In a direct line, the town is about 150 miles from Baghdad, but we usually followed a circuitous route to 200-220 miles in order to keep within gliding distance of inhabited territory.

Today Kirkuk is well known as one of the main oil fields of the Iraq Petroleum Company [at the time D'Arcy Greig wrote this chapter forty years later. Ed.]. In those early days, however, the only visible signs of oil were the odd holes in the ground from which local inhabitants used to fetch crude oil in buckets and five-gallon drums, to distil their own kerosene. There was also the 'Burning, Fiery Furnace' of Shadrach, Meshach and Abednego. This was a patch of fissured ground measuring roughly seven to ten square yards, from which issued burning gas from every crack. It seemed practically impossible to extinguish and although one could shovel sand into the fissure the flame would only go out momentarily. The fiery furnace had no doubt been burning for thousands of years, and from our point of view it provided us with an excellent 'lighthouse' during night flights. Sad to relate, towards the end of that decade, when the oil company made its first bores in this locality, the ensuing drop in subterranean pressure finally extinguished these flames which had burnt from time immemorial. Kirkuk is also the traditional burial place of the Prophet Daniel. I last visited Kirkuk in 1935, and by then the whole area was a vast hive of industry from which emerged the pipe lines to the distant Mediterranean ports of Haifa and Tripoli.

In common with many other parts of the Northern Hemisphere, the summer of 1921 in Iraq proved to be the hottest in living memory, the shade temperature at Baghdad rising to 126° and 132° at Basra, resulting in many fatal cases of heatstroke. On 7 July, at the height of the heat wave, a guest night was held to celebrate Ralph Sorley's promotion to flight lieutenant, which had come through forty-eight hours previously. After dinner we raided the Aircraft Park, captured their two field guns and presented them to 8 and 30 Squadrons respectively. The CO of the park was furious, so in due course the guns were returned and deposited outside his bedroom window. This was one of many similar incidents which were to culminate in a superb effort the following year.

An event of historical interest this very hot summer was the proclaiming of the Emir Faisal, son of the Sherif Hussein of Mecca, as king of the new state of Iraq. This alteration to the status of the country did not seem to have any profound effect on us except for the annoying fact that we had to register our private cars and motor cycles and obtain number plates and driving licences! The Iraq police had always taken a very sympathetic interest in our sometimes wild peregrinations. I well remember an occasion when riding my bike across a very crowded Maude Bridge. My handle bars became entangled with the flowing draperies of an unfortunate Arab woman, dragging her with considerable violence to the ground. In the ensuing hubbub a policeman appeared who, instead of asking for my licence, proceeded to beat hell out of the woman who was still prostrate, and yelling her head off. However, the chap evidently understood his job, for the woman immediately ceased her wailing, got to her feet, and made herself scarce without further delay.

Early August saw us getting steamed up operationally once more. This time the first orders were for a detached flight at Kirkuk, to operate in the Sulaimania area further to the north and north east. Four Bristols were to go, the pilots being Reggie, Tempo, Ralph and Eric Brewerton. I was also going but in a new capacity – 'Intelligence'. I could not fathom what this entailed, except it was clearly understood that I had to conduct a convoy of motor transport containing bombs, ammunition, wireless and other impedimenta, from Baghdad to Kirkuk. Being in charge, I decided to do my conducting by motor bike. The trip involved an overnight journey by rail up the right bank of the Tigris to the railhead at Maiji, about 100 miles south of Mosul. We would then head north by camel track for about fifteen miles to the Fatah Gorge, a narrow cleft in the Gebel Hamrin through which the Tigris flowed. At the gorge the river was crossed by ferry and the journey then continued by camel track again, across seventy-five miles of desert, away to the north east.

We loaded our convoy which consisted of one Leyland lorry, two Crossley tenders and a trailer, plus my Triumph bike, on to the train during the afternoon of 5 August, the train getting away at 10 pm that evening. On arrival at Baiji at 6.15 am the following morning, we unloaded and were on the track to Fatah by 8.15, arriving at the gorge at 10, after a very unpleasant drive over very rough ground and in a raging sand storm. It took an hour to negotiate the ferry, in which time the wind had dropped and with it the dust.

I had loads of confidence in my ability to find my way around the country and considered myself something of a homing pigeon. I had no qualms therefore, when setting out at the head of the column across miles of featureless desert. After a brief look at the map upon which most regular caravan routes were marked, I made periodic compass checks to confirm our heading. Fortunately the desert was hard and smooth, so the going was quite good apart from the fact that our speed was restricted to that of the slow-moving lorry.

The intense heat of the recent extreme weather had passed but it was still pretty scorching. After an hour or two we encountered a number of intersecting tracks not marked on the map and as the day wore on I began to get a bit apprehensive and not quite so confident as I had been earlier on. Then, to make matters worse, the track split, a feature also not marked on the map. After checking the two branches with my compass, I decided on the one with the most northerly heading, so off we went again. By late afternoon there was no sign of Kirkuk and to my alarm the desert started to take on a rather hilly aspect and I realised that we were lost and obviously to the north or even north east of Kirkuk. Dusk was approaching when we struck an Arab camp on the bank of a swift flowing river, the Lesser Zab.

The men at this camp were most helpful, realised our predicament and gave us a guide. We had not been long on a south-easterly course when the convoy was spotted by Eric Brewerton, who had been sent out in one of our aircraft to look for us. It was just about dark when we sighted the lights of Kirkuk. By speedometer reading we had covered 120 miles from Fatah instead of the seventy-five, so my desert navigation was not so hot on this occasion.

Apart from unpacking the gear from our transports, erecting our radio station and getting into wireless contact with Baghdad, I did not have an opportunity to learn more about my intelligence job because within forty-eight hours of our arrival, Reggie Smart and I were recalled for special duty. I flew down in the rear cockpit, with Reggie in front, leaving my camp kit and motor bike. At Baghdad we found that the special duty was night flying practice prior to proceeding with yet another detachment to Mosul, for night bombing operations at the time of the next full moon.

The next day but one I flew back to Kirkuk to collect my kit, and, if possible, my bike. This presented a bit of a problem but eventually we solved it by removing the wheels and stowing them in the rear seat, then we roped the frame of the machine to the Scarff gun mounting above the seat. I was about to rope my roll of camp kit plus one suitcase to the bomb racks, when I was asked to fly back as escort to Cordingley, who was returning an aircraft to Baghdad for a change of engine.

The engine of Cordingley's aircraft was slowly leaking water from a defective cylinder water jacket, so would in consequence need careful 'nursing' on the flight, so I offered to take his kit in order to minimise the weight in his Bristol. As my rear seat was full of motor bike, Cordingley's kit had to go on my third bomb rack. When eventually ready for flight, my Bristol Fighter seemed festooned like a Christmas tree. Most of the bike was 'outboard' above the fuselage, a large suitcase under the bottom centre section and two valises containing camp beds, blankets, etc, beneath the bottom planes. Such was my profound faith in the flying qualities of the Brisfit, that I did not really anticipate any serious difficulty in flying to Baghdad with this untidily disposed load. I should have known better.

That take-off was a shattering experience. I had taken the precaution of taxying well beyond the normal boundary of the airfield before turning into wind, but when I opened her up the machine ran on and on, without gaining speed, and showing no immediate inclination to leave mother earth. I eventually reached the end of the take-off area, well clear of the further boundary when, in desperation I yanked back fairly sharply on the stick. The machine responded valiantly and staggered into the air, the turbulence caused by the dangling baggage setting up violent buffeting around the tail. Well, it was one thing to get airborne but quite another to gain some altitude. It seemed quickly evident that the 275 hp of the Rolls-Royce Falcon engine would be severely overtaxed in attaining either speed or height. I finally managed a very wide gradual turn to the south not daring to throttle back, and decided that any attempt at landing back at Kirkuk would risk a serious crash. There was nothing for it but to head for Baghdad, with my airspeed indicator registering between 50 and 60 mph. Every time I eased the stick forward to gain a bit more speed, we just went down hill. The aircraft just scraped over the Gebil Hamrin and two and a half hours later, still flying at full throttle, I found myself at 1,000 feet over Baquba, thirty miles north of Baghdad. As the fuel was practically exhausted and with a wide expanse of level desert below, I made a fast approach with plenty of engine and returned to earth without further trouble. I contacted Baghdad and a supply of fuel arrived late in the evening. Thus ended a rather stupid episode. When I got back to base the following morning, I found that Cordingley had had an uneventful flight back but could not understand why he had seen nothing of his escort.

The night flying practice was uneventful, the pilots on this occasion being Reggie, Carpenter, Brewerton and myself. We left for Mosul on 16th August and I remained with this establishment until 4th September. Mosul is a very large town about fifty miles south of the Turkish frontier. To the north and east the country is mountainous and flat on the other points of the compass. Just across the Tigris to the east of the town lie the ruins of the ancient Assyrian city of Ninevah, with Nebi Yunis, the village named after and containing the tomb of the Prophet Jonah, just beyond. The 'whale' in the story of Jonah symbolised the vice-ridden city of Ninevah which 'swallowed' him and then coughed him up when he had learnt the error of his ways.

No.55 Squadron with whom we messed, were quartered in a large square fort-like building with a central quadrangle, no doubt of Turkish origin, situated between the airfield and the south of the town. We were looked after by the chaps of 55, a number of whom flew with us on one or two day raids, whilst we were familiarising ourselves with the fairly extensive target area. Some of us returned the compliment by flying as observers in their Ninacs, an event which proved disastrous for Carpenter who, on our second day at Mosul, went with Hugh Walmsley. On the return flight from the target, the rear cockpit burst into flames owing to the unaccountable explosion of a Verey cartridge and Carpenter burnt his hand extinguishing the conflagration, so could play no further role in these operations.

During this period I took part in five raids by day and three by night, the targets being towns named Batas, Herir and Rowanduz. The last was situated at the end of a precipitous gorge of the same name. In clear weather finding one's way over mountainous country is, I think, an extremely simple matter. Personally I have a fairly photographic brain and normally have little difficulty in memorising the main features and knowing where I am. However, on my third night raid things did not go quite to plan. On all three night raids we had been a bit hampered by low lying mist. The three aircraft, Reggie, 'Brew' and myself, took off at five-minute intervals and if conditions in the opinion of the

leader were unsuitable, he would fire a red light as a signal for immediate return to base. The first two raids went according to plan.

This third night, however, take-off was postponed owing to mist on
the airfield, so we returned to the mess. At 11 pm or thereabouts, we'd
just had a nightcap and were off to bed when news came through that
the mist had suddenly cleared, so off we went to our aircraft, eventually
getting airborne at around 11.30. For some reason or other I swung a
bit to starboard upon leaving the ground and on reaching 500 feet noticed a fairly heavy ground mist as far as the eye could see to the west
of the Tigris. The first range of hills, the Gebel Maklub, were visible,
so I set course in a steady climb, towards the target. The full moon
had not reached its zenith, so the glare rather accentuated the general
haze above the ground mist. On reaching the hills I noticed that the
valleys were carpeted in white vapour and I realised that locating the
target might prove difficult. The air was warm and smooth, and the
moonlit mountains enshrouded in slight haze, seemed quite enchant-
ing. I was in a state of reverie, possibly moonstruck and seemed not
to bother much about the passage of time. Suddenly I was aware that
the visibility at the height at which I was flying – 11,500 feet – was not
as good as it had been and I took a quick look vertically downwards
and noticed a mass of something rough looking, like corrugated iron,
passing by very rapidly just below the aircraft. The truth dawned on
me with a violent jolt – I was literally skimming along just clear of a
mountain range and well beyond the target area. I gingerly turned on
to the reciprocal bearing and with the moon at my back had a clearer
view of the country with was decidedly unfamiliar.

I had not been conscious of any drift on the outward flight, so reckoned that the reciprocal bearing on which I was now headed would
bring me back to Mosul. This assumption proved to be correct and
soon familiar peaks and crests loomed up ahead. The time was now
about 1 am, and I spotted, only a mile or two to port, what seemed to
be the glow of a camp fire right at the bottom of a valley which was
now fairly clear of mist. I knew I was not near the target but assumed
that I was still over hostile territory, so decided to make the glow a
present of the dozen 20 lb bombs I carried. I flew straight and level
over the glow and released all the bombs in rapid succession, then resumed my course for base. A few minutes later I saw a terrific 'Brock's

Benefit' going on about fifty miles ahead, obviously from Mosul airfield. They were sending up a succession of the latest signal rockets at regular intervals, a type which burst into clusters of white stars at 4,000 feet. I landed at 1.45 am with only a few minutes petrol left and found myself in for a ticking off. Apparently Reggie had fired off a red light within a minute or two of take-off, owing to the poor visibility, and he and Brew had returned home. I had obviously missed seeing the light owing to my swing to starboard when clearing the flare path and had kept everyone up, in a fearful flap, for over two hours.

A day or two later, a report came in on the political grapevine, on my bombing effort. The glare which I had sprinkled had come from an inter-tribal confab at a friendly village. They were in fact considering whether or not to join the rebels when I suddenly arrived overhead. In the midst of these deliberations it seemed to them that the wrath of Allah had descended amongst them from on high, killing two men and wounding another, plus numerous casualties amongst the sheep and goats. This totally unexpected visitation from above and in the middle of the night, was altogether too much for them, so they decided to remain friendly!

Some days before my return to Baghdad I joined a party which visited the ruins of Ninevah and then went on to Nebi Yunis, to have a look at Jonah's tomb. We did not find much of interest at Ninevah, in fact the city seemed to be just one vast and very high rectangular mound which at that time appeared not be have been seriously excavated. Jonah's tomb was a small mosque-like building. We were permitted to enter and view the sarcophagus after first removing our shoes. It was in a fine state of preservation. One could not make out whether the keeper of the tomb was a Mahommedan or Christian priest; he seemed to be of the former persuasion. Many of the ancient prophets are recognised alike by Hebrew, Christian and Islamic faiths.

Before finally leaving the subject of Mosul, I simply must refer to:

Our holy Balloonatic Ace,
Grows coarse pubic hair on his face.

This uncomplimentary quotation is from a rather rude little rhyme written about the CO of 55 Squadron, when he subsequently became CO of the Balloon School at RAF Larkhill, on Salisbury Plain. Vivian Gaskell Blackburn [4] had only recently taken over from Nicholas, who brought the squadron from Constantinople and with whom I flew a raid at the beginning of the year. 'GB' as he was known for short, had the distinction of being one of the only two officers in the RAF, not counting HM King George V, who was permitted to wear a beard, the other being C R Samson, the naval pilot who had covered himself in glory very early in the Kaiser's war, by his daring raids on Cuxhaven and other German ports, not to mention his attacks in charge of an armoured car outfit in France and Belgium [5]. Nobody seemed to know why GB had a beard. Various people suggested that he was subject to impetigo and could not shave. I suppose the real truth was that he, like Samson, had originally been a bearded naval officer and had been granted the privilege of retaining this facial adornment after the amalgamation of the RFC and RNAS on 1 April 1918.

Samson was a man of fire and brimstone, GB was not. This might possibly be the reason for GB being the subject of a great deal of harmless banter from time to time. At Mosul he was known as the 'Sacred Flying Officer', his quarters in the mess being flippantly referred to as the 'Holy Sepulchre'. This brings me to an amusing little anecdote, the veracity of which I am afraid I cannot vouch for, as I heard the story from a member of 55 who subsequently served with me at the Central Flying School.

Shooting parties were a very common form of winter recreation all over Iraq. At the end of one big shoot at Mosul, GB, who had been doing a bit of stalking on his own, eventually returned to the main party, joyfully carrying an enormous pelican which he declared he had shot among the tamarisk on the banks of the Tigris. He stated that a pelican not only was a rarity in Iraq, but was also considered to be a great delicacy. Some unkind person was overheard to say that it had probably died of old age and that GB had stumbled across it. However, in celebration a big guest night was laid on in honour of this bird.

The local army and political notabilities were all invited to this dinner and at the appropriate time the bird was brought in on a large silver salver, carried by two Indian bearers. In its roasted state it looked more magnificent than ever, its back end simply bulging with what was, no doubt, the most delicious stuffing. The offering was placed in front of

GB who rose and with much ceremony, picked up a carver and fork, thrusting the latter into the fattest part of the bird in order to secure a good stance before carving. The moment the fork penetrated the bulging skin there was a loud hissing noise like a deflating tyre and the most appalling stench permeated the entire room. Everyone present made a dash for the exits, the dinner party breaking up in chaos. As far as I know, the perpetrator of this atrocity was never discovered, neither did I hear of the technique employed. The general effect cannot have been the product of natural decomposition, and a far more likely reason was the insertion of a football bladder into the bird's rear end, then filled with some nauseous compound. Anyway, a good joke, perhaps carried a bit too far? Had the event occurred a few years later, I would have said that it was quite up to Atcherley standard [6].

No.55 Squadron was not the only unit to have a new CO this year, for a very colourful personality had taken over 30 Squadron at Baghdad West. This was Raymond Collishaw, a much decorated and lively Canadian being now in control. His medal ribbons rather overwhelmed our Eric Wormell who invariably referred to 'Colly' as the 'Spectrum'. [7]

At the end of September, Charles Goring took Ray Collishaw and myself on a three-day track reconnaissance to Nirjanah and back. We travelled by Rolls-Royce tender, the chassis being that of Charles's famous armoured car Harvester, a new chassis from England having replaced the 1912 veteran for the more arduous duty of carrying steel plating and machine guns. There had been a link between Charles and this particular car, and when recalling his various exploits, Charles always talked of 'Me and Harvester'. The trip was good fun and we got in a spot of shooting. During the last thirty miles of the return journey, we had to change seven tyres, a sweaty job as the weather was still extremely warm. Ray was a cheerful chap who loved hectic parties and noisy guest nights.

By the end of October, six of our Bristols, under the command of Tempest, had flown to Sulaimania in Kurdistan, for a five-day detachment, in order to carry out a series of demonstration flights. The other pilots with him were Ffoulkes-Jones, Beilby, Willie Pruden (a new arrival) and myself. Sulaimania, a town of about 10,000 inhabitants, in a broad valley between two mountain ranges, was a very pleasant spot, the airfield being about 3,000 feet above sea level. We all stayed with Major Goldsmith, the political officer, whose house of Turkish design was most comfortable.

Goldsmith's predecessor, Major E B Soane, had won fame throughout the country as an able and ruthless administrator who was both admired and feared by the wild tribesmen. Of all the tales told about him, an alleged example of how he instilled the rudiments of hygiene into the Kurd can bear repetition. The Kurd and the Arab had, in those days, simply no idea of sanitation. If a man wished to do his 'daily duty' he just squatted down in the garden, courtyard or roadway. In warm weather, the atmosphere in the vicinity of towns and villages was, in consequence, almost unbearable, let alone the amount of food contamination by flies which must have taken place. Soane had proper communal latrines built and issued appropriate orders as to their use. If, at any time, he found a Kurd squatting at the wayside when within easy reach of a latrine, the offender would be made to remove his turban, place the 'deposit' therein, and convey it to the latrine.

The various demonstration flights in formation were, on the whole, uneventful. In our spare time we shot a number of black partridges and foregathered with the levies in the mess. One demonstration flight is worthy of mention, as it took us some distance over poorly mapped territory and in rather bad weather. We took with us as guide, a chap named Cook, the political officer from Rania, a town in the next valley to the north west of Sulaimania. Cook always wore native dress and was indistinguishable from the Kurds, except of course, when he opened his mouth. The first snows had fallen in the mountains, and the sky that day was heavily overcast. The last leg of the flight took us through a long and narrow valley called the Naw Dasht. The mountains on each side were precipitous, the crests being hidden in unbroken cloud, the general effect being claustrophobic, rather like flying through a gigantic tunnel. We emerged again over the Rania Plain through a gorge at the bottom of which flowed the Lesser Zab. A landing was made at the village of Sersian where we received the hospitality of the local chieftain.

None of us had ever before been dined by a Kurdish sheik. For me, this occasion still ranks as the best of all such functions attended during a total of eight and a half years I spent in the Middle East. We all had very hearty appetites and the assembly took place under a large awning where hosts and guests sat cross-legged in a circle on the ground. A gigantic copper tray containing what looked like a mountain of rice was set down in the middle and we plunged our right hands into the middle and proceeded to do justice to the spread. The rice had been spiced and cooked to perfection and contained many chickens, dates, almonds, and sultanas, the combination being simply delicious. I regret to say that when I eventually rose to my feet, the sensation of abdominal distension was almost unbearable. We all returned to Baghdad the following day.

[1] Squadron Leader Charles Henry Nicholas AFC, received the DFC later in 1921. His AFC had been gazetted in June 1919 for services in Egypt. He also received the French Croix de Guerre, and the Egyptian Order of the Nile, 4th Class in 1919. By 1935 he had risen to group captain.

[2] Edmund Roger Tempest was twenty-six at this time and yet another WW1 fighter ace, with seventeen victories in that conflict flying SE5s with 64 Squadron. His brother Wulstan won fame for shooting down the Zeppelin L31 in October 1916.

[3] Later Air Vice-Marshal Amyss Eden Borton CB CMG DSO AFC. A former soldier and WW1 airman, in 1918 he completed the first England-India flight. Retired from the RAF in 1933 and became a director of Napier & Son. Died in August 1969.

[4] V G Blackburn had learnt to fly before the war, holding Aviator's Certificate No.617, dated 10 September 1913.

[5] Commander Charles Rumney Samson RN, had also learnt to fly pre-war, in fact Certificate No.71, 25th April 1911. He later became Air Commodore CMG, DSO & Bar AFC Ld'H. Died in February 1931 aged 47.

[6] Reference to Richard 'Batchy' Atcherley, who we shall meet in later chapters.

[7] Ray Collishaw had received the DSO & Bar, DSC, DFC for his prowess as a fighter pilot in WW1 with both the RNAS and RAF. Shortly after the end of WW1, he commanded a fighter squadron fighting the Bolsheviks in South Russia. He eventually attained the rank of air vice-marshal CB OBE when he retired in 1943. He died in 1975.

6

A NEAR DEATH EXPERIENCE

At the end of November, early December 1921, two weekend shooting trips were organised to the jheel at Abu Djisera. Five guns went on the first expedition. We travelled by rail trolley, leaving Baghdad at 2 am on Sunday morning, arriving at our destination two and a half hours later. It was still dark when we started wading through the reeds and as dawn broke, a heavy mist formed. However, the birds were on the move and flying low. That day we secured the record bag for that jheel. I cannot remember the number of duck and snipe we bagged, but we got thirty-eight geese. I was lucky in getting a 'right and left' on geese, an unusual event, so I was told. We all shot well except Jimmy Lawson, who didn't hit a thing! Right at the end of the day, we were wending our way back to the railway when a gaggle flew by almost out of range. All five guns let off both barrels, and after a slight pause, one solitary goose came fluttering down to the ground, whereupon one of our Arab beaters quickly retrieved it and, grinning from ear to ear, presented it with a great flourish to Jimmy.

The following shoot was carried out in great luxury. Our railway friends provided us with a hospital coach containing fourteen bunks, the coach being attached to the Saturday evening train to Khanikin, and shunted into a siding at Abu Djisera, where it was picked up the following evening by the same train on its return journey to Baghdad.

We were all provided with bearers, food and drink, so we made merry on the outward trip. Tempest brewed a marvellous punch to his own recipe. As far as I recall it contained the following ingredients: two handfuls of almonds, two more of raisins, half a nutmeg, a stick of cinnamon and a few cloves. To this was added a bottle of claret, a bottle of gin, a half-bottle of port, the whole mixture being brought slowly to the boil. The primus was then extinguished and a tumbler full of good brandy added to the sizzling mixture, which was then lit. The final rite before serving being the addition of twenty-one lumps of sugar melted in a colander over the flames of the burning liquor. You can take my word for it, it was a comforting potion and we all spent a dreamless night.

The shoot the next day was not up to the standard of the previous one. My total bag for the day was one goose and three ducks. However, I did see a simply enormous wild pig, but we did not get a shot at it.

Whilst on this lighter vein, another anecdote would not be out of place. The City of Caliphs contained two cinemas, the Central and the Royal. These were fairly regularly patronised by those of us who were keen on following the adventures of Pearl White, that famous heroine of the silver screen, whose innumerable hair-breadth escapes from a nasty death were an outstanding feature of the exciting serials of the silent era. Well, one evening, one of my chums who shall remain nameless in this story, and myself, decided to go to the Central. After parking our motor bikes we joined the queue at the booking office. Whilst thus occupied, a small boy of uncertain nationality, but probably Armenian, sidled up to my companion and informed him that he knew some nice ladies in Baghdad, and if my friend so wished, an introduction could be arranged, subject of course, to a modest fee, payable in advance – in this case 40 rupees.

My chum's eyes glinted in anticipation as his hand dived into his pocket in search of the necessary pieces of silver. The boy said that the introduction would take a little time to arrange, but if we turned up at the same time the following evening, he would, without fail, be there to conduct us to the place of assignation. The lad pocketed the cash and made off up New Street. Being very doubtful about the whole transaction, I kept an eye on the lad, till he disappeared down a dark alleyway.

The following evening we were back at the cinema on time, but of course, there was no sign of our young confidence trickster. However, I suggested to my pal that, as I had noted the direction in which he had disappeared the previous evening, no further harm could possibly result from a little exploring. We therefore turned down the same dark alleyway and were soon lost in a labyrinth of unlit passages. The search had to be abandoned and we endeavoured to find our way back to New Street. On reaching a fairly wide alley that headed in the right direction, our attention was suddenly arrested by sounds of merriment, a gramophone and a mixture of male and female voices engaged in a very odd conversation in pidgin English. As there was a familiar ring about the male voices, we located the house in question and then hid in the adjacent doorway to wait events.

Presently, the door opened, a head appeared and following a furtive glance to left and right, a figure emerged and made off down the street. After a short lapse of time this procedure was repeated, and in all, four or five figures came out. All were members of our own squadron, our elders and betters at that! Our curiosity now being thoroughly aroused, we approached the entrance to the house and, after a brief listening period, knocked on the door. We were admitted to find that the occupants were two Russian ladies, one young and quite attractive, the other just a little bit on the antique side. Both were somewhat scantily attired. Well, well, what goings on! Having barged in, in this manner, I was filled with confusion and embarrassment and did not know what to say. My immediate impulse was to get out and beat it for home. However, the ladies, who were doubtless two of the many refugees living in the city, did not object to our intrusion and offered us refreshment. My chum was not the least put out and made the best of a bad job of his regrettable financial transaction. Of course, we never ever saw that Armenian boy again.

We are now in the second week of December, and Christmas mail this year will reach England in record time owing to the introduction of the Cairo-Baghdad Air Mail Service. Three Cairo-based squadrons were responsible for this service, 45 and 70, which were equipped with Vickers Vimy twin-engined bombers, but in the process of converting to Vernons, the passenger-carrying variant of the Vimy, plus 216 Squadron's DH10s. The DH10 was much smaller than the Vimy, had very good lines and was fully aerobatic. Throughout its history the firm of de Havilland has, with one or two exceptions only, produced good looking aircraft of high performance and good handling qualities. One of the exceptions was the DH6 trainer, the type on which I learnt to fly during the war. This machine certainly was an ugly-duckling, blunt and square and with a maximum speed of 60 mph. In a strong cross-wind it flew just as fast sideways as it did forwards, hence its nickname 'crab'. Oddly enough DH's first prototype jet fighter was named 'Spider Crab', afterwards changed to Vampire. For various other reasons the DH6, in both service and training units, were also known as 'The Clutching Hand', the 'Sky Hook' and 'The Flying Coffin'.

The DH10 was what the Americans would call a 'three-place ship'. In the nose the observer, complete with front gun, behind him and just in front of the airscrew discs was the pilot. Behind him a 98 gallon fuel tank, then the bomb-bay, followed by another 98 gallon tank and finally, and by this time behind the main planes, sat a rear gunner. This description is just a preamble to an account of the most tragic personal experience of my flying career.

The incoming mail on the weekend of 11th December had been brought in DH10, No.9048, flown by Flying Officer 'Lofty' Wilson, a giant fellow. On the afternoon of the 13th, Lofty was carrying out an engine check preparatory to the return flight to Cairo, when, on extending an arm over the side of the cockpit to draw attention to something or other, he had a finger chopped off by one of the revolving propellers, and so off he went to hospital. Tempest, as soon as he heard of this mishap, at once saw an opportunity for visiting his old unit, 216 Squadron, and for spending a jolly Christmas in the fleshpots of Egypt. So a signal was sent to Middle East HQ, requesting authority for him to fly the mail from Baghdad the following weekend in 9048. Approval came through within forty-eight hours.

On the Saturday morning, the 17th, I heard that Tempo was going to take up the DH10 for a short test flight, so asked him if I could come along too. He had no objection and suggested that I might prefer the rear seat of the machine rather than the exposed front gun position, to which I agreed. We took off shortly after 11.30, swinging slightly to port during the take-off run and initial climb. We cruised around for about fifteen minutes and being sat behind the two 400 hp engines, their rhythmic roar making a deep and what was to be a lasting impression on my mind. I glanced along the length of the fuselage ahead of me and could just see the top of Tempo's head above the pilot's cockpit, but a gaunt figure with a sickle was at the controls. At last the throttles were closed and the landing approach began.

The leeward side of the airfield was approached in a cross wind glide, a final and rather steep left-hand gliding turn into wind being made at an altitude which I estimated as being around 200 feet. It is difficult for me to say exactly when I became apprehensive but I began to sense something. I did not feel too happy about that final turn and had the impression that Tempo had left it a bit late. I would have been greatly relieved had he corrected this apparent error by opening the throttles and carrying out another circuit. However, it was not to be. We had reached the stage of flattening out for the touch down, the left wing was still depressed and we had a pronounced drift to starboard. It was then that I realised that unless the engines were immediately opened up, a crash would become inevitable. We had no intercom so Tempo could not tell me what he was up to, and I couldn't speak to him. By this time we were longitudinally on an even keel but still drifting. I reckoned that we would hit with the port landing wheel and wing tip first, swipe the undercarriage off and slither to a stop, to the accompaniment of all the usual sounds of rending timber and metal.

The initial stages of the crash followed this pattern, but the slither came to an abrupt stop, the machine tilted vertically on its nose, throwing me half out of my cockpit. I would have come completely out but a portion of broken aeroplane caught me in the back, pinning my body firmly against the Scarff gun mounting. At this instant, something I hadn't anticipated happened. There was a sudden 'woomf' and my world was transformed into a sea of flame. The searing blast removed my moustache and I could feel my face and hands crackling. By merciful providence my feet found a solid footing and I pressed down with goodness knows how much force in excess of my normal strength, and I shot through the fire and dropped over the centre section of the machine and onto the ground. I was now free of the wreck but my overcoat was on fire, so I ran like a stag, tearing frantically at the buttons until the flaming garment was on the ground.

I then turned back towards the aircraft which was now a raging furnace. To search for Tempest would have been futile, and as I was standing there hoping the poor chap had been instantly knocked out, there suddenly emerged from the inferno an animated torch. It was Tempo. He had obviously been soaked through by the contents of the two petrol tanks and went up like a torch. The horror of the scene before me baffles description. I yelled to Tempo to throw himself on the ground, at the same time retrieving my greatcoat that was no longer burning. Reaching Tempo's body I did my utmost to smother the flames only to have my coat flame up again. It was quite hopeless.

Time seemed to come to a standstill. Would the fire tender and ambulance never arrive? I was so distraught that I started running in tight circles; being so utterly unable to help a friend in dire distress nearly threw me off balance. Suddenly the scene changed. There was the ambulance and fire tender, together with the figure of Long John Beilby, spraying Tempo with an extinguisher. The poor chap was sitting on the ground supporting himself upright with one hand, every stitch of clothing except helmet, goggles and field boots having been burnt from his body.

We were both given first aid at station sick quarters and then sent forthwith by ambulance to No.23 British Stationary Hospital at Baghdad North, accompanied by Doc. Montgomery. Tempo knew he could not last long and kept pleading with the Doc. to fetch a priest. His voice was little more than a hoarse whisper, as he had been inhaling fire during his struggles to get clear of the burning aeroplane. Mercifully he died about six hours later [1].

There has been considerable conjecture as to the cause of the crash. A popular theory being that Tempest had not adjusted the reach of the rudder bar. Tempo was a chap of a little below average height, whereas Lofty Wilson had been 6' 4". In my opinion this theory is faulty. If Tempest experienced trouble with his rudder control, it is reasonable to assume that he would have carried out a more cautious approach, than the one responsible for the disaster. I'm afraid he fell into that trap which is for ever open for the experienced and able pilot – over confidence. He made a spectacular approach across wind, which he misjudged and ended up with insufficient forward speed and in the wrong attitude at the critical period immediately prior to touch down.

Looking back over the years, my only occupational dreams which ever assumed nightmare proportions were those involving flying in bad weather, or of losing control, or a combination of both. This, I think, is understandable, as I have done my fair share of 'sticky' flying, much of it being undertaken before the advent of instrument flying and radio aids. Today, in addition to many instrumental, electrical and mechanical devices in aircraft, a pilot when caught out in bad weather, can fly along a radio beam and on reaching his destination can ask for a 'talk down' through any overcast.

In the pre-instrumental era I can recollect many occasions when I have approached near panic, particularly when flying in bad visibility whilst over rugged terrain. On reaching this state of mind I have invariably prayed very hard and have offered up thanks when that welcome break in the clouds appeared, the storm abated, the fog lifted, that distant chink of light has shone dimly through the murk, or a successful precautionary landing been carried out.

Although physically quite sound, apart from my second degree burns of hands and face, I was glad of the comfort of the hospital bed. I felt reasonably hearty the following day and the MO told me that I was to be taken to the operating theatre the next morning to have my blisters and cinders removed, a minor operation entailing the use of a general anaesthetic.

I came to fairly late on the Monday afternoon, feeling simply awful. I attributed my discomfort to the after effects of chloroform. I could not face eating and the next morning I felt infinitely worse and was running a temperature. The thought of food was still revolting and moreover, my left hand had started to throb very painfully, and the dressing needed changing every four hours. By the afternoon the glands in my left armpit became painful and I noticed that the veins in my arm were turning pink. I thought to myself that perhaps it was only shock and would soon pass. Sleep was quite out of the question and by evening I had to rest my throbbing hand as high as I could raise it on the headrest of my bed in order to alleviate the pain.

On Wednesday morning my temperature had gone up, there was now a pronounced lump in my armpit, the veins in my arm had turned scarlet and the back of my left hand was a suppurating mess. I realised that the limb was thoroughly septic, the change of fomentations being increasingly painful. In the afternoon, and as I had eaten nothing since Sunday evening, the ward sister came up and said: "Is there simply nothing that you fancy?" I pondered a moment and then there suddenly flashed into my mind a story I had heard about my father, when I was a small boy. At the turn of the century, my father, a planter in British Guiana, had saved the life of a man who was dying of either Yellow Jack, or Black Water Fever, by feeding him on champagne. My father luckily having a case of this delectable wine in his possession.

"Yes," I suddenly replied to the sister, "a bottle of champagne, please!" She gave me a peculiar look and on recovering her composure said: "Well, it's an odd request, but I'll go and consult with the doctor." In no time at all she returned with the desired bottle. Did that champagne taste good? The feeling of comfort and well being increased with each succeeding glass until the last drop had gone. A gentle glow suffused my entire being and I relaxed into a deep slumber, or more bluntly, I something-well passed out. As I'd had as much sleep as I had had food for three days, my state of coma was, I think, quite understandable. However, I slept like a log for the rest of that day and without a break throughout the night, not even stirring when my dressings received their periodic change.

I awoke the next morning feeling a new being. My temperature was back to normal, the feeling of discomfort in my armpit and hand had appreciably declined and I did justice to a hearty breakfast. For 'elevenses' the sister brought me an egg-nog and that evening I had another bottle of 'champers'. Thereafter the egg-nog/champagne routine became firmly established until my discharge from hospital on 17th January. A day or so later all signs of sepsis vanished, the purulent mess on the back of my left hand giving way to the granules of healing tissue.

At the first opportunity I asked the MO what his reaction was to my request for champagne. "Well," he replied, "I thought I'd better give way to the poor blighter's whim, as I'll probably have to amputate the limb tomorrow." Amazing! There are, no doubt, people who might say that the champagne urge could well have been a telepathic impulse 'across the grave'. My father had died in 1913, and as a boy of sixteen he had lost his left arm as a result of an accident. Who knows? A more down to earth explanation might be: an association of ideas, governed by a craving for alcohol. Whatever the answer, there is no denying the beneficial results of this happy thought.

So, 1921 was drawing to a close as I lay in hospital. On Christmas Day the sisters and nurses held a thé dansant [tea dance], to which they pushed me around in a wheel chair. I felt a bit of a prune sitting there, but a lot of the chaps were there also, so I survived the ordeal. It was certainly a very different celebration from the hectic one of the previous year.

On New Year's Eve, the matron, who was blessed with the odd nickname 'Whizzbang', disguised me as an Arab and smuggled me out of the hospital to attend the Old Year Fancy Dress Dance at the Alwiyah Club, a new establishment down the river near Hinaidi, which had only been open for about a year. Again I had to do a lot of hanging around owing to my bandages, but nevertheless managed to enjoy myself, not getting back to my ward until around 3.30 in the morning.

Although I entered this hospital under such tragic circumstances, the efficiency and kindness of the staff there was such that the spirit of gloom that had come over me was quickly banished, and my recovery, both physical and mental, went rapidly without a hitch. Adieu, 1921. [2]

[1]Edmund Tempest was twenty-seven years of age, and he is buried in the Baghdad (North Gate) War Cemetery.

[2] One thing Greig does not speak of during this year is the award of the Distinguished Flying Cross. The citation for his DFC was promulgated in the *London Gazette* on 28th October 1921, and reads:

For gallantry and devotion to duty. All through this period of hostilities this officer has proved himself to be a very keen and daring pilot, and has on every possible occasion engaged the enemy from very low altitudes with excellent results.

7

THINGS THAT GO BANG IN THE NIGHT

My final year with 6 Squadron in Iraq began upon my release from hospital. All three years had their notable features. 1920 saw the Arab Rebellion, an uprising which firmly established the value of the Royal Air Force as a highly mobile and effective weapon in dealing with small wars, whether employed in concert with other forces or acting independently. 1921 was the year of the 'Fordson Farrow', the Cairo-Baghdad Air Route and finally 1922 would go down in history as the year in which the RAF was to assume the chief role in maintaining order in the new kingdom of Iraq. All armed forces, army levies, etc, coming under the control of a RAF commander-in-chief.

When I arrived back, I still suffered for some time from my burnt hands, especially the left one. I had great difficulty in clenching my fist and the skin across my knuckles kept splitting. Massage did some good, but the trouble did not finally clear up until the summer, at which time I spent four weeks leave in Egypt. Daily immersion in the briny Mediterranean did the trick and I had no more trouble. In later life it took an expert observer to spot any disfigurement resulting from these burns.

On the first day of February, my twenty-second birthday, I appeared before a Medical Board and was passed fit for full flying duty and I got into the air the following day. From the psychological angle I suffered no apparent ill-effect from the crash. Although I seldom sleep a night through without dreaming, I cannot recall having once dreamt about crashing in flames. I've had plenty of such dreams but always as a spectator, never a victim, the reason probably being my freedom from personal responsibility in this accident.

Very early in this year I was faced with having to make an important decision. My short service commission was nearing its end and I was due to return home for transfer to the reserve. There were roughly half a dozen of us in the same boat in the squadron and although we had all been recommended for permanent commissions none of our names had yet come out of the hat. About the end of February we received orders to report to HQ for an interview with Group Captain Borton, and all six of us were ushered into the presence of the group commander.

'Biffy' Borton was simply charming. After expressing extreme regret that, in spite of the strongest recommendations, none of us had received a PC, he went on to add: "As you all realise, the next few months will see an almost complete change over in the flying personnel in this country and I am of the opinion that the retention of a small nucleus of 'old hands' to show the new chaps round, would be most desirable. I think, therefore, that if any of you were to volunteer to serve an extra year out here, there might possibly be a good chance of getting a PC. This is just my personal opinion of course, take it or leave it, but let me know in a day or two what you decide to do."

To quote a later idiom, we all felt very 'browned off' and left HQ fully resolved not to stay for the extra year. After vacillating for a couple of days, I changed my mind and decided to stay on. I was the only one to reach this decision, the others all returning to England. In the following autumn all six of us were at last granted permanent commissions. However, I never regretted my decision, as the following months turned out to be eventful and interesting.

The change over in personnel to which Borton had referred , had in fact already started. The two Vimy Squadrons, 45 and 70, had moved over from Egypt to the new airfield at Hinaidi. With these 'heavies' came three officers destined to achieve fame during WW2, Squadron Leader 'Bert' Harris [1], Flight Lieutenant Saundby [2] and Flight Lieutenant, The Hon. Ralph Cochrane [3]. Harris became CinC of Bomber Command in 1942, Saundby his chief of staff, while Cochrane became AOC of No. 5 Group of Bomber Command, part of which was the famous Dam Buster Squadron, 617.

Among those who came to 30 Squadron was Sam Kinkead, a delightful and much decorated South African who, five years later, flew with the British Schneider Trophy team at Venice, 1927, and who was to lose his life the following year whilst making an attempt on the 3 Kilometre World Air Speed Record [4]. 'Kink' was now a flight commander under his former naval CO, Ray Collishaw.

Other very notable arrivals at this time were the members of the first output from the RAF College, Cranwell, a batch of young newly commissioned officers. With the first intake of cadets at Cranwell were a few ex-midshipmen who had graduated from the Royal Naval College, Dartmouth. Owing to their previous experience these 'ex-snotties' only had to do one year at Cranwell before commissioning into the RAF. One of them, Hugh David, had arrived at 30 Squadron fairly early the previous year. At the time of their arrival they seemed very juvenile to us old stagers still in our early twenties. However, none of them had completed a full course of instruction on service type aircraft, consequently all had to undergo an instructional period on either Bristols or Ninacs before qualifying to pull their weight in their squadron.

Among the full-time graduates who now arrived were: George Mills, Douglas Macfadyen, and David Bonham-Carter. Of these Mills and Macfadyen were destined to become commanders in chief before eventually passing to the retired list.[5]

With two exceptions, I cannot recall time and place of my first meeting with a couple of others of these new arrivals, first being the new flight commander to replace Tempo. 'Bunty' Frew was a fellow Scot, with an even better war record than his predecessor [6]. I became acquainted with Bunty at the bar of the Alwiyah Club one Saturday evening. The second acquaintance occurred on a Sunday morning during the same period, and within days of my leaving the hospital. I happened to go down to our hangars, probably to borrow some tools, and spotted a complete stranger examining our aircraft. He was in civilian clothes and immaculately turned out. I walked up to him to say good morning, and to find out who he was and what he was up to. I felt somewhat disturbed when he immediately addressed me in a rather pompous and condescending manner, making what I thought were rather pointed enquiries about the squadron. Crumbs, I thought, I had better tread carefully, this chap must at least be a wing commander from HQ. I treated him with due deference then went on my way. The following morning at breakfast I saw him again, this time in uniform and bearing a flying officer's stripe. Such was my first meeting with A T K Shipwright, a 'card' if ever there was one.

Alan Shipwright soon settled in with us and proceeded to crash a number of aeroplanes, mostly through bad luck. We were to become good friends later on and did quite a lot of operational flying together. During WW1 he had been shot down and taken prisoner. Incarcerated in a PoW camp at Holzminden, he made a number of unsuccessful attempts at escape, on one occasion being carried out of the castle in a large sack full of garbage [7].

Another 'card' to arrive on the squadron was Flight Lieutenant C S Richardson, a tall, lanky chap who looked as though he had stepped right out of the Edwardian era. His style of dress when out of uniform was markedly 'old world' – Norfolk jacket, tight breeches, and a necktie pulled through a gold ring rather than tied in a knot. He had a very long moustache and his general bearing reminded one of Viscount Lascelles who married Princess Mary on 28th February of that year. Consequently he at once became known to us all as 'The Viscount', or just plain 'Lassy'. His manner was somewhat ponderous but he was a good shot and not lacking in a sense of humour. Everyone liked him and occasionally pulled his leg [8].

Mid-March to mid-April saw the gradual exodus to Egypt of all my chums of Arab Rebellion days, mostly those who had come out with me early in 1920. The exception was Reggie Smart who remained in the country for some months, was promoted to squadron leader and posted to HQ for a while before finally going home. There were a number of hectic farewell parties, culminating in a final 'hell of a do' for the CO, Ralph Sorley, Ma Briggs and Jimmy Lawson, on 11th April.

Two days before this final goodbye, a Sunday trip to Hillah to explore the ruins of Babylon was arranged. We went by rail trolley kindly provided by 'Railways' as usual, and we were amply supplied with provisions. The ruins, which I had frequently seen from the air, were not particularly impressive, certainly nothing to compare with the gigantic relics of Ancient Egypt.

By early evening we had walked back to the trolley and were enjoying a bottle of beer, when a strange apparition accompanied by a small dog, was seen approaching along the railway track from the direction of Baghdad. It turned out to be a man dressed in tattered garments. His hair and beard were long and unkempt, his skin burned a deep mahogany and there seemed to be a wild look in his eyes. He wore no socks and his footwear was in an advanced stage of disrepair. He addressed us in English with a very strong American accent and gave his name as Hippolite Martinet. The whole effect of his presence was bizarre in the extreme. We offered him a beer, but after pondering for a moment, he replied: "Thanks fellers, tea is best for hiking but perhaps not so refreshing. Beer is very refreshing but is not good for hiking." The term 'hiking' was a new and strange one to us all. However, he squatted down and took a long swig at the bottle.

The strange Mr Martinet then told us his story. He was a native of Seattle and had been practising dentistry in the city. Over two years previously he had contracted a serious illness. From his description it might have been TB. His doctor told him that he had not long to live, should stop work immediately and spend as much time as possible in the fresh air. He went on to add that he thought the best way was to go on a long hike. To cut a long story short, he set off to walk the 3,000 odd miles across the USA to New York. His progress to begin with was slow and painful but as time went by he felt himself gradually being restored to normal health. He there and then decided to walk around the world. How his journey was financed was not related, however, when he reached Cherbourg, he set off on foot across Europe. At each large town he arrayed himself as a sandwich-man, with two boards upon which was inscribed the words 'globe trotter'. He also sold signed postcards of himself. At Constantinople he found a little dog, which accompanied him through Asia Minor to Damascus where he joined a caravan crossing the Syrian desert to Baghdad. When we met him at Hillah, he had been walking for two years. We rather wondered whether the little dog was regarded as a companion or an 'emergency ration'.

Well, Hippolite had some more beer and when we left him to start our return journey, he was still soliloquising on the respective hiking merits of tea or beer. When we last heard of him, India had been reached. He had covered the desert of Syria, and the wild land of Iraq without molestation. The Arabs no doubt regarded him as mad and left him in peace, as the code of Islam maintains that the mentally afflicted are entitled to the divine protection of Allah.

Back again at Baghdad we had just forty-eight hours to prepare for Ed Rice's farewell guest night, which of course, would include the firing of our Turkish field gun. A new armament officer had arrived in the squadron, Hatcher, by name. He was a man after my own heart, having a predilection for bangs and fireworks generally. He provided me with all I required, the charge being loaded into a very long 'sausage' of aeroplane fabric. The whole operation of mixing, took the best part of a day. To provide a good flash the mixture included a large quantity of magnesium powder, so that a photograph of the explosion could be taken. The barrel and rifling of the poor old gun were well and truly lined with rust, this ensuring that the charge, when rammed home, was really securely tamped down. The vacant space left in the barrel was stuffed absolutely solid with old socks, trousers, etc, obtained from stores, and was all well rammed home with a pole. The gun was then wheeled into position on level ground. Necessary adjustments were made by daylight, so that all I would have to do before firing, would be to open the shutter of the camera, closing it again after the explosion.

High spirits prevailed throughout the evening. After dinner the usual preparations were made for seeing off the train, which was due to leave before midnight. This included the loading of beer into the transport, also a secret weapon which I had thought of that day – a large keg of soft soap. The time at last came for firing the salute. It was known that I'd loaded 'double for luck', so everyone moved off to what they hoped was a safe distance, except 'Lassy' who remained by the mess entrance gently swaying in the breeze, with another large glass of rum cupped in his hand. I opened the shutter, lit the fuse and moved back again to the camera. The explosion was stupendous. The gun fired at both ends as the breech-block blew out and sailed into the mess, landing with a crash on the floor, fortunately just missing Lassy who, looking rather dazed, announced in a slow, very audible and very deflated manner: "I won't have any more, thanks." He then dropped his glass and promptly fell flat on his back.

Alas the gun had fired its final shot, as the lock mechanism had been completely shattered. As though to make the best of this last effort, the wadding had torn through our telephone wires, severing all communication with HQ in Baghdad.

At the station the farewell party was soon in full swing. Verey lights being fired off and corks popping to a chorus of a weird assortment of songs. These occasions always appeared to cause a certain amount of alarm amongst the station officials. Whilst these worthies, including the engine driver and fireman, were engrossed in watching proceedings, I got hold of my keg of soft soap, liberally plastering the rims of the locomotive's driving wheels and with what was left, I spread over the rails for a distance of five or six yards. At long last the time for departure drew nigh and as the strains of Auld Lang Syne were wafted into the night sky, the guard blew his whistle and the driver opened the throttle valve. To the accompaniment of clouds of steam, a tumult of sound was emitted by the engine as the driving wheels spun probably faster than they had ever done before, the train however, remaining absolutely motionless. The driver momentarily shot off steam and a loud cheer went up as he once more, without success, attempted to get forward motion. The Iraqi staff were in a frenzy, such a thing had never happened before in the whole history of the railway. However, amid all the shouting and gesticulating someone had the savvy to spot the problem and sand the track, so at long last the train slowly moved off on its journey to Basra.

The photo of the gun's final bang came out very well considering that I was not using panchromatic film. Lassy, who claimed to having been a master gunner in the artillery, was wildly enthusiastic about it all, declaring that it was the only photo in existence of a gun parting company with its breech-block. "It is unique, old boy," he cried, "You must let me send a print to the Shop." Actually the photo has never gone further than my personal album.

The following day, Monday, Reggie Smart, Sibley (a newcomer) and myself were detailed to fly to Basra with two army officers from GHQ, and a RAF specialist on tropical diseases (Squadron Leader Tredgold). We took off after lunch, with the intention of refuelling at Amara, as strong head winds had been forecast. The wind was actually much stronger than anticipated and beyond Kut our ground speed came down to a crawl. About twenty miles short of Amara, it was clearly evident that we were about to run out of fuel, so Reggie went down for a precautionary landing, closely followed by Sibley and myself. Reggie unluckily hit a ridge which broke a longeron, putting his aircraft out of action. We pegged all three machines down for the night and set out in the direction of the nearest village, Kumeit, a short distance away.

One of the GHQ officers could speak fluent Arabic, so all was well on that score. We were greeted by the local head man, Sheik Nejem, who promised to put a guard on the three Bristols and invited us to share his house for the night. A report was telephoned through from the local police post and arrangements made for petrol to be sent up by barge the following day. We then adjourned to the sheik's modest residence.

Much has been written about the traditional hospitality of the Arab. Sheik Nejem certainly maintained this to the highest possible degree. There was something about him that differed from the normal run of Arab and Kurd, and he had a very merry twinkle in his eye. During the evening meal he held forth on the customs and habits of the British and apologised most profusely for his inability to provide us with whiskey. Being a Mahommedan we naturally attributed this deficiency to his religious scruples. However, we were mistaken, for he went on to add: "I did have some whiskey in my house, but am sorry it has all gone, but I do have something else which I know the British like very much." He left the room for a moment and returned proudly displaying two bottles. One was Worcester sauce, the other, Eno's Fruit Salts. He had evidently learnt one of the cures for a hangover.

The sheik then commented on Reggie's saxophone case. Our squadron band was making two final appearances in the Basra area before Ed Rice and Co. left the country, hence the reason Reggie was carrying his instrument. Old Nejem was most fascinated by the appearance of the 'sax' when the case was opened and requested a tune. We all cringed with horror, although Reggie's musical skill was of passable standard when playing in the band, as a soloist in a confined space he was a bit rough and ready. However, nothing daunted he proceeded to play. The sheik's face was a study in polite attention and I so wish I could have read his thoughts. It is, of course, quite possible that he enjoyed the impassioned rendition of Swanee River, or whatever tune it was, but soon afterwards it was time to turn in.

Some years later, when studying for my first promotion examination, I came across a passage in the manual of hygiene and sanitation which reminded me forcibly of the two nights spent in the sheik's house. It read: There is no disease known to medical science which is attributable to the bed bug. Well, within a minute or two of getting between the blankets, we were attacked by regiments of these pests, closely supported by a squadron or two of fleas. These parasites do not worry the Arab in the least, but our two nights were absolute hell.

The following day we dismantled Reggie's Bristol and with the help of a team of Arabs, manhandled all the components down to the village pier. The through railway from Baghdad to Basra follows the course of the Euphrates. There was a single line along the Tigris from Baghdad to Kut, but transportation from there to Basra was by barge and river steamer. In the late afternoon a boat arrived from Amara with petrol for the two serviceable machines, and while attempts to load the damaged kite onto the boat were tried, it was to no avail as the vessel was too small.

After a second night Reggie and Sibley came aboard and we all waved farewell from the bridge to Ed, Ma, Ralph and Jimmy as they sailed by in the *Varsova*. The famous band was no more. On arriving at Baghdad, our senior passenger, Colonel Dent, arranged with GHQ

to send a case of a dozen bottles of John Haig whiskey to Sheik Nejem.
In due course the following letter was received from his headquarters:-

> *General Headquarters,*
> *British Forces in Iraq.*
>
> *13th June 1922*
>
> *To:-*   *Major Middleton West MC*
>   *Flight Lieut Smart DFC*
>   *Flying Officer Greig DFC*
>
> *Reference the case of whiskey sent to Sheik Nejem of*
> *Kumeit by us. The sheik has written his acknowledge-*
> *ment and thanks and puts the resources of Kumeit at*
> *our disposal.*
> *   Will anyone who knows Squadron Leader Tredgold's*
> *address inform him or let me know where to write.*
>
> *Yours,*
> *W Dent.*

The final blowing up of our mess gun might have provided the inspiration or impetus, for within twenty-four hours of our arrival back at
Baghdad from Basra, 'Babe' Hudson, another newcomer to the
squadron, had organised the ultimate episode in the history of the field
guns belonging to the Aircraft Park. The reader might recall that on a
number of occasions we 'captured' these weapons and usually presented them to one of the other units at Baghdad West. Although the
officers of the park regarded these incidents with good humour, their
CO definitely did not.

Babe Hudson, a very large and good looking young man, who was
always bubbling over with fun, organised this event with meticulous
attention to detail, the plan being to remove the guns unobserved and
tow them down to Hinaidi, eight miles away, and present them to 8
Squadron. They were now positioned outside the main entrance to
the Aircraft Park HQ and at night were under the almost constant
scrutiny of one of the sentries patrolling the camp. Moreover, the airfield was surrounded with barbed wire, the only exit being past the
guard room.

Careful reconnaissance of the airfield perimeter wire between the guard room and the junction of the camp road with Maude Avenue, revealed a spot where, with the removal of one section of wire, it would be possible to drive a vehicle from the airfield on to the road without much difficulty and without being seen from the guard room. Arrangements were therefore made for one Leyland lorry to be left that evening outside 6 Squadron's hangars. At about 10 pm, it was moved to the most convenient position on the airfield within reasonable distance to the HQ.

We were split into two handling parties, one for each gun and one member was detailed to engage the sentry patrolling the Park area in conversation whilst the guns were rapidly man-handled onto the airfield. This all went without a hitch and the guns were secured to the rear end of the lorry. A circuitous route without lights to the appointed spot along the perimeter was completed, where a section of wire was removed and then replaced. When clear of the airfield and well on our way to Baghdad, the entry party broke noisily into song.

As we clattered across Maude Bridge, Babe Hudson was lustily singing a popular contemporary air: - If what they say is a positive fact, Oh, death where is thy sting. It might almost be prophetic, as within six weeks Babe had been gathered to Abraham's bosom [9].

We arrived at 8 Squadron's mess just after midnight and woke up the CO, Beery Bowman [10]. Why he was known as Beery I cannot imagine, as nothing in his appearance or conduct ever justified such a nickname. The connection must have been purely alliterative. [The name was given due to his often florid complexion. Ed.] Bowman donned his dressing gown, told us where to deposit the guns, generously opened up the mess bar and provided refreshment. We did not stay long but it was nearly 4 am when we at last reached our own beds.

Oddly enough, not a murmur came from the Park and we heard the following evening that Geoffrey Bowman had given orders for the wheel hubs of the two guns to be drilled and riveted. They never returned to Baghdad West, and thus ended the hectic history of these two ancient relics.

Following the departure of Ed Rice we had to get acquainted with our new CO, Squadron Leader E R Manning MC. Rice and Manning were as different as chalk and cheese. While the former was a tubby man with an ebullient personality, Manning, an Australian, was in contrast tall and thin and rather taciturn. He was, however, an efficient CO and in time we found that his natural reserve masked a very kindly nature. If any member of the squadron got into trouble, Manning would do his damndest to get him into the clear again [11].

From a personal point of view I had a strong feeling after my 1920 chums had left the country that the squadron was going to the dogs. After a month or two the outlook became substantially more optimistic. A cross-section of the new community revealed similar qualities to the old bunch. We did not, however, have a replacement for the piano-playing Jimmy Lawson.

On 16th May we had a tragic example of failure to observe that well proven maxim — When taking off never attempt to turn back with a konking engine. I was resting in my room after lunch when I heard a Bristol leaving the ground. Suddenly the even note of the engine changed to the staccato crackle indicative of acute fuel shortage. I dashed out onto the verandah, where I could see that the aircraft had reached a height of about 2,000 feet, its engine still spluttering. Had the pilot pushed his stick forward to keep up his speed and gone straight ahead beyond the airfield boundary, the result at worst would have been a damaged undercarriage. Instead he held momentarily to a level course, steadily losing height, then started a gentle turn to the left, obviously with the intention of landing back on the airfield. The Bristol stalled, fell into a left hand spin and struck the ground vertically, bursting into flames on impact. Thus died Flying Officer Hooton and his passenger, AC2 Butler [12].

I flew up to Sulaimania on the 25th, on detachment for two and a half weeks, with Bunty Frew in command. We were to co-operate with two columns of levies, one from the town, the other from Halebja, a town about forty-five miles to the south east. They were converging on an area in the vicinity of the village of Bani Banok, high up on the steep slope of the Hawraman mountain range that formed part of the frontier between Kurdistan and Persia. We were after recalcitrant Hawraman tribesmen who were stirring up trouble. The two columns were to meet and form an advanced base at Khurmel, close to the foot of the range.

The morning following our arrival I flew out with Captain Makant of the levies as my observer, to report on the progress of the converging columns. We kept each column informed of their respective positions by dropping messages, until they eventually met as planned. The next day, I landed at Khurmel with radio equipment and an operator, Corporal Dyer, to establish a ground station. The landing ground marked out by the levies was simply microscopic and had it not been for a high prevailing wind we might have had some difficulty in getting down. Luckily this strong wind lasted more or less throughout the period of operations.

On the morning of 31 May, Babe Hudson flew out to the column, taking with him Drudge, the photographic officer from HQ at Baghdad. Drudge, complete with camera, had flown up the previous day with Trevor Cripps and Lucy of 30 Squadron. On completion of their reconnaissance to Bani Banak they flew back to Sulaimania. I was on the airfield at the time of their arrival and watched the aircraft come in. Babe approached in a series of tight S-turns, the final one being carried out just short of the airfield and at a very low altitude. The Bristol was just about at its maximum angle of bank and pointing head into wind when it stalled and came down with a sickening crash on its port wing tip very close to where I was standing. In company with others I ran to the wreck expecting to find both occupants dead. Both were unconscious, Babe having sustained a very nasty, triangular, depressed fracture of the skull right in the centre of his forehead. To our astonishment, Drudge bore no visible sign of injury. After disentangling them from the wreckage, they were conveyed to the local native hospital, a very primitive building, with a solitary Indian doctor and staffed by Kurdish women.

The cause of the crash was pretty clear. The gliding turns carried out were accurately executed but tight enough to cause a high wing loading due to centrifugal force – 'g'. Had this approach, for example, been carried out in England under temperate conditions near sea level, a normal landing would have resulted. However, there were two factors which Babe did not allow for. (a) The altitude of the airfield, approximately 3,600 feet above sea level, and (b), the sub-tropical temperature of a hot, sunny day, which, acting in concert, reduced the buoyancy of the atmosphere, thus raising the stalling speed to well beyond normal.

An urgent signal requesting medical aid was at once despatched to Baghdad and within a few hours one of our own doctors, Spud Murphy, arrived. After a quick examination, Spud radioed Baghdad to send a specialist, this second medic arriving the same evening.

During the afternoon Bunty and I bombed Bani Banok, after which he flew down to Khurmel for a conference with the levy staff and remained there overnight. He sent a signal that all available aircraft were to bomb the mountain base at 06.00 hours the next day, in close support of the levies, who would be carrying out their main assault.

So the following morning I carried out two sorties. On the first my bombs exploded near the column, narrowly missing the GOC, General Nightingale. Early in the afternoon I bombed up once more and loaded some cans of petrol in my rear seat in lieu of an observer. After releasing my bombs over the target I landed at Khurmel to hand over the petrol to Corporal Dyer and to await further orders. No further bombing was needed but my services were required in a most unusual capacity. During the withdrawal down the mountain side, one of the British officers attached to the levies, Lieutenant Mott of the 3rd Dragoon Guards, had been shot through the spine by a sniper and died instantly. The GOC wanted me to fly the body back to Sulaimania for proper burial. I agreed on the understanding that a signal would be sent warning all those directly affected at Sulaimania. I did not want to arrive on the airfield un-announced in these macabre circumstances.

Mott was a very tall man, I should judge about 6' 4". By this time rigor mortis had set in, consequently the stowing of the body within the limited space available in the rear seat of a Bristol Fighter, presented quite a challenge. He could not be hung from the bomb racks; we tried! We eventually found the solution by adjusting the Scarff gun mounting to its maximum elevation and strapping the body to it in a standing position. The whole effect was grimly grotesque in the extreme, but there was no other alternative.

After taxiing the machine into position for departure, I paused while the levies were formed up along the line of take-off. I waited until the ranks had been properly dressed, with rifles at the slope. As I opened the throttle, the order to present arms was given, this final salute being completed as the Bristol sped on its way. To anyone not knowing of the circumstances, and viewing from a distance, it looked for all the world as if a senior officer was standing upright in the back of the aeroplane, acknowledging the salute.

Although the flight back only took about half an hour, it was certainly the weirdest I had ever experienced. That tall, inert figure, with head thrown back by the blast from the propeller, apparently standing rigidly upright immediately behind me, the eddies caused by the body sending cold draughts down the back of my neck. There was one unfortunate occurrence which we could not have anticipated however. The result of the officer's wound had meant immediate death, so the body, in consequence, had not bled to any appreciable extent. The rush of the slipstream now acted as a suction pump and by the time I reached my destination the aluminium-painted fuselage, from rear cockpit to the rudder, was sprayed with blood. To make the situation even worse, the radio message warning of my unusual arrival, had not been received. Therefore, as I taxied up to my screw pickets at the edge of the airfield, two airmen wandered up. The expression on their faces when they saw the state of the machine and then my passenger, was beyond description.

The following day, Bruce Sutherland and Johnny Leacroft [13] of 8 Squadron flew a couple of medical orderlies up from Baghdad to assist in looking after Hudson and Drudge. In addition to his passenger, Johnny had several cases of beer on board his Ninac, for our detachment, as we had run completely dry. The airfield had a very pronounced slope to the south and at the time of their arrival a slight and variable southerly breeze was blowing. Under these circumstances the aircraft should have landed UP HILL despite the fact that this would have been down wind. The DH9a was a much heavier and less handy machine than our Brisfits, consequently it required more room in which to land. It must also be borne in mind that wheel brakes were still a thing of the future. All breaking effort was only provided by the drag of the wooded tail-skid at the rear.

Sutherland, who came in first, elected to land by the wind-sock, which of course, meant down hill. He touched down satisfactorily but so close to the southern boundary that he over-ran the limits and dam-

aged his undercarriage. We all hoped that Johnny – with our precious
beer – would profit by this incident and land up hill. No such luck.
Down he came into wind, held off too high, stalled and crashed. It was
truly a terrible moment. We were not the least bit anxious about
Johnny, it was the fate of the beer that was uppermost in our minds!
When we had raced to the scene, both occupants were still smiling and
miraculously – and thankfully – not one bottle of beer had been broken.

Much to our regret, Babe Hudson died on 6th June. It had not been
his first skull fracture. He had been wounded in the head in 1916, suffered a fracture shortly afterwards, and had also been wounded when
finally brought down in 1917. He had lived this time just six days, and
that having lasted so long after the early onset of meningitis was, we
were told, due in some measure to the plate in his head, which allowed
for the expansion of the inflamed brain tissue. We buried him next to
Mott and two WW1 German airmen, the committal service being conducted by Squadron Leader Saul from HQ, as no chaplain was available.
The service was an ordeal, as, for some reason or other, Saul solemnly
ploughed through all the alternative prayers, in the order for burial.
We thought it would never end [14].

Drudge had no broken bones, but had been extremely concussed,
plus bruises and sprains. His left leg had sustained a hammering too.
The shock, very understandably, had thrown him very much off balance
and he suffered from a number of strange delusions. We visited the
hospital each day and I can well remember him confiding in us that
the doctors were most incompetent. They had, he whispered, removed his left leg and grafted on a Kurd's leg in its place. On another
occasion he told us the new leg was square. However, he eventually
recovered and served on until retiring as a wing commander in 1927.

I will always remember that primitive Kurdish hospital and the un-
stinted care and devotion lavished by the Indian doctor and the somewhat wild-looking Kurdish nurses, on our two unfortunate comrades.
The operations at Bani Banok were now over and the levy column
moved on towards Penjvin, some miles to the north west. My final detail before returning to Baghdad was to take Major E B Noel, the political officer from Halebja, on a reconnaissance beyond Bani Banok. He
especially wanted to look at a place called Weiss. According to my map

this was on the Persian side of the Hawraman mountains, where a forced-landing, in addition to salvage and recovery difficulties, might well be awkward politically. However, nothing daunted, we ventured north, crossing the range at 15,000 feet. Noel was obviously keenly interested in the terrain but I failed to observe exactly what he was looking for. I was however, absolutely fascinated by an oval, deep blue jewel glittering in the sun, thousands of feet below at the bottom of a valley – Lake Merican. This was a large expanse of water, with nothing comparable on the Kurdish or Iraqi side of the frontier. Lakes, waterfalls and rushing mountain streams have always given me a thrill. In this instance the sight of the lake was so unexpected that it must have made a profound impression on my subconscious mind, for many years later, I had a very vivid dream in which I was sailing serenely through space, unencumbered by any mechanical contrivance, pull of gravity or any other mundane sensation. Suddenly my surroundings became strikingly familiar and there down below me was my lake. I immediately went into a terrific dive, flattened out and skimmed the surface of the water like a swallow catching flies, zoomed up the mountainside again, and awoke to find myself still comfortably in my bed. Perhaps, when we shake off our mortal coil, travel in this manner may be a reality? If so, all the trouble of getting steamed up to fly to the moon, Venus and Mars, on a front end of a squib and all trussed up in a space suit, really seems rather pointless.

At the end of the third week in June, the CO tackled me quite casually outside the mess one evening to say: "I've just heard that a passenger on next week's mail run to Cairo has dropped out. You've been out here nearly two and a half years without leave, so I've put you down to take his place. Four weeks holiday should do you good." I thanked him and said that I would be more than pleased to go. He then added that he had a married sister living in Alexandria and would give me her address and a letter of introduction.

With one passenger and crew, with Flying Officer P M McSwiny, Vickers Vernon J6865 took off from Baghdad at 5 am on 24th June. Two hours later we landed by Ramaidi, having covered eighty miles against a 45 mph head wind. Dust was blowing, so we could not continue till the next morning.

We took off once more after dawn on a very tedious journey, with wind and dust making things difficult. Just beyond Wadi Hauran we lost sight of the Fordson Furrow, also a lot of altitude, so we landed in the desert to hold a conference. After some discussion as to our best course to fly, to find the track again, we took off once more. The Furrow was soon relocated and the Vernon plodded steadily westward, practically making no forward progress at all. After flying for seven and a half hours from Ramaidi we found ourselves over 'J' landing ground and short of petrol, so down we went. Our average speed for that day was exactly 40 mph. After rigging our ground aerial, we radioed Amman for fuel, then prepared to camp till morning.

The desert at this point is 2,000 feet above sea level, consequently when the sun went down there was a very sharp fall in temperature and we shivered all night. Early next day two Ninacs arrived from Amman with petrol, and it was not long before the Vernon was on its way to Ziza, the final refuelling point a few miles to the south of Amman. This flight took exactly two and a half hours. The east-bound Vernon was also at Ziza, with Reggie Smart as one of the passengers returning from leave in Egypt.

It was early afternoon before preparation for the final leg of the flight was completed. It was also hot and with a light breeze blowing from the west, so we had to take off towards the mountainous ridge bordering the valley of the Dead Sea. Our attempt at leaving the ground at Ziza stands out very nearly at the top, if not the actual pinnacle of really frightening experiences. The Vernon was a fairly large machine, powered by two 375 hp Rolls-Royce Eagle VIII engines. As we rolled across the ground it soon became pretty obvious that our total of 750 hp was not going to get us off satisfactorily under the conditions of wind, temperature and atmospheric density prevailing at that time of day, the altitude of Ziza airfield being about 3,000 feet above sea level.

I was sitting in the second pilot's seat alongside Philip McSwiny. After an immensely long run the wheels at last lifted from the runway, but that was about all. McSwiny looked worried, and my apprehension increased to abject terror, as the rising ground kept only just clear of our undercarriage, and I was convinced we were going to crash. In a frenzy, I grabbed the second control column just as McSwiny started to edge the machine round in a very flat, skidding turn to the left. He could not apply any bank as there was so little clearance that to have done so would probably have pushed the wing tip into the ground. We literally slithered round in an enormous left-hand circuit and managed to land again in one piece. We both heaved a mighty sigh of relief.

I immediately went up to Reggie and asked if I might return to Baghdad with him as I could not face the prospect of another take-off like the one I had just experienced. I got no change at all. "Don't be a bloody fool, Greig, nobody will be taking off till dawn tomorrow, when the air will be cool. Go to the mess and have a few noggins, you'll soon forget all about it." This was very wise council, the few evening noggins completely restored my confidence and the following morning in the cool and denser air, the old Vernon leapt into the air, cleared the Judean Hills with ample margin, and we arrived at Heliopolis four hours and twenty minutes later.

I have purposely described this flight as it affords an interesting comparison with present-day air travel. The distance from Baghdad to Cairo is about 850 miles, which we took three days to complete, the actual flying time being sixteen hours and ten minutes. By modern air liner it only takes a fraction of this time.

[1] Later Marshal of the Royal Air Force, Sir Arthur T Harris GCB OBE AFC. Army and RAF in WW1, served as a fighter pilot on the Western Front in 1917, and commanded a Home Defence Squadron in 1918 (AFC). C-in-C Bomber Command 1942-45. Died in April 1984.

[2] Later Air Vice-Marshal Sir Robert H M S Saundby KCB KBE MC DFC AFC. Another soldier and then fighter pilot in France 1916-17, who also flew in Home Defence, whence he shot down Zeppelin L48 on 17th June. Retired in 1946 and died in September 1971.

[3] Later Air Chief Marshal Sir Ralph A Cochrane GBE KCB AFC. Son of Baron Cochrane of Cults. Served in the navy and RAF in WW1. Served as ADC to King George VI and Queen Elizabeth II. Retired in 1952, died December 1977.

[4] Samuel Marcus Kinkead from Jo'burg, had an Irish father and Scottish mother. RNAS from 1915, then RAF in 1918. Awarded DSC & Bar, DFC & Bar in WW1, followed by the DSO for service in Russia 1919. A very successful fighter ace.

[5] Later Air Chief Marshal Sir George H Mills GCB DFC. Bomber Command in WW2 (DFC). ADC to the Queen 1956-63, when he retired. Was also Black Rod till 1970. Died in April 1971. Air Marshal Sir Douglas Macfadyen KCB CBE. Group captain WW2; AOC British Forces, Aden, 1952-53, then commandant RAF Staff College 1953-56. Retired in April 1959 and died in July 1968. His son also became an air marshal.

[6] Matthew Brown Frew had received the DSO MC & Bar and Italian Silver Medal as a fighter pilot in both France and Italy in WW1. A Bar to his DSO came for service in North Kurdistan 1931-32 and after more distinction in WW2 he retired as Air Vice-Marshal Sir Matthew, KCB CB AFC in 1948. Died May 1974.

[7] Lt Shipwright flew Spads with 19 Squadron and was shot down by the German ace Offstv Klein of Jasta 18 on 16th August 1917. Klein ended the war with sixteen victories, Shipwright being his first.

[8] By 1939 Colin Spencer Richardson MBE had risen to group captain.

[9] Although Hudson may have been a newcomer, he was an experienced fighter pilot of WW1. Flight Lieutenant Frank Neville Hudson had been a soldier and pilot and had won the Military Cross in 1916. Wounded twice and finally shot down and taken prisoner, he had been Mentioned in Despatches after the war for gallantry whilst incarcerated by the enemy. He was seriously injured on 31st May 1922 and died on 6th June.

[10] Geoffrey Hilton Bowman DSO MC & Bar DFC CdG, was yet another successful WW1 fighter pilot who had achieved over thirty victories. Retiring as a wing commander in 1934 he served again in WW2 till 1941. He died in March 1970, aged seventy-eight.

[11] Edye Rolleston Manning came from Sydney. Served in the British army before moving to the RFC, where he won his MC in 1917. He would be awarded the DSO in 1924 before retiring in 1935. In WW2 he served in the Far East with the RAF becoming an air commodore. He died in April 1957, aged sixty-eight.

[12] Lionel Conrad Hooton MC & Bar, soldier and pilot in WW1. Won his first MC in March 1918, flying AWFK8 two-seaters in France, the Bar coming later that summer. He had also served in Russia in 1919. He was five days short of his thirty-first birthday.

[13] Both men later became group captains. Robert Bruce Sutherland DFC served in Egypt in WW1. He retired from the RAF in 1947. John Leacroft MC & Bar was yet another soldier turned airman, who had flown as an observer

and fighter pilot in WW1, and again another high-scoring ace. He retired in 1937 but served again in WW2. He too lived in Bexhill until his death in August 1971.

[14]Later Air Vice-Marshal Richard E Saul, CB DFC. DFC awarded at the end of WW1. Commanded No.13 Group of Fighter Command during the Battle of Britain, then AOC Egypt 1943. Retired in June1944; died November 1965r.

8

MY LAST YEAR IN IRAQ

My leave in Egypt followed the pattern expected of most young men returning to civilisation after two and a half years in the wild. Although the change probably boosted my morale, I doubt whether I derived much benefit physically from burning the candle at both ends. However, as previously mentioned, my daily swim in the Mediterranean at Aboukir completely healed my hands. Our return flight to Baghdad was accomplished without trouble in two days, flying time being twelve hours and twenty-five minutes, with a staggering average speed of about 70 mph.

After Egypt the heat of Iraq was of furnace intensity. It was now the fourth week of July and as the reader might well imagine, our chief form of recreation in the hot weather was our evening swim. Way back in 1920 we started to use a large island in the Tigris, known to us as Pig Island, as these animals were reported to exist there, although we never saw one in the dense scrub. We would drive down to the river bank after tea, take a boat across where we had a sandy beach, although in truth it was more mud than sand, where we had it entirely to our-

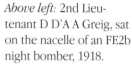

Above left: 2nd Lieutenant D D'A A Greig, sat on the nacelle of an FE2b night bomber, 1918.

Above right: The author had a passion for motor cycles, shown here on a Douglas model "while in Iraq.

Left: The FE2b; it was this type of aircraft in which the author went to war.

Bottom left: The author shown here on another Douglas motor cycle. This picture was taken in Iraq, 1921.

Right: The author with yet another motor cycle, though this time he is pulling B Flight personnel out to dispersal. Jimmy Lawson is at the front.

Below: A 6 Squadron Bristol Fighter over the desert.

Below right: 6 Squadron's mascot, 'Jane', Iraq.

Bottom: Officers of 6 Squadron, Baghdad, in 1922. Front l to r: Roberts, author, Briggs, H G Smart, Squadron Leader E A B Rice MC, R Sorley, Lawson, S D Culley DSO, Langley. Rear: E J Ffoulkes-Jones, J W Cordingley, L C Hooten MC, A E Beilby, Pruden, Brewerton, Beach.

p left: The squadron often escorted DH9 bombers of 30 Squadron, like the one seen here flying
ove the Iraq desert.

ove right: The author seated in a Bristol Fighter. It was not his usual machine but is the second
om the right in the line-up of BF2bs (below).

ove: Major Charles Goring MC in a Rolls-Royce armoured car.

low: A line-up of 6 Squadron's BF2b machines. The tail markings denote the flight; A Flight had
nnants, B Flight had card suits, and C Flight had chequered tail-fins. The machine on the far right
H1558, often flown by the author.

Top left: Tea-break out in the desert. The author took several trips with the army out into the desert looking for native rebel tribesmen.

Top right: Flight Lieutenant E R Tempest MC DFC, killed in a DH10 crash with the author in the rear cockpit, 21st January 1921.

Middle left: Another version of a Rolls-Royce armoured car. Note the Browning machine gun, solid tyr and the protective doors (open) in front of the radiator.

Above: The Avro 504 (2293) that shed its No.8 piston causing Bowen-Buscarlet and the author to for land, Salisbury Plain, 9th October 1924.

p left: A post-war Sopwith Snipe. The author flew Snipes at the Central Flying School.

p right: The author seated in a Grebe II monoplane, J7288. This machine later flew with 25 quadron in 1929.

iddle: Grebe II J7288 – note the 'blood wagon' on the right in the background.

bove: Instructor and pupil using the Gosport tube to communicate.

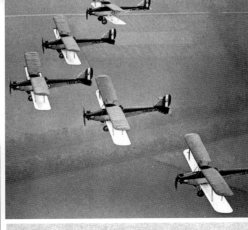

Above: Flight Lieutenant J A Slater MC DFC, whose footprint was marked on the Up-avon Mess ceiling the night before his death, in November 1925.

Above right: Greig's display team, flying DH Genet Moths. The author is leading, with Atcherley and Beilby on his right, and Waghorn and Stain-forth to his left.

Right: Making a for-mation loop, the au-thor leading. Again Waghorn and Stain-forth (J8819) are on his left, and Atcherly and Beilby are on his right.

Bottom: Waghorn on a roll (J8816).

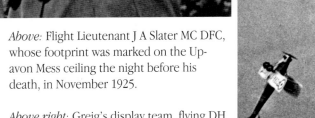

Above left: A Gloster Gamecock of 23 Squadron. Flying one on 27th April 1927 the author failed to recover from an induced spin and was forced to use his parachute to bale out.

Above right: Taking Moth G-EBSI to Copenhagen in September 1927. This picture shows the stop at Hamburg, with the author and his friend Claude Frowd checking things in the foreground. Note the hangar with the name of Bäumer. German World War I ace Paul Bäumer's aircraft works were here, although he had been killed during a test flight two months earlier.

Left: Squadron Leader W H 'Scruffy' Longton DFC AFC, killed during the Bournemouth Air Races on 6th June 1927.

Below: G-EBSI had been repainted overnight to the Danish T-DALF. The bearded man is the new owner, arctic explorer Peter Freuchen, and his young son.

Above: The Fokker F7 (H-NADX) in which the author and Claude began their return to Croydon from Copenhagen on 27th September, with Claude's head deep in a sick-bag.

Above right: DH Moth G-EBTD, fitted with a new Halford engine, tested by the author at Stag Lane on 11th January 1928.

Middle: The 1927 Schneider Trophy team, Venice. L to r: Flight Lieutenant H M Schofield, Flying Officer O E Worsley, Flight Lieutenant S N Webster, Flight Lieutenant S M Kinkead DSO DSC DFC, Squadron Leader L H Slatter OBE DSC DFC. It was Sammy Kinkead's death in 1928 that led to the author becoming officer commanding the RAF's High Speed Flight. Behind them is a Supermarine S.5.

Bottom: Flight Lieutenant S N Webster, the pilot who won the Schneider Trophy in 1927, seen here with R J Mitchell and his Supermarine team.

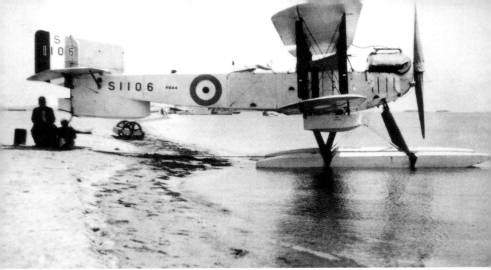

Top: A Fairey IIID Mk II Flycatcher. It
s a similar machine in which the au-
or first made a water take-off after
ning the High Speed Flight, on 7th
y 1928.

Above left: A Gloster Napier IV (N222)
nich the HSF had on strength.

Above right: Supermarine S.5 (N220)
king off. This aircraft was flown sev-
al times during the build-up to the
29 race.

Right: It was in a Supermarine S.5
(N220) that the author achieved the unofficial world speed record of 319.57 mph, on 4th Novem-
er 1928. Here is Greig climbing into it.

Above: The author seated in his S.5.

Above right: The ground crew hold the Supermarine S.5 down as the engine is run-up.

Right: Two giants of the aircraft industry sit side by side, R J Mitchell of Supermarine and H P Folland of Glosters.

Below: Personalities of the 1929 team. Reginald Mitchell, the famed designer of a Supermarine (a father of the Spitfire), George Stainforth, A H Orlebar, D'Arcy Greig DFC AFC and AVM 'Topsy' Holt.

Above: Augustus Henry Orlebar AFC, team leader for the 1929 race.

Top right: Greig in the S.5. Note the windshield in the up position prior to take-off.

Above right: Reginald Mitchell, the author and Harold Perrin of the Royal Aeronautical Club.

Below: The victorious 1929 Schneider team. L to r: H R D Waghorn, T H Moon, Greig, A H Orlebar, G H Stainforth, and R L R Atcherley.

Above: Not getting one's feet wet. The author about to be carried to his seaplane.

Top right: Greig being towed out to the start-line in '5'. In front is '8' flown by Batchy.

Above right: The author's N219 being put into the water on her trolley, with Calshot Castle in the background.

Below: At the 1929 race. D'Arcy Greig on the left, his brother Billy far right. The lady is Laura Dean, soon to become Mrs Greig.

Top left: Waghorn's S.6 (N247), in which he won the 1929 race at Calshot, which was numbered '2' on the day.

Top right: The author during the 1929 race at Calshot in N219 '5'.

Above: At the pontoons, 7th September 1929, awaiting the final tow to take-off positions. Aircraft '4' is a Macchi M.52R flown by Wing Officer T Dal Molin, '7' is a Macchi M.67 flown by Lieutenant R Cadringher, and '10' is another M.67 piloted by Lieutenant G Monti. Next is '8', a Supermarine S.6 (N248) flown by Atcherley and '5' is the author's N219.

Above right: The course of the 1929 race.

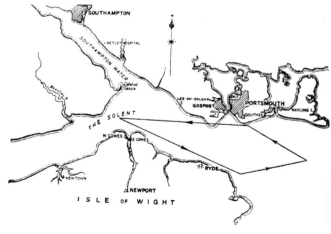

Right: Greig, slightly oiled-up, and Waghorn, after the race.

Middle: A cleaner Greig at Calshot, aboard a pontoon.

Bottom: Wing Commander Greig, seated centre, front row, when officer commanding 75 Squadron in 1939.

Top left: The author showing off his experimental g-suit, Canada, 1940.

Top right: Calgary, Canada, October 1941. Greig is at the back during a visit by the Duke of Kent. Far right is Wing Commander Sir Louis Greig KBE MVO (no relation), who had been an aide to Prince Albert (later King George VI) in World War I.

Above left: Group Captain Greig back in England.

Above right: Air Commodore Greig during an army exercise in World War II.

Above: Greig is presented with a certificate to mark the fiftieth anniversary of the winning of the Schneider Trophy, by Sir Dermot Boyle. The trophy is in the background. On the extreme left is AVM F W Long CB.

Right: At a reunion of old pals: Dermot Boyle, the author and 'Batchy' Atcherley.

Below: Air Vice-Marshal S N Webster CBE AFC and Air Vice-Marshal F W Long CB with the author at a function in 1979. Sidney Webster had won the Schneider Trophy in 1927, while Frank Long had been a member of the 1931 team.

selves. The Tigris contained some very large and rather bony fish. On one occasion, Hatcher (our AO) and I hit on the idea of trying to collect some fresh fish for the mess, by a simple expedient of dropping explosives into a deep pool to stun them. We had no gun-cotton in the bomb dump so decided to use Mills grenades.

One evening we duly armed ourselves with a few of these and joined the usual bathing party. Everyone was most interested in our experiment and the bank was searched until we found what appeared to be a very deep pool, overhung by a vertical drop of about six feet. Hatcher was to be the bomb thrower, the retrieving of the stunned fish being my responsibility. The safety pin was withdrawn from the first grenade and Hatcher dutifully lobbed it into the water a few feet out from the bank. Normally the bomb should have exploded after five seconds, but nothing happened.

We waited a while longer for the detonation but there wasn't a ripple on the water. I therefore decided to dive in and retrieve the dud, if I could find it. The pool was indeed deep and I must have gone down some fourteen feet before striking the bottom. After grovelling in the inky blackness for only a second or two, my hands contacted a hard metallic object. It was something much larger than a grenade and I experienced a little difficulty in bringing it to the surface. Returning to the light of day I held aloft a 16 lb Hales anti-personnel bomb, an obsolete type once dropped by aircraft. It obviously had not long been in the water as there was no sign of rust, and its yellow paint was still in good condition.

We didn't try another grenade but returned to camp to report our find. We discovered that the local ordinance depot had, only a few days previously, dumped several tons of obsolete or unserviceable explosives into the same pool. If our grenade had not been a dud, the chances are that the explosion would have set off the whole lot and blown us all sky high! We thanked our lucky stars that our guardian angels had been kind enough to spit on the fuse.

We were now at the end of August 1922 and no further mention had been made of Kerim Fattah Beg for more than two months. This does not imply that this gentleman had been keeping out of mischief – quite the opposite. Shortly after the Bani Banok expedition, KFB, with a following of about forty horsemen, met by appointment Captains Bond and Makant of the levies, ostensibly to come to terms, instead, they were both shot in the back. At the time of the incident, Sutherland of 8 Squadron, was sitting blissfully by his force-landed DH9, a broken connecting rod sticking through its sump, only a mile or two from the place of the murder. Luckily for him the raiding party never spotted his downed machine.

KFB and his gang managed to evade the levy column and aircraft that attempted to find him, so they eventually reached the Towandez area. After a short lapse of time he returned with a very strong following and was soon within a few hours march of Sulaimania, threatening the only lines of communication by which a retirement could be carried out from the town. The rebels really had their tails up, as only a short while back a levy column had been routed by Pishder tribesmen on the Rania Plain, the tribesmen being successful in capturing a considerable quantity of booty, including mountain guns, machine guns and ammunition. A strong levy force was now operating in the vicinity of Koi Sanjak, a town situated in the mountainous country to the north west of Kirkuk and on the southern ridge that overlooked the Rania Plain. 8 Squadron was detached to Kirkuk to work in concert with 55 Squadron at Mosul, in support of these operations.

On 3rd September I was ordered up to Kirkuk and attached to 8 Squadron to act as an air taxi and general 'dogsbody' to the levy column to the north. Early the following morning I was ordered off to Koi Sanjak to pick up a badly wounded officer, Captain Teague, and fly him back to Kirkuk. Before taking off on this assignment the passenger's seat was loaded with boots and medical comforts for the levies. A Rhesheba (the black wind of Kurdistan), a strong north-westerly wind, violent and gusty, was blowing across the Koi Ridge and as I was landing, a severe gust dropped my Bristol heavily on one wheel, resulting in the collapse of the starboard centre-section struts, and the breaking of a cross-bracing wire in the front bay of the fuselage.

Normally, this mishap would have meant an immediate grounding of the machine until completion of repairs. However, I reckoned that with careful handing the Brisfit would hold together. The gale-force wind reduced our take-off run to a few yards only, which was all to the good, but the vibration due to the damage, was pretty severe until the wind took the full weight of the aircraft. So long as the engine was running smoothly the aircraft felt quite normal. Throttling back to reduce speed had the effect of producing a low amplitude vibration as though the Bristol was trying to flap its wings! However, I and my wounded passenger landed safely at Kirkuk without sustaining further damage. As I got out, an airman informed me that Flight Lieutenant Massey, the detachment adjutant, wished to see me.

On my way to report to the HQ tent, I wondered what I had done wrong this time, but on arrival Massey handed me two telegrams, one from my squadron and the other from Wing Commander [W F] McNeece, of Group HQ. Both wires were to congratulate me on being awarded a permanent commission. My reaction on receiving this news was one of intense satisfaction and relief. I could now banish from my mind the prospect of having to look for a job in civilian life in about three months time.

There are many who maintain that the first 'airlift' in air force history was the evacuation by 70 Squadron, of about 600 personnel from Kabul, in Afghanistan, at the end of 1928 and early 1929. This is not the case. On 5th September 1922, and within a space of just a few hours, sixty-five government officials, Assyrian levies and friendly Kurds, were flown from Sulaimania to Kirkuk. The preparations for this evacuation had been completed with the utmost secrecy. My CO, Squadron Leader Manning, was in charge of the operation which was carried out by a mixed bag of aircraft, Ninacs, Bristols and two brand new Napier-engined Vernons of 70 Squadron. If I remember rightly, the Vernons were flown by two stalwarts of the 'heavy brigade' – Ted Hilton and Tom Horry [1]. My own Bristol was undergoing a rapid repair, so I was landed with the job of reception officer at Kirkuk. For a short while I was kept busy, booking in the oddest collection of passengers. Some Ninacs seemed to have complete families within the confined space of their observer's compartment. There were Indian 'Babu' clerks, Kurds and Arabs, in fact anyone who was liable to get their throat cut when KFB and his merry men took over. The last to land were the evacuating party, Manning, Reggie Smart, and 'Gobbo' Gibbs [2].

Later that afternoon there was another job for me, for two Britishers still remained in the danger area. Major Noel and 'Mongoose' Soden of 1 Squadron [3], had been on leave and climbing mountains in the Penjvin district and were due back at Haleja, about forty to fifty miles beyond Sulaimania, that day. Manning detailed me to take Sibley's Bristol, fly to Halebja, pick them up and fly them to Baghdad. As there were no night flying facilities at Kirkuk, the chances were that it would be dark before I could get them back. The flight out would take about an hour and a half and I would have to allow at least two hours for the trip back with the extra weight. I did not care much for the prospect, even with an extra fuel tank under the rear seat, there would be little margin for error and Sibley's Bristol was not fitted out for night flying except that the ASI and compass had luminous dials. I took off at 4.30 pm feeling very gloomy about the whole affair, but was overjoyed when, about twenty minutes later, the engine started to spit and vibrate badly. I carried out an immediate about turn and got back to Kirkuk without further incident.

Early the next morning I made a fresh start for Halebja, this time in my own machine and with an escort of two 8 Squadron machines flown by Beery Bowman and Flight Lieutenant 'Porky' Park [4]. Park's DH9 burst a tyre whilst taking off, so Bowman and I carried on without him. As arranged the previous day, I was to land and pick up the two passengers, but this time bring them back to Kirkuk. The escorting Ninac was to orbit the airfield and come to my assistance in the event of trouble.

I landed and met Noel. The news of the Sulaimania evacuation had not yet filtered through, so the inhabitants were still friendly. However, there was an unforeseen and very awkward situation, for Soden was not at Halebja, but languishing in a tent four miles away, with an attack of jaundice. I felt that this unexpected complication required the attention of a senior officer, so I decided to signal by popham panel to Bowman, to come down and join us on the ground.

The airfield was small and sloped steeply to the west, and a light wind was blowing from the west. I knew that Bowman was an excellent pilot quite capable of getting his machine down in this very restricted space, provided the landing was made up hill. I therefore put out the usual signal for indicating the desired direction for landing, ground strips in the form of a letter 'T', with the head of the tee facing up hill.

To my utter consternation, Bowman proceeded into the wind but down hill, overshot, and climbed away again. Once more he came in the same way and again was forced to overshoot. If only we had ground to air radio in those days. By this time I was in a frenzy, and feeling completely helpless. He made a third and final attempt in like manner. On this occasion his judgement was perfect and to make sure of getting down, he switched off the engine. The Ninac touched down with his propeller stopped, right on the eastern boundary, ran straight down the slope to the west, over-ran the farthest limit, and trundled into a ditch where it stuck, with its tail pointing to the sky.

On reaching the wreck I found Bowman venting his spleen on the unfortunate aircraft, hurling rocks at it and cursing wildly. He had mistaken the meaning of my signal and thought he was supposed to land down the long arm of the tee, a most unfortunate error. Noel reckoned that the best thing to do now was to walk up to the town, about a quarter of a mile away, and try to sort things out in comfort.

The town of Halebja and its surrounding district had a distinction almost unique in the Moslem world, the local ruler being a woman. In the eyes of Mahommedans, a person of the inferior sex. The Lady Adila was a member of a ruling family of considerable standing and was known to us as 'The Old Lady of Halebja'. However, as Noel had been on good terms with her in his official capacity for some years, we all repaired to her house where the demands of traditional hospitality had to be satisfied before we could get down to the serious discussion about what to do next.

We had just started an early lunch when a very excited Kurd rushed into the room announcing that news of the Sulaimania evacuation had come through, and that the local inhabitants were all for KFB. Worse still, my Bristol Fighter had been smashed up by a mob. This was a little disturbing to say the least, but we carried on with our lunch in typical British fashion, secure in the knowledge that so long as we remained under the lady's roof we would be quite safe.

In the postprandial discussion which followed, the Lady Adila strongly advised Bowman and myself to remain in her house until nightfall when she would provide us with a couple of horses on which to ride to the frontier, forty miles away. This suggestion filled me with horror as I was no horseman and the idea that I should ride a hard-mouthed native steed, sitting on a Kurdish saddle, in pitch darkness over rugged mountain terrain, just turned my bowels to water! Eventually, Noel suggested a quiet walk to the airfield just to see the extent of the damage to the Bristol. We all agreed that this was a good idea, and the Lady Adila said she would come with us to ensure our safe conduct.

That walk was a masterpiece of nonchalance. We strolled down the road lined with what appeared to be bunches of cut-throats just itching to slit our gizzards. We chatted away with Noel who was wearing a lounge suit and swinging a walking stick. It really seemed most odd. On arriving at the Bristol we found that the wrecking report had been a gross exaggeration. The fabric on the lower wing had been torn and a few ribs broken, and all removable flying gear, including my helmet and goggles, had been stolen. Having found the aeroplane to be perfectly flyable, it only remained to settle upon a plan to meet existing contingencies. Finally, it was decided that Bowman and I would fly back to Kirkuk straight away, that Noel would return to Lady Adila's house and then make his way back to where Soden was located, and that in forty-eight hours time aircraft would fly out to a rendezvous somewhere on the Halebja Plain, where we would pick them up. We studied my map, fixed an area for the RV, handed over ground strips for marking a landing area, then started the Bristol in which Beery and I flew off without further ado.

For the trip to the RV, two Bristols flown by Bunty Frew and myself would be escorted by two Ninacs flown by Park and George Daly [5]. The prearranged day turned out to be a dud owing to a dust storm, but the following day was clear. Bunty and I took off to the RV, the two DH9s to the rear. We spent some considerable time searching from a low altitude but neither of us saw any ground strips or any sign at all, so after a time we reluctantly gave up and flew home. As we were about to land I noticed that our escort was no longer with us, neither did they turn up immediately after we had landed. About half an hour or so later, both machines came in, with Noel and Soden as passengers. The two pilots had spotted the ground signals just as Bunty and I set course for base and as they were unable to catch us up, went down and did our job for us. Did Bunty and I feel small? We went around for days with our tails between our legs, feeling that we had let the side down. Eventually we flew back to Baghdad on the 13th.

For some time to come the rebels went from strength to strength, the Pishder tribe, with the aid of Turkish personnel (mainly Bashi Bazouks), money and arms, forced the levies to evacuate temporarily, both Koi Sanjak and Ranis. The DH9 squadrons were kept very busy during this period, and started operating very effectively with bombs fitted with long delay fuses. As a demoralising weapon, they were first class, and the Kurd could just not fathom the heavy explosions that suddenly took place when no aircraft had been heard or seen for many hours.

Towards the end of this month, Air Vice-Marshal Sir John Salmond [6] arrived from England to become CinC, Iraq. Among the various changes that took place was the transfer of the armoured car units to the RAF. My old chum Charles Goring had to discard his army uniform and don RAF blue. On 2nd October, I was detailed to fly Sir John on his first tour of inspection around the northern outposts of his new command. We left for Mosul the next morning, the flight being un-eventful, save for the fact that a Vernon carrying his kit, force-landed, and he had to make do for the next twenty-four hours with what he had with him in my Bristol. Sir John next flew with 55 Squadron on the 4th, to four outposts north and west of Mosul. Later that day I was informed that early the following morning Sir John wanted me to fly him to Erbil, another quick inspection, after which we were to take off in time to join in a bomb raid on Koi Sanjak by 55, 30 and 8 Squadrons.

The town of Erbil is one of great historical interest, its origin being buried in the depths of antiquity. It was old when Alexander the Great marched through on his way to India, and in those days was known as Arbela. Through the centuries it has survived the devastation of war, earthquake and famine. The main part of the town is built on an enor-

mous circular tumulus largely consisting of the ruins of previous buildings. As a landmark it is unique and can be clearly seen from a great
distance.

As a contribution to the raid, we loaded eight 20 lb Cooper bombs
on my Bristol before leaving Mosul at 6.45 am. We reached Erbil in
time for breakfast and I had barely left the machine when Charles Lit-
tledale, chief of police of the area, spotted my camera and claimed my
attention with the following greeting: "Hello, Greig, you've got a camera, so are just the chap I'm looking for. We've got a hanging on at the
serai and there's just time to take a picture of it before you eat." I had
learnt by now that this was a country of surprises but this one took the
biscuit. However, always willing to please, I jumped into his car. Fortunately, Sir John had already been taken care of by senior officials, so
I was quite free to go until the time came to rendezvous with the Ninacs.

On arriving at the serai, I found that the hanging was over, the felon
being a Kurd with a long record of highway robbery and murder. The
execution had not been carried out in the conventional manner, no
trap or scaffolding being available. However, it had been dealt with
very effectively. The condemned man, his hands tied behind his back,
his feet fettered and an ammunition bag placed over his head, had been
pushed off the wall of the fort. They had allowed sufficient slack in
the rope to allow for an adequate drop. I took the required photos,
which turned out very well, and was then conducted to the mess.

When Sir John and I took off, the Ninacs from Mosul could be seen
approaching, so our time was just right. The formation overtook our
machine a few miles from the target, so the raid was already in progress
when we reached the immediate vicinity of Koi. I regret to admit that
the accuracy of the bombing was of a rather low order and I became
acutely conscious of the CinC's displeasure. I could almost feel the
wrathful emanations filtering through from the rear cockpit. I must
admit quite frankly that the current methods of bomb-aiming were decidedly haphazard, few pilots taking really serious interest in the bomb-
sights then in use. Reliance was placed almost entirely on individual
technique. In the Bristol was a type of fixed sight on the floor of the
pilot's cockpit, consisting of a condensing lens and one or two cross-
wires, but it was not much use.

My old friend Arthur Beilby, had evolved a remarkable system of his own, for which he claimed a quite exceptional degree of accuracy. His method was to approach the target head into wind at an altitude of 3,000 feet, wait until it had disappeared behind the leading edge of his bottom plane, then recite 'The Lord's Prayer' at normal speed before pulling the bomb-release toggle! With regard to the present occasion, I waited until the whole area was partially obscured by dust and smoke before making my run in and releasing the eight bombs. I think this subterfuge paid off, as there was no adverse comment from behind me.

Immediately after the raid, a conference presided over by the CinC, was held at Kirkuk. Sir John had some very caustic comments to make on the obvious lack of training in the use of bomb-sights, Ray Collishaw and 'Mary' Coningham [7] the two subordinate commanders present having to bear the brunt of this admonition. The following morning I completed my tour with Sir John, my landing being made at Kingerban and Khanikin where inspection of the levies and APOC workshops was carried out. Baghdad was reached in time for lunch.

Owing to the almost continuous operations now taking place in Kurdistan, two Ninacs were based on Mosul whilst 6 Squadron's Bristols, augmented at times by other units, continued to work from Kirkuk. Consequently, at the end of the summer, semi-permanent accommodation was erected at the latter airfield. This took the form of a large serai constructed of mud bricks, into which the aircraft were wheeled at the end of each day's operations. Against the eastern wall of this edifice, rather rough and ready but nevertheless quite adequate, was mess accommodation put up with 140 lb tents erected along the northern wall. The only privileged person who was allowed to live at the house of the political officer was the detachment commander.

I spent practically the whole of my remaining time in Iraq on detachment at Kirkuk, an arrangement which suited me admirably. The Squadron had moved over from its old home at Baghdad West and had taken up residence in the brand new buildings at Hinaidi. Although the mess and quarters were quite luxurious, I missed our primitive mud huts of the preceding two and a half years, with their many memories of jolly parties and hilarious goings-on.

The move to Hinaidi also coincided with a tightening up of discipline, including the inauguration of proper daily working plus weekly ceremonial parades. This was not at all to my liking. To my everlasting shame I must confess that throughout the length of my service I had a deep dislike for drill and ceremonial, for the simple reason that I was completely lacking in aptitude in this capacity. If anyone could be relied upon to get out of step, halt on the wrong foot, give the wrong word of command or end up with the rear rank where the front rank should be, that was me all over. I can recall a singularly painful episode when, one Friday morning, I was detailed to command A Flight on parade. I was stricken with terror, as this meant leading the flight, and if it had been C Flight I could have followed the movements of the other two in front. Gobbo Gibbs, now our very efficient adjutant, was officer in charge of the parade. The flights were formed up in the usual manner, I believe column in flights might be the correct term, with me standing on my own and right out in front. Another failing was that I was never any good at interpreting the extraordinary sounds that issued from the vocal cords of officers and senior NCOs, when giving the executive order of command for some movement or other. On this particular occasion some such noise emanated from Gobbo, who was somewhere right out on the flank. I was in a state of desperation and I suppose such situations frequently result in desperate measures, for on the spur of the moment I raised my voice in a frenzied shriek, with: "A Flight, by the right, quick march." I stepped off smartly with my left foot and headed for the hangars. After a moment or two, it sunk through to my paralysed brain that I could not hear the rhythmic stamp of marching feet following my wake. On glancing nervously over my shoulder, I observed some distance to the rear, an immobile line of airmen in the final stage of having been dressed by the right. I miserably retraced my steps, showing bags of swank, but feeling a complete prune! I never lived that one down.

I suppose it could not be expected much better from a peculiar mentality such as mine, which sees in a guardsman's bearskin, a pregnant tea-cosy, and in the RAF full dress hat of the period between the wars, a baboon's bottom with a feather stuck in it.

Two flights of four Bristols left Hinaidi for Kirkuk on 4 October, with Bunty leading one and myself the other. We refuelled on arrival and immediately set off on a raid on Rania, with two more during the afternoon. Ray Collishaw was OC of the detachment. The next day our forward supply dump at Kingerban went up in smoke and 2,000 bombs and 10,000 gallons of petrol were destroyed, so not a good start. However, bombing continued for the next four days before a temporary halt had to be called due to our loss of supplies.

This period witnessed the advent of a new weapon, the 'baby incendiary bomb'. They really were babies, each weighing only a few ounces and about the size of two 12-bore cartridges. The BIs were carried in canisters of about 250, the complete cluster from each being released simultaneously. They were excellent for the destruction of fields of standing corn, hay stacks, and houses that had already been damaged by high explosives.

The Kurds also, were showing some initiative in the use of weapons, no doubt ably instructed by their Bashi Bazouk friends from over the Turkish border. Machine guns captured by the Pishder tribe a month or two earlier were used against us. Their best effort, however, was the adaptation of captured mountain guns for anti-aircraft work. Personally I never saw any shell bursts, but among others, Harry McLaren Reid reported bursts in the vicinity of his machine [8]. Another 'dodge' was to post riflemen high up on the mountain-side where they could take pot-shots at us as we flew by.

Nevertheless, despite all this 'frightfulness' only one fatality due to enemy action took place in this locality during the remainder of my time at Kirkuk. Sopwith Snipes of 1 Squadron were working with us, and on the morning of 24th October, Flying Officer F S Harrick of this unit was reported missing. He had last been seen diving on a camp near Ranis. All available aircraft searched the area for the next forty-eight hours but to no avail. We eventually heard that his Snipe had been brought down by machine-gun fire and had dived through the roof of a house in Rania.

During the last week of October, my pyrotechnic collaborator, Hatcher, arrived from Baghdad. One afternoon when off duty, I went for a walk with him towards the rising ground near to the north of the airfield and discovered what seemed to be a line of wells at regular intervals, of about fifty yards or so, running in a straight line from the direction of the hills towards the town. They were roughly twenty feet or so deep and at the bottom was a stream of clear water. Although we did not realise it at the time, it must have been an artificial channel connecting a spring up in the hills, into the town. Such devices are fairly common in the more arid regions of Persia where they are known as Qanats. The only one which we found was probably of great antiquity. However, what interested us was the fact that the stream contained fish.

We at once decided to attempt fish bombing, our previous effort at this sport back at Baghdad having been abortive. No grenades or guncotton slabs were available, so it seemed that our project was doomed before it had begun. Fortunately, I had a brilliant idea – why not try a 20 lb Cooper bomb! The Cooper was a fragmentation bomb designed to go off immediately upon impact with the ground and had been used a good deal against German troops, transport and airfields, in WW1. To make them safe to handle and to eliminate risk of explosion if accidentally released from an aeroplane in the process of taking off, the following safety devices were embodied in the nose-cap. Firstly a small aluminium wind-vane had to complete twenty-five revolutions once dropped, before the striker was properly aligned with the percussion cap of the detonator, and secondly, a small copper rivet securing the striker to its socket, the force of the blow upon the nose-cap having to be of an intensity sufficient to fracture the rivet.

At the first available opportunity we returned to the line of wells, complete with one Cooper. We selected a boring with vertical sides and no protuberances to impede its fall. The plan then was to run to a hole downstream after dropping the bomb, so as to retrieve any dead or stunned fish that floated by. I removed the nose-cap, rotated the wind-vane till the striker was properly aligned, gave it a sharp tap to sheer the copper rivet, inserted the detonator and replaced the cap. The Cooper was now in a thoroughly dangerous condition. Without further ado, I stood at the edge of the boring, the bomb in my right hand extended to arm's length, Hatcher firmly gripping my left wrist. On completing a count of three, I released my hold on the Cooper, and Hatcher tugged me away from the hole with all the force he could exert.

There was a splendid explosion, followed by a fountain of water that shot into the air. We had been so intent on our nefarious task that we failed to notice the approach of a sleepy looking Kurd, mounted on an equally drowsy horse. The animal, its head down and proceeding at a very slow walk, was only a few yards away when the fountain of water blasted its way into the firmament. The effect of this unusual phenomenon upon the poor beast was stupendous. It took off like a rocket and in no time was out of sight, the rider on its rump, hanging on for grim death.

This momentary diversion took our attention away from the boring, from which issued plopping noises, indicating the partial collapse of its walls. We rushed down to the next well, to see the water, that hitherto had been crystal clear, was now the consistency of pea soup. I regret to say we found no fish, our only trophy being the empty shell of a solitary crab.

Between the episode of the Cooper bomb and my departure from the country, I was only implicated in one spot, or series of spots, of pyrotechnic skulduggery. One afternoon when shopping in Kirkuk bazaar, I found a stall with Chinese fire-crackers on sale, and couldn't resist buying several bundles of them, although I had no definite clues as to what I could use them for. However, it was not too long before I overcame this problem, receiving sudden inspiration, from which I fashioned a fiendish plot. I disentangled one bundle and proceeded to experiment with individual crackers. The object was to find a way of exploding them underwater – but not, this time, for catching fish. The fuses were of thin, twisted paper, containing a 'fizz' mixture. By trial and error I eventually found that by allowing the fuse to burn till the flame reached the casing, then casting the squib into a bucket, an under-water explosion would result. It had, of course, to be timed to perfection, not least because there was only a three-second delay between the flame reaching the casing and the ensuing bang.

As stated previously, all members of the detachment with the exception of the CO, slept in small tents pitched in the serai. We used camp beds and what is more important in this instance, camp baths made of canvas, rigged in a low, collapsible frame. Most of the chaps had their daily bath in the evening, either before supper or at bedtime. By now, the evenings had drawn in, illumination within the tents being provided by paraffin lamps. Owing to the shadow cast against the tent fabric, it was relatively simple to see what the occupants were up to whilst one strolled casually by, and if bathing, the sitting victim made a very clear silhouette. What could be simpler when taking the air in the evening, than to touch off the fuse of a cracker with the glowing end of a cigarette, lift the fly of a tent and drop it into the bath?

It was not long before a general air of apprehension prevailed each evening at bath time – it was all too easy. An exploding cracker under a bare bottom didn't really hurt but it was inclined to be a trifle startling. Any way, the general effect provided entertainment for any onlookers, which was all that really mattered. I did not have it entirely my own way and at times I was the object of well deserved pretty rough treatment. I recall on one occasion being tied to a chair and forcibly fed with some extremely hot curry! However, on balance, I think it was worth it.

We continued to harry the Kurd unremittingly throughout November and December. On the first day of November we had a particularly successful sortie with our baby incendiaries, the smoke from burning stacks and houses in the vicinity of the target hanging like a pall at several thousand feet. I had little sympathy for the Kurd, for he was a barbaric foe who did not understand handling with a velvet glove. The only thing he did understand and admire, was the big stick.

Civilisation is something which takes a very long time to sink in. One can educate the 'wild and woolly', provide him with modern amenities, motorcars, machinery, the lot, and gradually adorn him with the trappings of culture, but all too often it turns out that under a very thin veneer, the savage is still furtively lurking. Let us digress for a moment and jump ahead to the late 1950s. Iraq, by then was a modern and independent kingdom. A spark of rebellion kindles a conflagration and young King Faisal and Nuri Pasha were both brutally murdered. Nowadays, all too often it seems that common sense is being sacrificed upon the altar of political expediency.

Having got that profound statement off my chest, let us return to

14th November 1922. Our CO, Squadron Leader Manning, arrived up at Kirkuk together with Flight Lieutenant J M Robb, a new flight commander just out from England [9]. Robb had come to us from 24 Squadron at RAF Kenley, where for a year or two he'd been kept pretty busy flying to and from Paris with various wise and learned gentry, whose job it was to prepare the treaty which could guarantee future immunity from Teutonic aggression!

At the end of November I heard that I was to be posted to Egypt instead of returning home. I was simply furious as I had nearly completed a year over the normal tour for Iraq. Fortunately, HQ was very sympathetic and promised to do all they could to get matters put right.

December proved to be a very chilly month, especially when under canvas, and our tents were stiff with frost each morning. The 140-pounder [tent] would hold just two people, and at this time I was sharing with young Bonham-Carter [10]. One could work up a wonderful fug very quickly by lighting the Primus stove. None of us considered living under these conditions in any way a hardship, in fact we thoroughly enjoyed life in general. We made our own Christmas decorations for the mud-brick mess and had an unexpected and uninvited guest for the festive season, in the form of a stray pigeon, that flew in one day and took a fancy to our mantelpiece. We made a great fuss of it, and so it decided to stay the winter. It had its own special niche to the right of the warm chimney stack.

On Christmas morning, Pa Miller, the political officer, and officers of the levies, called on us. We returned their call after lunch, but three of our party, Robb, MacFarlane and Bonham-Carter, had to dash off on a raid. In the evening we all mucked in and helped entertain the airmen.

Boxing Day was the day I carried out my last bomb raid before leaving. It might easily have been my last ever, as some fiendish marksman put ten bullets through my Bristol Fighter. Had I been forced down, I know either Bunty or our third man would have followed me down to rescue me. We were a very closely knit team and flying in formation with good and dependable chaps engendered a great sense of security over hostile territory. Finally on the 29th I said goodbye to Kirkuk and flew back to Baghdad.

One day in the second week of January 1923, I was again on the deck of the SS *Varsova*, sailing serenely over the bar of the mouth of the Shatt-el-Arab, and out into the Persian Gulf. I glanced at the slowly receding landscape and was pondering my three-year sojourn in the 'sweatbox of septic sores'. I thought to myself, Greig, that lousy old land has really done you very well. Three interesting, busy, entertaining and profitable years. So, hail and farewell, ancient land of Adam and Eve, of Ur of the Chaldees, of Abraham, Sennacherib and Belshazzar, Noah, and Sinbad the Sailor. But what future awaited my arrival in England?

[1] Later Squadron Leader Thomas Stanley Horry DFC AFC. Joined the RFC in 1917 and won his DFC as a fighter pilot on the Western Front in late 1918.

[2] Later Air Marshal Sir Gerald E Gibbs KBE CIE MC & two Bars. Another successful WW1 fighter ace who had flown in Macedonia. After a successful career, he retired from the RAF in 1954 and died in October 1992.

[3] Frank Ormond Soden DFC & Bar had been a successful fighter pilot in France during WW1, with twenty-seven claimed victories. He had also served in South Russia in 1919 and the Bar to his DFC was awarded for operations in Kurdistan in 1922. As a wing commander in WW2, one of his jobs was station commander of RAF Biggin Hill in 1941. He died in February 1961.

[4] Walter Henry Park MC DFC served in Egypt, Gallipoli and Macedonia in WW1 before training as a pilot. He won the MC in 1918, followed by the DFC for operations in North Russia in 1919. For his work during the evacuation of Sulaimana he received a Bar to his DFC. Returning to England in 1927 he was on the staff at ADGB but died in October 1928 after a short illness.

[5] George Dermot Daly DFC, was a wing commander by WW2 and retired as an air vice-marshal CBE, in 1949. His 1922 DFC was awarded for operations in Kurdistan.

[6] Later Marshal of the RAF, Sir John M Salmond GCB CMG CVO DSO Ld'h CdG. The son of a knighted major general, he had been a soldier before WW1 and moved to the RFC in 1912. In 1918-19 he commanded the RAF in the field, and later rose to chief of the air staff. He died in 1968.

[7] Having spent much of his youth in New Zealand, Arthur Coningham had become known as 'Maori', which in turn became 'Mary'. In WW1, as a fighter pilot, he had received the DSO MC and DFC. In WW2 he commanded the Desert Air Force 1941-43, then AOC 2nd TAF 1944-45. Knighted for his work, he was lost on a flight to Bermuda in 1948.

[8] By 1939 Harry Redvers McLaren Reid was a wing commander. In 1923 he was awarded the DFC for two actions in Kurdistan on 15th February and 19th June of that year. He retired as a group captain in 1948.

[9] Later Air Chief Marshal Sir James M Robb KBE GCB DSO DFC. A Scot like Greig, he had been a successful fighter pilot in France during WW1, and following a period with 6 Squadron in Iraq, took command of 30 Squadron (1923-24), where he received the DSO. In WW2 he commanded ADGB/Fighter Command and retired from the service in 1951. Died in December 1968.

[10] Later Air Commodore David W F Bonham-Carter CB DFC. In WW2 he served with 5 Group, Bomber Command and OC RAF Waddington (DFC). AOC RAF Hong Kong (1951-53) after which he retired from the service in February 1953. Died in May 1974.

9

A LONG LEAVE, THEN 24 SQUADRON

In due course, the *Varsova* reached Karachi, where I transferred to HM Troopship *Braemar Castle*, an ancient relic of the Union Castle Line which, so I was told, saw service as a troopship during the Boer War. The 'old girl' was lightly laden and I was given a deck cabin, luxurious travel for a very junior pilot.

The voyage to Egypt was enjoyable. On the morning of our arrival at Port Said, I was standing by the deck with all my luggage ready for disembarkation, when the ship's adjutant, Hugh Walmsley [1], emerged from his office and informed me that a signal had arrived cancelling my posting to Egypt and that I was to carry on to the United Kingdom – Heaven be praised.

Owing to a heavy influx of troops due for home, my deck cabin was given to a senior officer and I was banished to a really horrible affair down in the bowels of the ship. The new cabin was shared with two very cheerful Irishmen, Mickey Noonan and Denny. Despite this congenial company the rest of the voyage was sheer misery. The cabin was badly ventilated and on the first night out I developed chronic asthma, a complaint from which I had suffered as a child. This is mentioned solely because I was destined to be severely handicapped periodically by this wretched malady throughout the rest of my service on the active list. We eventually sailed up Southampton Water on the afternoon of Monday, 13th February, but did not disembark until the next morning. I noted that this was the exact same date I had departed from England three years previously.

I quickly reported to Air Ministry and was granted six months accumulated leave, and reached my home in Bexhill-on-Sea on the evening of the 14th. The next couple of weeks or so were spent in searching for a second-hand car, and I eventually found one to my liking in London's Great Portland Street, a Hillman 'Speed Model'. It was resplendent in shining aluminium, with a magnificent straight-through, copper exhaust pipe on the outside of the body. The shining body and copper pipe probably clinched the deal, for although the engine made a magnificent 'burble' I noticed on reaching open country that the rear axle produced an aggravating whine which increased to a shrill scream when a speed in excess of 45 mph was reached. However, this misfortune was accepted philosophically and plans were made for a few visits with this conveyance.

On my arrival home a letter from Ed Rice, my former CO, giving all the latest news of 6 Squadron, was awaiting me. Ed had just re-formed 11 Squadron at Andover, had Ma Briggs with him and Reggie Smart was at the nearby Central Flying School (CFS) at Upavon, as chief flying instructor. A westerly course for Salisbury Plain was therefore decided upon, a locality with which I was entirely unfamiliar.

I stayed a few days at Andover and whilst there drove over to Upavon one morning for lunch with Reggie. It was a dreary day in early spring, a low rack of cloud at about 800 feet with a steady drizzle. Much will be written about Upavon in later chapters, but brief comment on first impressions would not be out of place now.

The road from Andover passes directly through the camp at Upavon, the main airfield being to the south of this road, with a smaller, subsidiary field to the north. As I slowed down on entering, my attention was riveted by a solitary Snipe aircraft, the only machine in the air. The pilot was performing a series of absolutely perfect rocket loops, the machine momentarily disappearing in the overcast at the top of each loop, and flattening out from the ensuing dive just about level with the hangars, not more than about thirty feet from the ground. The judgement and smoothness of each manoeuvre were superb. I was simply enthralled, and having never flown a 'scout', I envied the pilot his prowess. I later learnt that the chap in the Snipe was Flying Officer 'Pedro' Mann, who had a reputation of being probably the finest pilot in the RAF at that time [2].

The CFS was formed at Upavon in 1912 and in a contemporary issue of *Aeroplane*, the editor, the one and only C G Grey, referred to the school as being built on the top of a mountain. This was, of course, a bit of an exaggeration, the eminence being about 500 feet above sea level, with the undulating terrain of Salisbury Plain stretching away to the south as far as the eye could see. The officers' mess is on the northern slope of the camp and separated from the south aerodrome by a small pine wood. It was to this building that I now repaired in order to meet Reggie for luncheon.

The Upavon Mess is unique. Its construction began prior to WW1 and was completed in 1915 when it took the place of the original mess, a temporary, wooden affair. The building is of stone and with the exception of one small room, at that time used as a ladies' room, was built on one floor but owing to the slope, on two different levels. It faces north with a magnificent view of the Vale of Pewsey to the Marlborough Downs.

One approached the entrance up a flight of broad stone steps. The hall is imposing, with a short flight of marble steps spanning the whole area and leading to the domestic offices. To the left of the hall, a passage leads to the cloak rooms, card and billiard rooms, the walls of this area being hung with photographs of prominent personalities in the history of the unit, and group pictures of various courses. There are two doors to the right, the first giving direct access to the main anteroom, then through a further door on the west wall, to a second and smaller room. A broad 'plate rack' runs around the walls of the main room, above which were mounted trophies of the chase.

The second door to the right of the hall leads to a covered court of ample proportions and having a roof and west wall of glass, also a parquet floor. Suspended from the roof trusses were numerous baskets of growing plants and flowers. This area functioned as a ballroom in addition to a splendid sun lounge, for it stretches the full length of both ante-rooms, to which it has access. The south wall of the court leads by way of two entrances up a short flight of marble steps to the dining room on the upper level of the building.

My initial entry to the dining room completed a picture which can only be best described as 'dignity combined with an atmosphere of good, solid, comfort'. It was a long room, with a fireplace at each end, and large bay windows facing south. An unbroken line of polished mahogany tables ran the length of the room and between these and the bay windows was a short impressive sideboard covered with a massive array of food. On it were sirloins of beef, broiled ham and chicken, legs of lamb and pork, fish and an infinite variety of cold viands. Behind the sideboard stood the man responsible for the provision of all these things, a figure of dignified military bearing, of middle age and dressed formally in civilian attire. "A slice of undercut, Sir, or perhaps you would prefer a little cold salmon?" I noticed that Reggie and other members of the mess, addressed him as Mister Watts. However, to the commandant, Group Captain Holt [3], he was 'sergeant major'.

Before returning home I attended a guest night at Andover. Shortly after dinner some extraordinary noises were heard emanating from the ante-room. A crowd surrounded the piano and seated at it was a young pilot officer with a face like a fish, who was giving an impassioned rendering of grand opera – 'Pagliacci' I believe. As he sang in a very strident tenor voice, his face seemed contorted with intense agony, the words being in a completely unrecognisable language. He was an unquestionable master at the ivories. Such was my first meeting with 'Cod' Forster, a chap who could entertain by the hour and who could 'take over' the band in any London night club, without giving offence to the normal conductor. Unfortunately, he lost his life a couple of years later in a car crash in Iraq; a great loss to the community [4].

Towards the end of April my leave was rudely interrupted by a letter from the Air Ministry informing me of my selection for the second Air Pilotage Course at Calshot, commencing in May and ending in July. It regretted the interruption to my leave but stated that I could take the balance outstanding on completion of this course. Feeling a little put out, I nevertheless reported to Calshot, not having a clue as to what the course involved. It turned out to be a course on dead reckoning navigation. Strictly speaking, I should draw a veil over this brief interlude, as my general performance was far from creditable. I received my first shock upon discovering that some knowledge of trigonometry and logarithms was essential, so being never any good at maths, it was just like returning to school. Moreover, we were expected to do home work in the evenings. Personally I found the delights of Bournemouth to be far more attractive. However, with the passage of time, it eventually sunk into my thick skull that a 'fix' could be something other than an awkward situation, that a 'gnomonic projection' had no connection whatsoever with Fairyland, and that the 'saturated adiabatic' was not a nickname of our instructor in meteorology.

The practical side of the course was pleasant, as it involved excursions around the English Channel in Felixstowe F5 flying-boats [of 480 Flight at Calshot]. These ancient relics were masterpieces of the cabinet makers – sorry, I mean boat builders – whose craft-hulls were beautifully finished mahogany. But they were grossly underpowered by two Rolls-Royce Eagle VIII engines, and if there happened to be a flat calm at time of take-off, they frequently refused to unstick. On such occasions the pilot had to taxi frenziedly up and down the Solent and around in circles in order to disturb the surface of the water before trying again, but even then they sometimes failed to get airborne.

I can recall one exercise in which the quality of my navigation was of a remarkably high order. F5 No.N4035, piloted by Flight Lieutenant O'Brien, was detailed on 11th June 1923 to co-operate in naval manoeuvres being held twelve miles south of Portland Bill. The flight plan entailed: take off from Southampton Water, climb to operational height (1,500 ft) over Calshot, check wind speed and direction, set course for St Alban's Head, then head out to sea to rendezvous with the fleet. O'Brien, generally known as 'OB', was a placid Australian with a very dry sense of humour.

We took off at the appointed time and OB flew up and down the Solent whilst I checked the drift and got the apparently correct wind reading, after which I set to with dividers, chart-board, then the course and distance calculator. Having arrived at a course to St Alban's Head I passed it to OB, then busied myself in the cockpit, calculating the course to steer from there to the RV point. I took far longer than the normal time in arriving at the answer, and happened to glance back casually at OB. To my astonishment he was grinning from ear to ear as though enjoying a good joke. This disturbing phenomenon caused me some apprehension and on glancing anxiously ahead, I was absolutely shattered to see the spire of Salisbury Cathedral dead on our track. With an expression of utter scorn and a shrug of his shoulders, OB did a quick turn to port and it was not long before we were once again over the Channel.

At last came the final examinations, an aggregate of 60% being required for a pass. The kind-hearted staff gave me 61%, so with a light heart I resumed my interrupted leave.

While on my course I had traded in my Hillman for a new car – an HE. This was a rakish contraption with a clover-leaf body, a very noisy exhaust, a performance which did not come up to expectation, but a truly marvellous, close-ratio, four-speed gear box. Cars were still in the pre-synchromesh era but the ease and rapidity of the gear change on this car was quite phenomenal. The makers, now defunct, were the Herbert Engineering Company of Reading, and the designer a clever Cornish engineer by the name of Sully.

As the end of my leave approached I received posting instructions from Air Ministry. My new home was to be 24 Squadron, Kenley, James Robb's old unit. I duly reported on 1 October and to my joy found myself in a squadron similar in spirit to No.6 in Baghdad, a super bunch of chaps, the CO being Squadron Leader E R L Corballis [4]. However, he was due for posting and left the unit a few days later, his place being taken by R S Maxwell, whom I had previously known as a flight commander in 55 Squadron.

Also at Kenley was 32 Squadron, equipped with Sopwith Snipes, and our group HQ was under the command of Air Commodore E L Gerrard [5], one of the pioneers from the very infancy of the flying services. Gerrard left Kenley later in the month, being replaced by none other than the redoubtable Air Commodore C R Samson. Maxwell, or 'Max' as he was usually known to us, was one of those chaps who, in wartime, was a magnificent leader. Under all conditions he had the respect and affection of all ranks but in common with many of his type he might not always have seen eye-to-eye with higher authority. If I may digress for a moment, he was eventually retired from the RAF as a group captain on 1st April 1941 but that was not the end of Max. At the beginning of 1943 I had only just returned to England, and upon calling at the RAF Club a day or so later, I spotted a tall, bearded Fleet Air Arm lieutenant-commander. There was something familiar about him and when he turned, I was astonished to see the ribbons of the Military Cross and Distinguished Flying Cross on his naval tunic. It was Max. After leaving the RAF he had offered his services to the Royal Navy and at our time of meeting he was an instructor in deck landings on aircraft carriers.

The flight commanders in 24 were 'Daddy' Lale, C N Lowe, the famous rugger international and W S Caster [6]. Among the more junior members were a few sterling characters including Eric Wormell, formally of 6 Squadron. In my opinion the leading light in the mess was Flying Officer Willett Amalric Bowen Bowen-Buscarlet [7], or 'Bus' for short, a name that conjured up visions of knights in shining armour, mounted on gaily caparisoned chargers. Bus had no charger but was nevertheless the owner of a 'fiery steed' called a Bertelli, a small racing car with a sleeve-valve engine. A member of Brooklands Automobile Racing Club, he had entered this car for the junior Car Club 200-mile race the following year. Unfortunately, at the last moment it cracked its cylinder block and had to be withdrawn.

Bus also had an exceptional claim to fame in being the designer of a very unusual and revolutionary aircraft called the 'Katashytoplane'. This brain child reached the drawing board towards the end of WW1, when, owing to the submarine blockade, our petrol supply was in jeopardy. It was to use a most unorthodox method of propulsion quite beyond my descriptive powers. Suffice it to say this aircraft never saw active service, but the designer, in keeping abreast with modern developments had, from time to time, embodied various modifications, so that in the event of a future national emergency, this machine would be able to play its part in our defence.

Leslie Hamilton was another character in the squadron [8]. A strikingly good looking young man and a magnificent pilot, with a fine war record. Although not a similar make-up to Bus, he also possessed an inventive streak. His epic discovery was that a toilet roll, launched from an aeroplane, would become completely un-rolled during its fall to earth. Unfortunately, Leslie did not always confine his experiments to the open air. I can recall one occasion when he was week-ending at the Grand Hotel, Eastbourne, and in a fit of exuberance launched a toilet roll from the top floor of the building, down the stairwell and into the main lounge. The manager, particularly as it happened on a Sunday afternoon, failed to appreciate the humour in this and poor old Leslie was asked to leave.

Leslie resigned his commission during the mid-1920s and became the personal pilot to Princess Lowenstein-Werthein. One day, not long after Charles Lindburgh made his historic non-stop, solo flight across the Atlantic to Paris, Hamilton and Colonel F F Minchin DSO MC, along with the princess, tried to be the first across from east to west but were never heard from again.

The work of 24 Squadron was varied and interesting, ranging from communication flying to ab initio instruction. It also provided 'Hacks' for officers working at Air Ministry. The aircraft were a mixed bag of Bristol Fighters, DH9a, and Avro 504K, plus three machines of a new type for trial and report, cumbersome contraptions called Fairey Fawns, a two-seat day bomber.

In view of the amount of instructional flying done by this unit, it was rather odd that I can recall only one member of staff, Flight Lieutenant Caster, being a properly qualified flying instructor. However, within a month or so of my arrival, Flying Officer Kay-Williams was sent to the CFS for an instructor's course and thereafter a succession of pilots went to Upavon to qualify.

Not long after getting into my stride in the squadron, I committed an act of gross stupidity during a flight between Tangmere and Hythe. When passing over Bexhill, I succumbed to a sudden impulse to 'beat up' the Bell Hotel, which stands at the top of the hill in the Old Town. The Bell was where I garaged my car when visiting my nearby home. The landlord was Jack Derry, a former regimental sergeant-major in the Royal Artillery. He was a very understanding chap who was always willing to cash post-dated cheques in time of emergency. Well, as the saying goes, I beat up the pub really good-and-proper. The following

Saturday, on my arrival home for the week-end, I was handed a note in which my presence was urgently requested at the local police station for an interview with Superintendant Whitlock. That's torn it, I thought!

I had hitherto avoided running foul of the police so was in a thoroughly strung-up state when reporting to their HQ. The superintendent, a large, rather heavily jowled man, looked me up and down for a moment or two before speaking. "Well, young man, you've got some explaining to do as I've some very serious charges to make. Among other things, I've received a complaint from all the local chemists that since your visit on Monday last, they've not been able to sell an opening medicine." [laxatives!] When I had recovered my composure following this statement, he added: "Strictly speaking, I ought to report you to your superiors, but if you give me your word that you won't do anything like this again, I'll forget all about it." I gave him the necessary assurance, his concluding remark being: "Cor, you didn't half stir 'em up – did 'em a power of good." I left the station with a very high regard for the East Sussex Constabulary and never again committed this particular indiscretion. Some others, but not one like this!

However, a matter of a few weeks later, I was once more in trouble with the local police. One Saturday evening a friend and I were returning very late in our cars from a party in nearby Hastings and as there was no traffic, decided to make a race of it to the Bell. On turning into the final stretch of about a mile and a half of straight road to the Old Town, I was leading by a fair margin so put my foot hard down to make certain of winning. I was going well when a police constable, hand upheld, stepped majestically into the beam of my headlights. It must be borne in mind that those were the days of an absolute speed limit of 20 mph. I regret to say I was not in the mood to stop for anybody and although I was not actually driving at the constable, he nevertheless decided that discretion was the better part of valour, and leapt smartly to the side of the road.

After garaging our cars at the Bell, we eased open the scullery window, climbed through, and set about plundering the larder. Jack Derry always left this particular window unlatched so that one could enter and obtain refreshment to ward off initial signs of starvation, should the hotel staff have gone to bed.

About twenty minutes later we had nearly finished our snack when our constable appeared at the window. There was nothing for it but to let him in. Police Constable Hyde, in full measure with that unruffled calm so typical of the British Bobby, a characteristic only to be found in the police force of this country. After interrogation and inspection of my driving licence, he informed me that I would be reported for driving a motor vehicle in a manner dangerous to the public, bid us a very civil good-night, and went on his way. He gave no indication of personal annoyance at my outrageous conduct and made no comment on the apparent fact that we had been burgling the larder, not to mention the bar after licensing hours. Anyway, nobody in the hotel was disturbed and in due course we made our usual exit via the back door.

My recent interview with Superintendent Whitlock was still very fresh in my memory, so the following morning, banking on his obvious benevolent disposition, I paid him a visit, hoping that perhaps a lenient view might be taken of my lamentable behaviour. Well, he was not sympathetic. Then, when it was stated that witnesses had said that I had been driving at between 40-50 mph, I foolishly replied: "Well, I wouldn't dispute that!" I knew immediately that I had made an error the moment I spoke.

In due course the summons arrived and was passed on to the Automobile Association to arrange legal representation. They briefed Mr H J A Hardwicke, a well-known local solicitor for my defence, and a plea of 'Not Guilty' was entered. I felt rather a naughty schoolboy up in front of the headmaster when I entered the magistrate's court, the chairman of the Bench being Admiral Davis, the father of one of my chums in the RAF. I also knew the magistrate's clerk, Colonel Langham.

There were two witnesses for the prosecution, apart from PC Hyde. The first stated that he saw the headlights and heard the roar of a very powerful car coming at high speed from the direction of Hastings. He estimated the speed to be 40-50 mph. Under examination by Mr Hardwicke, he admitted that there was no vehicular traffic other than the car following a short distance behind. Also, there were no pedestrians. Mr Hardwicke continued: "In your opinion the car must have been a powerful one on account of the loud exhaust noise. In actual fact it is only a small one of 13 hp, so I put it to you that when you first saw it, it had just turned the right angled bend by the Glyne Gap gas works and was accelerating on an upward gradient in low gear, and could therefore have been travelling at only a very moderate speed. The noise of the engine and the dazzle of the headlights might well have confused you." The witness agreed that this might have been the case. One down, one to go.

The second witness was given similar treatment, Mr Hardwicke handling the technicalities with consummate skill, really creating the impression that owing to the low horse power, upward gradient and a strong head wind, the car was having considerable difficulty in making any progress whatsoever. At this juncture an acquittal seemed to be a foregone conclusion. As Mr Hardwicke sat down, Superintendent Whitlock, who was seated on the other side of the bench, solemnly rose to his feet, fixed me with an unflinching gaze and asked me: "Do you recall visiting me the morning following the alleged offence?" After an affirmative from me, he continued: "When I told you witnesses said you were driving at 40-50 mph, do you remember that you commented that you wouldn't dispute it?" In complete and utter confusion, I replied, "That's a hot question to answer." The Bench retired and on their return said that a fine of £1 would be imposed with costs of 10/- [£1.50]

Before leaving court I was censured by Mr Hardwicke for letting him down badly, in failing to tell him about my chat to the Super. All in all it was excellent value for money – I should have been shot!

These brushes with the local Bobbies, formed the start of a long friendship between Super Whitlock and myself. He eventually became deputy chief constable for East Sussex. On retirement he returned and settled in Bexhill where he later died. He was a very human chap with a delightful sense of fun. His tolerance and understanding were reflected in the general attitude of the force throughout his parish. A rogue would get short shrift but a youthful misdemeanour would generally get away with a sharp 'kick in the pants'. The community at large could do with more of his type.

Meanwhile, at Kenley, here's a word about our mess, which at that time was a fairly large requisitioned house situated on the well-timbered slope of Whyteleafe Hill. In the early and mid-twenties it provided a pleasant home for the single blokes, some of whom lived in the main building, the surplus being accommodated in huts in the garden. The larger bedrooms in the house were made into dormitories to take a number of officers, only those of senior rank obtaining rooms to themselves.

Among the officers under instruction was a very charming squadron leader, an observer during WW1, by the name of John Kilner Wells [9], but known to us all as 'Bombardier'. J K Wells was thirty-nine years of age when he came to us to learn to fly and was almost a father figure to the rest of the mess. He and Buscarlet were chums and played a great deal of Mahjong together. He might well have been regarded as a steadying influence on our juvenile and high-spirited community, but I must say that on 5th November 1923, he strayed just a little too far from the 'straight and narrow'.

Following the honoured practice, a bonfire and fireworks party had been laid on, but on the day it turned out to be bitterly cold, and after tea it started to snow. We all felt depressed and disappointed until some genius said: "To hell with the gloom chaps, let's have the fireworks in the mess." Without a single intelligent thought as to the possible consequences, this suggestion met with instant and unanimous approval. Fortunately someone had the good sense to muster all available fire extinguishers in the hall before the detonation of the first thunder-flash gave the signal for the party to commence. In no time at all a delightful state of pandemonium reigned throughout the building and the hall curtains were ablaze. Luckily nobody was injured, despite the fact that stick-less rockets were snaking at high speed all over the place. The dense smoke and acrid fumes were, however, almost overwhelming and after a few minutes a temporary halt was called to clear the air and slake our thirsts, so we adjourned to the ante-room for refreshment.

Bombardier Wells was already there, quietly warming the seat of his pants in front of the fire, an expression of smug contentment on his face. All was quiet whilst we started on our mugs of ale, then suddenly, our elderly squadron leader announced in a very casual tone: "By the

way, chaps, there's a Verey cartridge in the fire." Now a Verey cartridge
packs a considerable punch. Everyone realising this made a dash for
the door, the last to leave being Bombardier. Luckily, the projectile did
no exceptional damage but the explosion of the propellant ejected the
entire contents of the fireplace onto the ante-room carpet. Fire extinguishers were at once brought into action and afforded almost as much
fun as the fireworks, which were once more in evidence. Eventually
came the explosion of the last of our squibs and the party quietly fizzled
out.

When the smoke finally cleared, the state of the mess had to be seen
to be believed – it was simply chaotic. The bulk of the damage was to
curtains and carpets, and while I can't remember the cost required to
return the building to its previous condition, we had had a remarkably
good run for our money. As if to round off an eventful party and no
doubt due in some measure to the excitement of the evening, a strange
case of somnambulism occurred before a fresh day dawned. As the
reader might readily appreciate, our mess being in normal times a private house, the toilet facilities were not really adequate for our large
population. To compensate for this deficiency, authority had provided
in ample sufficiency an item listed in the appropriate RAF schedule of
equipment as, 'Pots chamber, badged, officers pattern'. In the small
hours of the morning some of the occupants of one of the dormitories
were awakened by the sound of running water. As the lights were still
on an extraordinary spectacle met their gaze. Flying Officer 'Blank'
was standing erect in the middle of the room, sound asleep, whilst performing a natural function. From his stance it was obvious that he was,
or should have been, holding one of the said pots, but in his case it
was wholly imaginary. From the extent of the inundation, his need of
relief must have been great. Luckily there were no carpets on the floor
and the stout deal floor boards, tongued and grooved, provided adequate protection for the ceiling of the ante-room immediately below.

Numbered among our various recreational activities were frequent
visits to the West End, most of us being members of that well known
establishment at No.43 Gerrard Street, the domain of the famous night
club, Queen Kate Merrick. Personally, I was not a very good patron of
the '43', as I did not care for night clubs, but being the owner of a car,
I was frequently in demand as a taxi-driver. The '43' was a fascinating

place although there could be an element of uncertainty about one's welcome, which depended on the frequency and intensity of the occasional 'black'. I can recall one evening when to my utter indignation I received a completely unwarranted rocket from the owner and was requested never to darken her portals again. I took her at her word and forever after avoided this threshold of the underworld.

Our nocturnal visits to London resulted in one time-honoured custom — the breaking of the record from the RAF Club to the mess at Kenley, a distance of about eighteen miles, via Sloane Square, Chelsea Bridge, Nightingale Lane, Mitcham and Purley. In the early hours of the morning, incredible average speeds were recorded over this route, without a single regrettable incident.

Although I did a considerable amount of flying with 24 Squadron, there were very few highlights. First and foremost there was the introduction to that most famous of all training aircraft, the Avro 504K. Buscarlet enlightened me as to the mysteries of the Monosoupape Gnôme engine, whisked me around the sky and sent me solo.

In January 1924, during a railway strike, I flew HM The King's Mail in a DH9 to Bircham Newton, the nearest airfield to Sandringham. On the return flight from this mission the next day, London and the suburbs were enveloped in fog, but the forecast gave hope of clearance, so I decided to press on. If conditions proved to be impossible I could retrace my steps and land at Harlow. I found that to the north of London, the fog extended to Hatfield, so I climbed to 12,000 feet to clear the top of the murk, which was around 8-10,000. I set an approximate course for base, having decided that if at the end of ten to fifteen minutes I still could not see the ground, I would fly back. South of London conditions seemed to be as bad as ever but as I was about to turn, I glanced directly below and saw the faint outline of a chalk circle surrounding the identification lettering of Kenley, although I could see little else.

Although it was a foolish thing to do, I immediately throttled back the Ninac and began a steep left hand spiral, keeping my port wing tip firmly on the circle. It got very dark when I entered the pass but fortunately I did not lose that circle and arrived intact, with the visibility at ground level barely the length of our small airfield. Bad visibility was a condition one had to become accustomed to during the winter, care being taken not to get entangled with the civil aircraft operating from our close neighbour, Croydon Airport. The lack of radio and other aids, was to a great extent offset by the acquisition of a thorough knowledge of all prominent local landmarks, of which Crystal Palace was one of the most valuable as, on a southerly heading, the two towers taken in transit, pointed directly to both Croydon and Kenley.

The year of 1924 saw the amalgamation of four privately operated air transport companies in the birth of Imperial Airways, the forerunner of BOAC. Some time prior to this event, a civilian pilot who had been earmarked for an important appointment in this concern, was to report to Kenley in accordance with some freshly formulated regulation, to undergo a practical flying test to assess his competence. It fell to my lot to test this chap. On the morning of 13th March, to my utter consternation, Major H G Brackley reported to me [10]. I had never previously met him but knew him well by repute as one of the pioneers who had been flying on the London to Paris route from Cricklewood to Hounslow, since 1919. Having to test and report on his ability as a pilot was a most embarrassing and seemingly unnecessary task. However, the demands of bureaucracy had to be met, so off we went in a Bristol Fighter and flew around for twenty minutes. I am sure we both felt the awkwardness of the situation, but he carried out the various manoeuvres in expert manner and was most co-operative in every way. In due course he became air superintendent of Imperial Airways and continued for many years to be one of the really great figures in the aviation history of this country. His death by drowning whilst in South America was a sad loss to civil aviation.

In rounding off this chapter I will relate the story of an event that must rank as unique in the unrecorded history of the RAF. The 'Kenley-Northolt War'. One dull and gloomy afternoon in February 1924, we had just returned to our flight offices after lunch. The weather had deteriorated still further since the morning, with a low overcast and thick mist developing. The trees on the airfield's north boundary, about 800 yards distant, were barely visible. It was clearly unfit for flying so the aircraft were put away and the hangars closed. As we drowsily toasted our toes by our office stoves we became conscious of the dull roar of approaching aircraft. A few minutes later a flock of 41 Squadron Siskins from RAF Northolt, flying in flights, line astern, came in at tree-top height and buzzed over us.

The impact of this unexpected visitation was stupendous, and one could almost feel the scorn and contempt with which the Northolt pilots were regarding the weather-shy Kenley 'cissies'. It was at once apparent to all that something had to be done immediately to retrieve our honour and the atmosphere of languid somnolence changed in an instant to one of intense activity. A rapid improvised conference decided unanimously on an immediate raid on Northolt by all aircraft available.

The leading figures in what followed were Max and Buscarlet, and it was settled that the maximum possible load of toilet paper would be carried by each aircraft for liberal distribution over the target. Whilst the machines were being made ready, one of our officers under instruction, Flight Lieutenant F R Alford, took Bus to Caterham in his car to purchase lots of the necessary loo rolls from a local drug store. What the chemist must have thought of this extraordinary large demand I cannot imagine. By the time they returned to the tarmac area, an assortment of sixteen aeroplanes, Bristols, Ninacs, Avros and the three Fawns, plus three Snipes of 32 Squadron, were ready for action.

The Avros, being the slowest, were the first away, led by Buscarlet, the rest taking off at suitable intervals. Through the gathering gloom this odd armada tore across the housetops of Morden, Wimbledon, Richmond, Brentford and Ealing, and more by luck than navigation, arrived in one compact bunch over Northolt. The load of bumf was well distributed over the entire camp and we were back at Kenley within the hour, just before dusk turned to darkness. There was one casualty – Bus was missing. His engine had conked out over the 'enemy' airfield, forcing him to land there and be taken prisoner, condemned to clear up the bulk of the litter. Having done so, he was regally entertained in the officers' mess for the rest of the evening.

This raid did not bring an immediate reaction and it was some days before a formation of Armstrong-Whitworth Siskin fighters arrived once

more over Kenley. Their bomb load on this occasion being an assortment of old boots, and everyone needed to rush for cover. Again the
atmosphere simmered for a week or two until one evening, during an
excursion to London, Buscarlet spotted a couple of palms, aspidistras
or some such, in two wooden tubs outside the main entrance to the
Jermyn Court Hotel, and decided there and then that they were just
the very thing for planting in the circle on Northolt aerodrome. This
visit to London was prolonged into the early hours, until the street was
reasonably clear, whereupon the tubs were hastily loaded into the
dickey seat of his car and driven home. In due course the raiding party
set off with the tubs on board. They were successfully planted whilst
the bulk of the formation circled overhead.

The success of these operations so stimulated the blood of ancient
warriors which coursed through Buscarlet's veins, that plans almost
amounting to piracy emerged from his fertile brain. Why not a mass
flight to Gosport to capture a naval officer and bring him back to Kenley, or alternatively to Cranwell, and capture a cadet. A scheme was
actually well in progress for a further raid on Northolt and to land a
load of stray dogs and cats on the camp, when the great 'Sammy', our
group commander, stepped in and said that things had gone far enough
already. I'm sure he was right.

Personally, I only took part in the first raid, for on 17th March I left
Kenley for Upavon, to read – mark – learn – and inwardly digest, the
gospel according to Smith-Barry.

[1] Later Air Marshal Sir Hugh S P Walmsley KCB KCIE CBE MC DFC. A WW1
soldier and airman, he won the MC for long-range bombing sorties in 1918, and
the DFC for operations over Iraq in 1922. In WW2 he served with Bomber Command and Transport Command. Retired in 1952 and died in September 1985.

[2] William Edward George Mann was just a couple of months younger than
Greig and had been a successful fighter pilot in WW1, and had won the DFC.
Post-war he was an instructor at CFS, and part of the RAF aerobatic team.
Later became air commodore CB CBE. Died in May 1966.

[3] Later Air Vice-Marshal Felton Vessey Holt CMG DSO, son of Sir Vessey Holt,
of Holt & Co, the army's bankers. In WW1 Holt had invented the Holt Flare
System landing aid. When AOC Fighting Area, ADGB, he was killed in a mid-

air collision whilst a passenger in a Gipsy Moth, and a Siskin, on 23rd April 1931.

[4] Flying Officer Edward Beresford Forster, died 26th May 1928.

[5] Later Air Commodore Eugene Louis Gerrard CMG DSO, who had been with the Royal Marine Light Infantry pre-WW1. Commanded No.1 Wing, RNAS during the war and was later AOC Palestine in 1924, then AOC I Air Defence Group in 1927. Retired in 1929 and died in February 1963.

[6] Horace Percy Lale became a WW1 ace flying Bristol Fighters over France, for which he received the DFC. A Bar to this decoration was awarded for operations in Waziristan in 1920. After 24 Squadron he took command of 32 Squadron in April 1924. A future group captain, he died in April 1955. Cyril Nelson Lowe had received the MC and DFC in WW1 flying fighters, most of his successes being while with 24 Squadron. After his later service with 24 in 1923, he went on to command squadrons in Iraq, including Greig's old 6 Squadron. Lowe also played thirty-five times for the English rugby side. He also made group captain and died in February 1983. William Samuel Caster MC, army and RFC observer in the Middle East. On becoming a pilot he won his MC for bombing raids in 1917. Retired as a group captain in 1946 and one of his later jobs was helping in the development of Gatwick. He died in November 1979.

[7] By 1937, Willet Amalric Bowen Bowen-Buscarlet DFC, was a wing commander. He had received his DFC in 1931 for distinguished service in the Kordofan province of the Sudan, 1929-30. Temporary OC RAF Scampton in 1938 and in WW2 served in Malta, Turkey and Italy. Retired as Air Vice-Marshal Sir Willet, KBE CB DFC DL in 1946. Died in September 1967.

[8] Leslie Hamilton fought his war in Salonika in 1918 and also won the DFC as a fighter pilot. Leaving the service he was lost in June 1927 during an attempt, with Col. F F Minchin, to fly the Atlantic.

[9] J K Wells retired as a wing commander OBE AFC in 1935 and at the start of WW2 was a member of the Air Ministry's Ordnance Board, Woolwich. Recalled and served in the RAF 1941-45.

[10] Later Herbert George Brackley CBE DSO DSC FRGS CdG etc. RNAS & RAF in WW1. In WW2 he rose to air commodore and served with Coastal Command and Transport Command. After retiring in October 1945, he became assistant to the director of BOAC. Died in November 1948, aged 54.

10

CENTRAL FLYING SCHOOL

I was now sent to No.13 Flying Instructors' Course, at Upavon. One of the great pioneers of early flying was Robert Smith-Barry, who had learnt to fly in 1911. After service in France with the RFC early in WW1, he returned to England and convinced the 'powers that be' that there should be a school to teach would-be instructors to instruct. Until then, it was assumed that if someone could fly, that person could easily instruct others, whereas Smith-Barry argued that instructors should be schooled in the art. By the end of the war it was almost a badge of honour to have been selected to go to his School of Special Flying at Gosport.

So I was now a member of No.13 Flying Instructors' Course. With me were a few chums from Iraq — Ffoulkes-Jones of 6 Squadron, Trevor Cripps of 30, Bruce Sutherland [1] of 8, plus 'Slab' Porter and Joe Fogarty [2] of 84. The duration of the course was three months, the working week being from first flying parade on Monday till lunch time Friday, when all those not required for Sunday church parade or station duties were allowed weekend leave. A nice, gentlemanly existence.

The working day was divided into flying, lectures and discussion periods. The pupils received flying instruction in the mornings only. The afternoon we flew in pairs in dual control aircraft, taking turns to be instructor and student. Whilst these afternoon exercises took place our instructors went off to play golf or tennis, or to shoot or fish, depending on the season and personal inclination – jolly good old days.

Mess life was pleasant, dinner being a formal parade each evening during the working part of the week. Every Thursday was a guest night. A mess dance took place on the last Friday of each month, with an annual ball being a lavish affair in which Mister Watts, plus the co-operation of Harrods stores, really excelled himself.

The commandant, 'Topsy' Holt, at some time prior to our course, had started an interesting guest night custom. All members of the mess were required to assemble in the main ante-room before dinner, to take part in a thirty-minute debate. On the first guest night of our course, Topsy, in an opening address, informed the newcomers that the object of this exercise was to accustom young officers to public speaking. However, at one of these assemblies an atmosphere of almost uncontrollable levity arose as the result of an apparently equally uncontrollable condition.

The subject of this particular debate was 'poison gas'. After opening proceedings, Topsy called upon the station MO to describe the effects of various kinds of poison gas upon the human organism. Unhappily, our doctor, no doubt as the result of having eaten too many radishes for tea, was evidently suffering from acute discomfort when he rose to his feet, for his audience had to endure a learned dissertation frequently punctuated by gaseous eruptions, hiccoughs and the most audible tummy-rumblings. Not long after this demoralising occasion the guest night custom just faded away.

Our after-dinner activities followed the normal pattern. Those wishing to play cards or snooker went about their business, the remaining majority adjourning to the main ante-room to indulge in rough games, armchairs and settees being placed back to back for a follow-my-leader steeplechase. Teams also assembled for games such as 'High Cockalorum', 'Cockfighting', and 'Are you there Moriarty?' However, there was a stunt involving great skill which was peculiar only to the Upavon mess. A fairly wide plate rack surrounded the room, well above door level. At intervals a short distance above the rack, were mounted trophies of the chase. Members were challenged to climb onto the projecting ledge and then circumnavigate the entire room without falling to the floor. As the drop was fairly considerable, a catching party was always in attendance whenever an attempt was being made. Were it not for the trophies, the feat would not really have been too difficult, but when one considers that the various obstructions included the heads of an eland, a bull moose and a warthog, successful completion of the circuit was a feat of no mean skill. Of course, everyone expected contestants to fall, which they invariably did, but nevertheless the course was, on very rare occasions, successfully negotiated.

Having introduced the domestic side of CFS, we must now get to work. On reporting for duty each pupil was immediately issued with the two essentials of the course, a set of Gosport earphones, and a patter book, the latter being a Roneod copy of Smith-Barry's Gospel, amended and up to date, in other words, The Principles of Flying Instruction. The complete course covered basic flying in logical sequence from taxying to handling of the engine, to advanced aerobatics. The wording of the patter was framed in such a way as to ensure synchronisation of speech with control movements, and included the whys and wherefores, and the do's and don'ts of separate and combined control manipulation being explained simply and concisely for application whilst actually handling the aircraft in the air and on the ground. Detailed explanations, theory and airmanship formed that part of the syllabus carried out in lecture room or flight office.

An impressive preliminary, exclusive to CFS, was a daily event known as the 'instructor's ten minutes', when aircraft were tested prior to starting work. During this brief period all flying rules and regulations went by the board, the flying appearing at times to be almost subterranean as well as sideways, upside down and occasionally normal. This 'crazy flying' that was particularly well executed by Pedro Mann was, a year or two later, developed into an event for the annual RAF Display at Hendon, by two of the flight commanders at Digby, Joe Fogarty and Reggie Lydford [3].

The camp tailor having fitted the Gosport tubes to my flying helmet, I was all set to start. This arrangement was not electrical, but simply two cylindrical earpieces connected by flexible metal gas-tubing to a mouthpiece thus completing simple and fool-proof intercommunication between front and rear cockpits of the Avro 504K, our instructional aircraft.

I at once realised from preliminary scrutiny of the patter book how little I knew about flying. Casting my mind back six years, my original efforts at learning to fly seemed crude in the extreme. Seated in a DH6 behind an instructor whose only means of demonstrating control was by shouting, gesticulating and moving the stick and rudder fairly coarsely in correcting my errors, whilst I endeavoured to steer a direct and level course along a short but straight, railway line between Newmarket and the nearby village of Soham. At the time of my first solo, after just two and a half hours instruction, I had no knowledge of stalling, spinning, how to do a steep turn, how to carry out a cross-wind landing or a forced landing in the event of engine failure, nor how to execute the simplest aerobatic manoeuvres. All in all, I was quite clueless.

The Avro 504K in which we were taught was the most famous training aircraft in a long line emanating from that stable. A two-bay biplane of fairly ample proportions, it had a long fuselage terminating in a balanced rudder. The undercarriage was sprung on elastic and had a long, ash skid projecting below and in front of the propeller, its purpose being to prevent 'nosing over', and was commonly known as the toothpick. The engine was a rotary, a Monosoupape Gnôme of 100 hp. The compactness and light weight obviously contributed very considerably to the outstanding handling qualities of this machine, the control being light and very responsive. In the hands of a capable pilot the Avro could be practically landed on a postage stamp. In the opinion of Smith-Barry, a good pilot should have been able to cut his engine at 2,000 feet and judge his approach and landing so as to end his run between the hangar doors. Needless to say, this practise received no official encouragement.

The cockpit layout was simple. A control column, rudder bar and engine control lever. Instruments were an ASI, altimeter, compass and lateral inclinometer. Wheel brakes were still things of the future.

My flight commander, Flight Lieutenant B K D Robertson [4], assumed responsibility for me as his pupil. Brian Robertson was a fine example of what a good instructor should be. An excellent pilot, calm and precise, and possessing a more than ample fund of patience, while his manner at all times would be cheerful and full of confidence.

I did not find the course easy. Being inclined to be hesitant in my speech and a bit slow on the uptake, I had the greatest difficulty in synchronising my patter with control movements during the various demonstrations, and in fact, the course was well over half completed before I began to make any progress whatsoever. The sequence for a normal landing and forced-landing procedure gave me the greatest trouble. During the former I seemed never to be able to get the final phrase worked out satisfactorily, and would still be muttering into the mouthpiece: "Continue holding off by easing the stick steadily back until the machine sinks to the ground, wheels and tailskid together," when the aeroplane was already on the ground and practically at the end of its landing run! With a forced-landing demonstration, I found that for a very long time I simply could not keep up an easy flow of chat whilst concentrating on a tricky side-slip approach over a high bank of trees at the edge of the rather small, forced-landing field. At times I was almost in despair. However, the fact that I experienced such difficulty was, in itself, a valuable lesson, as it taught me to exercise tolerance and understanding when later dealing with pupils similarly afflicted.

I enjoyed the afternoon flying sessions with other members of the course and can recall an occasion when Joe Fogarty and I shared an Avro for about forty-five minutes. After a short period of exchanging patter, Joe made an enlightening and welcome innovation, when he suggested that I take the rudder control only, while he took the stick and fine adjustment. We would not talk to each other while doing this, and later we would swop controls. During the following minutes we had a splendid time, although the poor old Avro could not have known if it was coming or going, with all the violent and erratic skids, swerves, and so on. No doubt Joe received some inspiration for his future crazy flying at Hendon.

As the end of the course approached, I found that Brian's painstaking efforts with me were at last paying a handsome dividend, for not only had I gained confidence but also some ability. Eventually came the day of my final test by the CFI. To my total astonishment I was awarded the highest possible category and was informed that I would not be returning to Kenley but retained at Upavon as an instructor. I felt sad at parting with Kenley but very flattered by being posted to the CFS. Selection for service at CFS, or to one of the experimental establishments, was the highest possible tribute to one's prowess as an aviator.

One other pupil on the course was similarly complimented, Flying Officer Arthur Scroggs [5]. If I might be so bold as to venture a profound statement, Arthur and I were widely divergent types. He was extremely erudite and the holder of a university degree, a first-class mathematician and scientist, and, at that time, a staunch teetotaller and non-smoker. What we did have in common was a love of flying and a predilection for motor cycles. He later became the owner of a series of Trojan cars, curious box-like vehicles with two-stroke engines, epicyclic gears, cantilever springs all round, no differential and solid tyres. He gained many motoring awards with these contraptions both on the London-Edinburgh and London-Exeter runs. Despite a somewhat retiring disposition, Arthur was very popular with the rest of the staff and an absolute asset when some knotty problem required unravelling. He eventually acquired a unique nickname – 'The Water-cooled Slide-rule'.

Having completed the course on the 504K, it only remained for me to do a short conversion course to fighters, a type on which I had no previous experience. Pedro Mann, whose flying I had so admired on my first visit to CFS a year previously, took me in hand and sent me solo on a Sopwith Snipe.

My three months tuition was over. Even considering a small amount of amateur teaching during previous years, in addition to the high rating I now possessed, I did not consider myself to be a competent instructor, for I lacked experience, so only time would tell whether my new appointment was really merited. Actually, within the next year or so, a hard and fast rule was introduced which forbade the award of the highest category to any student on the instructors course however competent he seemed to be. He first had to prove his worth by serving a term as an instructor at a flying training school.

Many years later, when doing my second period of service at CFS, I assisted in a complete revision of the instructor's bible – The Principles of Flying Instruction. Among my personal observations I included the following. An instructor must study the psychology of his pupil to ascertain the best line of approach to his mentality. It is no use being a first-class pilot, possessing a complete knowledge of flying instruction, if one lacks the necessary temperamental qualities of patience, perseverance and sympathy. Whatever the pupil may do, an instructor should never display signs of apprehension, otherwise the pupil's confidence will be shaken. An instructor must be patient with the backward pupil and quick to check the overconfident one.

My final flight as a pupil on No.13 Course took place on the morning of 1st May 1924, and lasted just fifteen minutes. It was a memorable occasion as it was to take place during an event which brought down the wrath and indignation of the Air Ministry. A landing competition between instructors and members of the course, where the landing mark was the letter 'U' of the name Upavon, which was prominently marked in chalk on the south aerodrome. The lettering ran from south to north, the 'U' being the furthest point, about 150 yards from the tarmac. A small wooden stake was driven into the centre of the 'U', the winner of the contest being the one whose aircraft stopped with the point of the 'toothpick' nearest the stake, the approach having commenced at 1,500 feet immediately above the marker and with the engine stopped.

At first sight there might appear to be nothing unusual about a contest of this sort, in fact there would not have been, had the wind been easterly or westerly. There was, however, a fair breeze from due south. To appreciate the situation one must try to imagine the scene viewed directly north from the stake. At right angles to the line of vision, a line of hangars sat just beyond the Andover-Devizes Road, and with it a line of telegraph poles. Behind the road was the pine wood just south of the mess. One hangar stood on the direct line of approach into wind, but there were reasonable gaps to either side. The only other serious obstruction was an old barn located at the edge of the tarmac area, and just to the west of the direct line. To complicate matters further, the slope of the ground directly south of the tarmac fell away quite sharply and ended in a typical Salisbury Plain 'shallow valley'. Furthermore, during the approach to land, one blip from the engine would disqualify a contestant.

After the initial loss of height to position oneself for the final glide in from 500 feet, the following alternatives were presented. A straight approach ending in a sharp side-slip down the front of the hangar, or a variety of cross-wind approaches, all at minimum speed. The selection of this particular landing point was probably rather foolish, as one giving an unobstructed glide-in could easily have been arranged further to the west and clear the line of hangars. However, the point selected, being somewhat hazardous, definitely challenged one's skill and was, therefore, in keeping with the traditions of the school. In short, we were asking for trouble and certainly got it.

I cannot remember the total number in each team, probably about six to eight, the commandant and the CFI both being on the tarmac to act as umpires. In a very few minutes there was a remarkable array of lopsided and damaged Avros being pushed frenziedly out of the way of other approaching aircraft, and the telephone wires along the main road were all down. One pilot, hopelessly undershooting, struck a telegraph pole fair and square, swiping off the port planes and ending up minus undercarriage, just short of the tarmac. By this time the CFI was very worried and suggested to the commandant that the contest be cancelled. However, Topsy Holt, who was rocking with mirth, replied, "Nonsense, this is the funniest thing I have ever seen. Wheel out some more Avros!"

It certainly was an extraordinary spectacle, the poor Avros crabbing and swish-tailing in from all directions in a frantic effort to skid off all the surplus speed before violently hitting the ground. I was one of the lucky ones who did not break anything, but I got nowhere near enough to the landing mark. The really prize performance was put up by another member of the course, Ferdy Swain, who many years later established the world altitude record at Farnborough [6]. Poor Ferdy approached in a series of S-turns and with a completely stationary propeller. The final turn ended much too low and with the Avro headed for the old barn at the edge of the tarmac. He pushed the nose down to gain a little extra speed, then yanked the stick back to try to clear the roof. His undercarriage struck the ridge with a resounding crash and a shower of tiles, leaving the aircraft completely stalled and in a flat swerve in which it descended on to the roof of Nobby Clarke's car immediately below. The top of the car was ripped off and the machine came to an abrupt halt with its nose embedded in a mound of earth. Ferdy was quite unhurt but the mechanic in the front seat got a bit shaken up. The owner of the car, a large and genial Australian on the staff, was on the tarmac enjoying the fun. The amiable grin quickly left his face when he saw what had happened to his Barouche. The eventual winner was Rex Stoken, one of the instructors, but on aggregate, the pupils beat the staff.

This tale must surely create an impression of irresponsibility and seem tough on the taxpayer, but, after all, those old aircraft were not so very costly and all were repairable. We were a very juvenile service and one must always make due allowances for the very young. The era of the light and handy biplane might well be referred to as – 'The gay and carefree age of service aviation'. It was an age which, all too soon, would pass into history. The all-metal cantilever monoplane would quickly be heralding the advent of an 'Age of ever increasing responsibility'.

The events following the landing contest took a somewhat odd form and to my knowledge Topsy Holt did not receive a personal admonition, but Air Ministry did issue an order that in future forced-landing practice on the Upavon circle must not take place when the wind was in the south. As weekly orders went to every RAF unit, it must have been obvious to the whole service that some grave misdemeanour had occurred at CFS.

Holt was a remarkable character. A stern disciplinarian with a highly developed sense of fun, he feared nobody and was a man of substance, with many influential friends. He would not tolerate what might be termed unwarrantable nosing into the affairs of CFS, the integrity of the school came before all else.

I can recall an occasion when a wing commander from HQ visited us without prior warning, in order to investigate alleged heavy spending by members of the officer's mess. Moreover, he proceeded with his appointed task without having first made his number with the commandant. He had barely started operations when his presence was requested at Topsy's office, where an infuriated CO tore him to shreds, sent him off immediately from the station, then vented his wrath over the telephone to HQ.

On another occasion a signal arrived one morning to say that a certain very senior officer from the training branch of AM, was on his way by air to Upavon. I have no idea what this visit was about but Topsy was on the tarmac to meet the visitor. After alighting from his Bristol Fighter, the man was engaged in conversation for a mere minute or two, whereupon the chap climbed back into his aeroplane and flew back to Northolt. In no time at all word went round that another visitor had been sent off with a 'flea in his ear'.

In not quite the same context, another instance is worth mentioning. A young officer on the staff, somewhat irresponsible but possessing a very attractive personality, got heavily into debt and could not pay his mess bill. He was in such trouble that it seemed a court martial was inevitable. However, Topsy's pride in the good name of CFS, combined with an affectionate regard for this scallywag, resulted in unconventional disciplinary action, the offender being interviewed in Topsy's office and soundly berated. Topsy then settled the lad's mess bill, gave him some additional funds towards his other debts and told him he was never again to jeopardise the honour of the CFS in this manner. The rebuke and kindness went home and the scamp did not blot his copy book again.

Before leaving the subject of the landing contest, an instance springs to mind in which the winner, Rex Stoken, was involved. It also throws further light on the personality of Topsy Holt. Shortly after the turn of the year 1924-25, a boxing team from Upavon had to compete in the Southern Command inter-service championship at Winchester. Unit teams had to include representation of all ranks, and in this particular instance, the officers at Upavon had to enter a welterweight. It transpires that Rex and I were the only two in the mess who came within this class, so Topsy said very firmly that one or t'other of us should uphold the honour of CFS in this event, and if necessary toss for the privilege. Personally I felt in an awful quandary. I knew little about boxing, loathed being hit on the nose and lacked the moral courage to say so. Rex had just returned from winter sports in Switzerland and was on the top of his form. The fact that he too was no boxer was no concern of mine. I regret to admit that I behaved like an utter cad and solved the problem by pleading that my asthma would automatically preclude me from the contest. Rex very gallantly agreed to go to the contest.

To clinch the deal, Topsy invited him to a dinner party he was giving in Winchester, on the eve of the contest. Another guest, Lord Hugh Cecil, offered to foot the drink bill at the party. Needless to say, Rex dined and wined in magnificent fashion in this distinguished company and after a final brandy, was led like a lamb to the slaughter, to the gymnasium at Worthy Down. I occupied a ring side seat and in due course a very replete and somewhat flushed Rex stripped for action. His opponent in the opposite corner was a very alert and handsome young officer of very athletic appearance. He was announced as being the army welterweight boxing champion! I became conscious of a fiendish chuckle from Topsy. What a situation. Poor Rex, gorged with good food and with port and brandy practically dribbling from his ears, was about to face such a doughty opponent.

To give him his due, he lasted the three rounds and managed to bash his opponent's nose. To quote Rex's own words: "All I can remember of the fight was seeing Topsy roaring with laughter every time I got knocked around the ring." Sadly he lost the bout, but when all the points were added up at the end of the contest, it was found that the one point scored by Rex putting in an appearance, resulted in the RAF winning the championship. He was very sick immediately after the fight, but being a perfect gentleman he managed to refrain from depositing his dinner in the ring.

An established custom among the staff at CFS was the use of Christian names, except when circumstances dictated otherwise. A pleasant rule which never fell into any form of abuse, and of course, senior members such as the CO or CFI were never addressed in this familiar manner.

My first flight as an instructor took place on 17th June 1924, a familiarisation flight on a new, ultra light aeroplane. At that time ultra light aircraft were very much in vogue, the government the previous year having offered a prize for the best machine with an engine capacity not exceeding 750 cc's. De Havilland's built one for trials at Lympne that October.

The DH53, or the Humming Bird as it was called, was a small monoplane fitted with an inverted Vee twin Blackburn 'Tomtit' motor-cycle engine, and although this machine did not win the competition, a dozen were ordered by the RAF, and a few allotted to CFS for evaluation. From a strictly practical point of view, they were not much use, being single seaters of very limited endurance and performance. Flat-out at ground level they could just about reach 70 mph. However, they were a joy to fly and we had a great deal of fun. Personally I used to take a delight in stalking motor cyclists on the unobstructed roads on Salisbury Plain, approaching them from the rear, so as to give the impression of another motor cyclist about to overtake, before hopping over the head of the astonished driver. An ideal aeroplane too for contour chasing and weaving between clumps of trees.

In July the following year, two of our DH53s were on view at the Hendon RAF Display, and I had the job of flying one from there to Upavon. Shortly after taking off visibility deteriorated in a very unpleasant manner and by the time I reached the vicinity of Staines, it was really thick, and in no time at all I had lost my bearings and had neither compass nor map. Spotting a cross road, complete with AA box, I orbited the sign post in an unsuccessful attempt to read directions, so landed in a fair-sized field just to one side. Having regained my bearings, I got back into the machine and started the take-off run. At the far end of the field was a very substantial hedge, which I was approaching rapidly without any sign of the machine leaving the ground. The grass being on the long side was probably responsible for this, so in a matter of seconds I was faced with an imminent collision. To obviate this I held the machine on the ground till the very last moment, then pulled back very sharply on the stick. The aircraft responded sluggishly, staggered into the air and sank like an agitated hen, slap into the middle of the hedge, where it stuck firmly. Without much difficulty I extricated myself from this undignified position and examined the aircraft, noting only superficial damage to fabric and plywood. As nothing further could be done, I walked to the area equipment depot at Ascot, only a mile or two away, arranged for the collection of the machine, and then made my way by train to CFS feeling rather dejected.

The 14th course at CFS began, and when I was not required for instructional duties, I devoted a great deal of time in attempting to perfect my aerobatic skills in a Snipe. My initial conversion to this fighter had consisted of a short flight of twenty minutes in a dual control Snipe, with Pedro Mann, after which I was on my own to gain experience with the time-honoured method of trial and error. My progress with slow rolling and inverted flight I regarded as highly satisfactory, so much so, that I became rather bored with demonstrating my prowess at a safe altitude of 2,000 feet and above, so gradually reduced the height, eventually delighting in starting the roll from ground level following a dive down to the tarmac in front of the hangars.

One fine morning I was doing just this and diving down from the east, pulled up into a shallow climb. As I began the roll, and when in just over half an inverted position, something went wrong. I think one leg of my flying overalls got caught in some projection and I could not apply sufficient rudder at the crucial moment. The roll could not be completed, so in a state of panic I put everything in reverse, the Snipe eventually slithering and slipping on to an even keel, low down over the Avon Valley, and well below the level of the airfield. I had just cause to be thankful that the aerodrome had been built on top of C G Grey's mountain, for had it been otherwise, I would have undoubtedly ended up in smoke.

The start of the 15th course in October 1924, brought some interesting characters to CFS, the most notable being two naval commanders, C Harris and Cosmo Graham. The Admiralty had just come to the conclusion that senior officers selected to command aircraft carriers should have some practical experience of flying, and these two were the first selected. They were a delightful pair who fitted in remarkably well and joined in all our mess skullduggery. We were all sorry when they returned to their own service after having learned to fly Avros successfully.

Among the RAF contingent was Gerry Pentland [7], the wild Australian who had covered himself in glory during WW1, and my old mate Bowen-Buscarlet from Kenley. As Bus had given me my introduction to the Avro 504K only a few months previously, I naturally returned the favour and secured him as one of my students for the course. In addition to being a first class aviator, Bus was a possessor of a well modulated voice and his articulation was perfect. In a nutshell he possessed all the attributes of the ideal flying instructor. In fact, at the end of this course, both Gerry and Bus were retained as instructors.

During one period of instruction, we had an amazing but somewhat startling experience which brought home rather forcibly the very unpredictable behaviour of the Gnôme engine, and the value of Smith-Barry's teachings. We were up together in our Avro, practising low flying, and had just completed the demonstration and had handed over to Bus so he might repeat the lesson. It was a pleasant afternoon and from my position in the rear cockpit, I had a first class view of the back of my companion's head, plus the unbroken vista of Salisbury Plain beyond. We were flying along at a height of not much more than twenty feet, my pupil's voice, loud and clear, in my earphones. He was just giving me some patter about what to do at low level if the engine packed up, when – crash, bang – "Christ Almighty..." yelled Bus. The wildly vibrating Avro was completely dead, and was turning about 40° to starboard but Bus landed it intact on the upslope of the gulley. A cylinder had blown off, stripping the engine cowling in the process of departing into space, via the inter-plane struts. It was a remarkable coincidence, and I don't doubt a valuable lesson in a practical manner. Bus had shown good airmanship and kept a cool head, taking the correct and immediate action. [8]

A further amusing incident occurred from an engine failure during this course. A pupil, Flying Officer W N L Cope, proceeded one afternoon for solo flying practice in an Avro. He took with him, for a joy ride, a very young and raw cockney aircraft hand, who had never been up before. The wind was northerly and for some reason Cope elected to take off over the hangar, instead of taxying to the westerly end of the airfield. Cope's Avro was well and truly airborne by the time he reached the tarmac, but went directly over the hangar. The Mono started to bang and splutter with considerable violence, and it was clearly evident that complete engine failure was imminent. I could well imagine Cope's apprehension at the prospect of having to make a birdlike forced landing either in the pine trees or on top of the mess. He had not sufficient height to clear these obstructions to reach a nearby golf course and the joke was, the airman in the rear seat, completely oblivious to the somewhat terrifying situation, was gaily waving his arms to his chums on the ground. The inevitable happened and with a loud noise of much splintering, the poor old Avro pancaked on top of the trees, where it remained firmly wedged in the upper branches. Neither occupant had been hurt, and when they were eventually rescued, the cockney airman was simply bubbling over with pride and enthusiasm, because on his first flight he had been crashed by a 'toff'.

On the arrival of autumn 1924, the shooting season got into full swing, our Upavon shoot being very different from the very extensive rough shooting of Iraq. Topsy Holt exercised control and each shoot conducted by him, assumed the characteristics of a military operation. Although I did not realise it at the time, one of the afternoon outings in this season was destined to be a turning point in my attitude to killing for the fun of it. On this particular occasion, we were covering ground between Upavon and Netheravon. There was a very strong wind blowing and I held the gun to the extreme left end of the line. Conditions being as they were the driven birds were coming over extremely low and very fast. One covey caught me napping, and I missed with my right barrel as they went by. Just at that moment, a hare came bounding past and I let it have the left barrel. It was a rotten shot and only wounded the poor beast, which lay screaming, its hind quarters paralysed, just a few paces from me. I reloaded immediately and put the animal out of its misery. There was a quality about that hare's screams which did something to my conscience. The sound being not unlike a small child in extreme distress. It played on my mind for some time, and although I continued to shoot from time to time, the sport had lost its appeal.

Our close neighbour, No.1 Flying Training School, five miles distant at Netheravon, was responsible for the training of naval pilots and worked somewhat longer hours than the gentlemanly CFS, and they also started earlier. Their CO was Wing Commander W G S Mitchell, known throughout the service as Ginger Mitch, and who after retiring as an air marshal, became gentleman usher of Black Rod. He was a great character, fiery of temperament but with a strong sense of justice and humour. A good chap. [9] All this early morning flying on the part of our neighbour became rather a trial to CFS, as one or two pilots had a nasty habit of flying over in DH9s just as we were about to have breakfast, and spatter our tarmac and hangars with bags of flour and rotten tomatoes.

These visitations were by no means regular so we never knew when they were going to happen. Towards the end of dinner on 9th December, conversation got around to this question and what might be done about it by way of retaliation. I suggested a night raid. The port had been circulated and so everyone was in high spirits and good humour, so my suggestion was met with immediate acclaim. In the ensuing discussion it was decided that owing to the nature of the operation, nothing could be done without the commandant's authority.

The night being bright and clear, it was essential to strike whilst the iron was hot, so lots were drawn as to who should ring Topsy. One of the flight commanders, Flight Lieutenant J H Butler [10], drew the winning ticket and we all assembled in some apprehension around the telephone while he put through the call, fully expecting to receive a sound ticking off. Our fears were, however, quickly allayed. Topsy gave his blessing on condition that only one Avro was used.

In the mid-1920s, night flying did not feature in the CFS syllabus, consequently there was no night flying equipment. This defect was remedied by providing an electric torch for the cockpit lighting and mustering every available car to form a headlight flare path on the south aerodrome. As this nocturnal operation was being carried out on my suggestion, it was up to me to make the first sortie, taking with me a bomb-aimer, Flying Officer Tremeillen, an ex-pupil awaiting his posting to Egypt. With a fair wad of toilet paper, we took off in fine style and in a minute or two we were over Netheravon. It was the only occasion that I ever flew in mess kit! On reaching our target I pulled back the fine adjustment lever to starve the engine and make it pop and bang, and as the Avro was practically at roof-top height, we both leaned over the side and let off a series of moaning yells and cries of: "Help, help." The rolls of toilet paper then went over the side in smart order and we returned to hand over to crew No.2. I cannot remember the exact number of sorties made, but the whole operation was a great success and went off without any untoward incident.

The post-mortem the following morning proved to be interesting, as the first sortie evidently coincided with the end of the cinema performance, just as the audience was emerging from the camp theatre. They ran into a mass of fluttering paper and one lady was heard to exclaim something about a lot of pretty streamers! When, however, she grabbed one, her only exclamation was, "Oh." Apart from this, the initial impact was one of alarm, as we were genuinely thought to be an aircraft in distress. The fire party and ambulance had turned out and the provision of a flare path was underway before the leg-pull was fully realised. I gather there was a somewhat acrimonious exchange of words over the telephone between Ginger Mitch and Topsy, but the whole incident ended with good humour all round. Mitchell never forgot the affair and invariably reminded us of it whenever we met in the future.

Course No. 16 began in January 1925, Topsy's last as commandant. With this intake came my old friend Arthur Beilby, freshly home from 6 Squadron. Needless to say he became one of my students.

The early part of this year was not particularly noteworthy for disorderly conduct, apart from the temporary adoption of a new craze which I believe originated in the USA – wing walking. Although quite spectacular, there was really nothing to it in a slow biplane, with lots of bracing wires and struts to hang on to. The curious feature of this activity was that standing or sitting on the wing did not induce giddiness as can be experienced when walking along the top of a high wall, or standing on the edge of a cliff. I used to do a lot of it with Arthur and on one occasion sat on the lower wing tip, pretending to read a folded newspaper to seek the alarm of those on the tarmac at Netheravon. This exhibition was reputed to be responsible for upsetting the equilibrium of a Naval pupil as he was approaching to land, causing him to fly straight into the ground.

[According to Greig when talking to the late J W R Taylor (author of *C.F.S.*) these things were merely one CFS interpretation of the precept that 'nothing that a pilot may do in the air is dangerous if he knows what he is doing'. Greig liked nothing better than to be flown 20 feet or so over the roof-tops of some HQ while dangling his legs from the undercarriage or wing of an Avro 504K. Ed.]

This period witnessed the arrival of a new unit at Upavon, No. 3 Squadron, disbanded at the end of WW1 and now reformed. Equipped with Snipes, it was commanded by Squadron Leader John Russell [11], the great rugby football player. The personnel shared our accommodation, so we had a number of new faces in the mess.

The squadron adjutant was a flight lieutenant, a little under medium height, of chunky build and rubicund countenance, plus a puckish, toothy, grin. Very shortly after their arrival, Arthur Beilby was heard soundly berating a young pilot officer in the mess, for addressing a senior officer, to wit, this squadron adjutant, in an unduly familiar and disrespectful manner. The young officer, bubbling over with indignation, retorted: "But I wasn't being disrespectful, his name really is Cockey." [12] And so it was, Leonard Cockey, soon to become one of the most popular members of our mess, a keen shot and golfer, and a great motoring enthusiast, who in collaboration with Bus organised hill climbs and other trials in the locality.

At the end of No.16 Course, Beilby had acquitted himself well and was kept on as one of the staff. We were sad to lose Topsy, who went on to fill a higher appointment elsewhere. The new boss was Wilfred Freeman, different in both character and physical resemblance to Topsy [13]. A tall, clean shaven, good looking chap and reputed to be the youngest group captain in the RAF. He was undoubtedly a man of marked ability, destined to go far in the service. Possibly more serious than his predecessor, he nevertheless had a good sense of humour, an essential for a commandant of CFS.

The intake of pupils for the 17th course in May 1925, included three more naval officers for ab initio training up to solo standard. They were Commanders P L Melville, M S W Boucher DSO, and C R E W Perryman DSC. Boucher became my responsibility. Of all the pupils I ever had he was by far the slowest to go solo. I gave him twenty hours of dual instruction before sending him off on his own. However, he finally cottoned on and then became a very good pilot indeed. I well recall he used to strike an analogy between an Avro and docking a destroyer.

Perryman turned out to be a bit of a problem for he had no aptitude at all, and eventually he was handed over to me. He was a simply charming chap and for this reason we were all keen that he should, if at all possible, make the grade. One morning, much to my surprise, he made three successive and quite good landings. There is nothing like striking while the iron is hot, so when the Avro came to rest, I got out and sent him off on his own. Round he went, made a good approach and came down successfully all in one piece. Never have I seen a more happy chap and it being mid-day, we repaired to the mess to crack the traditional bottle of bubbly, in those days the instructor's perquisite following a successful first solo. That afternoon he flew his second solo, misjudged the landing and completely wrecked the Avro. He was quite unhurt but completely dejected and never flew again.

Not long after the final departure of our sailor friends, Boucher turned up and to everyone's surprise, requested a bit more than just qualifying on Avros, and had been to the Admiralty to pull a few strings. I sent him solo on Bristols and Snipes, he also flew the DH53, and eventually flew everything that the Naval Air Arm had to offer, and also qualified for deck landing. We last had a very brief meeting in early 1943, when as a retired admiral, he was in charge of the Air Transport Auxiliary at Prestwick.

[1] Later Group Captain Robert Bruce Sutherland DFC. Won his DFC during WW1 for service in Egypt. Retired in 1947.

[2] Later Wing Commander Francis Joseph Fogarty DFC AFC. Joe had also been decorated for operations in Iraq in 1922.

[3] Later Air Marshal Sir Harold T Lydford KBE CB AFC. Retired April 1956 after a distinguished career in the RAF. Died in September 1979.

[4] Robertson retired from the RAF as a squadron leader in 1932.

[5] Later Wing Commander Arthur Francis Scroggs, who as WW2 began, was part of the Directorate of Repair and Maintenance, having become a graduate of the RAF Staff College, and had qualified at a university course in engineering.

[6] Later Air Commodore Francis R D Swain CB CBE AFC. Received the AFC for his world altitude record in 1936. OBE and CBE in WW2. Retired in July

1954, died August 1989.

[7]Alexander Augustus Norman Dudley Pentland MC DFC. Flew Spads and Sopwith Dolphins in the war, claiming some twenty-three victories in air combat. Post-war he had served briefly in the RAAF, and then flew over the New Guinea goldfields, before going into the airline world. In WW2 he ran an air sea rescue outfit in the Pacific, and was awarded the AFC. He died in 1983.

[8]The date of this incident was 9 October 1924 and the No.8 cylinder had blown off, and in so doing had shredded the cowling. Luckily they were only twenty feet up and Buscarlet was able to make a rapid and successful forced-landing.

[9]Air Marshal Sir William G S Mitchell KCB CBE DSO MC AFC, had learnt to fly in 1913. An Australian, he was decorated for his services in WW1, both as a pilot and a wing commander. Ill-health forced his semi-retirement in 1941 when he became a Gentleman Usher. Died in August 1944, aged sixty-six.

[10]James Humphrey Butler retired as a group captain in 1946.

[11]Later Air Commodore J C Russell DSO.

[12]Later Air Commodore L H Cockey CB, retired in December 1945.

[13]Became Air Chief Marshal Sir Wilfred R Freeman GCB DSO MC Ld'H FRAeS. A pre-WW1 soldier he joined the RFC and was among the first airmen to land in France in August 1914. Awarded the DSO and MC, 1915 and 1916, and in 1945 was created 1st Baronet for his services in WW2. Died in May 1953 aged sixty-five.

11

AN INSTRUCTOR'S LOT CAN BE A HAPPY ONE

One sunny afternoon in the early summer of 1925, I was on duty at the hangars, whilst the pupils of the 17th course were doing their solos in patter jargon, when my attention was arrested by a superlative display of aerobatics being given by the pilot of a Snipe flying at fairly low altitude. It reminded me of a similar display I had seen at Hawkinge, about fifteen months earlier. On that occasion I asked another onlooker who was it, and was told it was a chap named Waghorn, newly arrived from Cranwell. On this occasion I checked at the flight office to find that the pilot I had just watched, was Pilot Officer R L R Atcherley, a pupil on the course. Atcherley and Waghorn were the top two products of the same period at Cranwell and both destined for great things, and about whom I shall be writing more later.

My chum Beilby seemed to have no relatives living in England, consequently he frequently accompanied me on weekend leaves to my home in Bexhill. During the summer a large hotel there, the Metropole, was due to be opened. In WW1 it had accommodated Canadian troops and had remained derelict ever since. However, new management were now in charge and it had been completely refurbished. A grand re-opening celebration at the weekend was being planned.

Beilby and I decided we had better muscle in. We pondered as to how to make the most of the party and the solution to our problem was rapidly reached. In newly reformed 3 Squadron was a Flight Lieutenant N C Saward, tall, dark and handsome, with very wavy black hair and a fierce black moustache [1]. He was known among his friends as either 'The Baron', 'The Count' or just 'Seaweed'. Our plan was to induce him to come to Bexhill, take him to the hotel and introduce him as an Italian count, scion of a noble Roman family. Saward was a chap never at a loss for words, so the idea appealed to him immensely although he could not speak a word of Italian, but was able to produce, as he ably demonstrated, a truly remarkable flow of fantastic broken English.

We arrived in Bexhill early on the Friday evening, the hotel was already functioning as such, but the special dinner and dance was booked for the next day. We lost no time in making our presence rather obvious and in the bar introduced our distinguished visitor to all and sundry, as the Count De La Dago, an outrageous and fantastic title that failed to arouse suspicion. Thanks to Saward's rather forceful and pompous demeanour, the title was accepted without question. Moreover, later in the evening the manager invited us to a dinner/dance the next evening and promised to reserve the best table in the dining room for our use.

Saturday proved to be a rousing success and we found ourselves to be the recipients of every conceivable kind of hospitality. The conductor of the orchestra, who had spent his youth in the city of Florence, was anxious to meet the count, so at what was presumably an opportune moment, he approached us to enquire about the count's taste in music. He bowed respectfully and addressed Saward in Italian. For one awful moment I thought we were sunk, but not a bit of it. The count, simulating extreme annoyance and irritation, turned to the unfortunate conductor and said in tones audible throughout the room: "I'm here to speaka da English – no to speaka Italian." The conductor, looking as though he had been shot, apologised and retired in confusion.

During the dance the count dated a number of young women, who agreed to meet us in the lounge on Sunday morning at noon. As we were due to return to duty that evening, someone during the morning session suggested that we might all troop over to Eastbourne for afternoon tea at the Grand. A procession of vehicles headed by my HE accordingly arrived there at 4 pm.

At last the time came for us to depart and whilst waiting for the bill, the count completely dropped his phoney accent and said: "By George, this has been the best weekend I have spent in years." For a moment there was an awful silence, followed by gasps from the ladies. I thought Arthur and I were due for a lynching, but then everyone laughed heartily and agreed that the leg-pull had been perfect. We avoided the Metropole for some little time after this episode, but before leaving the subject I must just mention one other event worth recording.

As Bexhill had been my home since 1914, I had a small circle of contemporaries with whom I used to foregather from time to time. One was a young naval officer with the name of Dick Eccles, who ultimately became Admiral Sir John, CinC, Home Fleet. As boys, Eccles and I were members of a gang which used to play hockey on push bikes on the roadway along East Parade, much to the discomfort of strollers and passers-by. In our weekend peregrinations at the Metropole, we made the acquaintance of, and eventually became firm friends with, an old boy in his 70s by the name of Stanton. Old Pa Stanton was a bit infirm, but young in spirit and thoroughly enjoyed the company of young people. He was very kind and such good company, and so appreciative, that we always got him to join us in our various jaunts around the district. During a weekend leave that winter, we collected him on the Saturday morning and after making the rounds, ended up in the lounge of the Metropole shortly before lunch time. Unknown to us poor old Pa suffered from a serious bladder weakness and had to wear an apparatus concealed down one trouser leg.

We were standing in a semi-circle of half a dozen, around an open fire, enjoying a pink gin, when suddenly there was a most awful trickling and splashing, and to everyone's consternation, an extensive puddle started to form around Pa's feet. The poor old chap had obviously forgotten to fasten the bung in his gadget properly, and his distress and embarrassment was pathetic to see. However, in true tradition, the senior service came to the rescue with the remark: "Good Lord, Sir, don't you worry, we'll all do it and keep you company." Eccles' timely exclamation saved the day and the atmosphere once more re-tuned to normal. The Metropole was an unlucky hotel, it never really paid and in WW2 it once more became a barracks and was seriously damaged by enemy action. It remained an unsightly ruin for about seven years after the war and was then demolished.

The year of 1925 began to witness the eclipse of two old-fashioned aeroplanes. In May, 3 Squadron began to replace its Snipes with Hawker Woodcocks, and on the 15th of that month, I flew in our first Woodcock from Brookworth. At the end of August and early September, a party of us made two journeys to A V Roe at Manchester to collect the first 504N, to replace our 504Ks. It was my first visit to the main works of A V Roe, where we were admirably looked after by the great 'Dobby', later to become Sir Roy Dobson. I had previously been a fairly frequent visitor, generally in company with Hamersley [2], one of our flight commanders, to a small experimental airfield of A V Roe at Hamble, the principal characters there being Parrot, the manager, Roy Chadwick, the chief designer, and H J L 'Bert' Hinkler, the famous test pilot. Hinkler went on to fly the first solo trip from England to Australia in 1928, and three years later, the first solo in a light aircraft from New York to London, flying a Puss Moth. Sadly he was killed in a crash crossing the Alps in 1933.

In general outline, the 504N was similar to the old 504K, the main difference being the replacement of the 100 hp engine by a 100 hp Armstrong-Siddeley Lynx radial, an extremely reliable, but much heavier engine. The old undercarriage, with its toothpick and rubber elastic shock absorbers, was replaced by one of hydraulic design.

Although the aeroplane handled well and was much easier to maintain, the increased weight naturally made itself felt in comparison with the old 504K. Gone was that feeling of lightness and also that bouncy undercarriage that always shouted at the pilot if he failed to make a good three-point landing. Aeroplanes were getting faster and in not many years hence would come the day when a well damped undercarriage would be an absolute necessity.

The late summer of 1925 was marked by an unusual event. The periodical intake of learner pilots into the RAF exceeded capacity to train them, so as an emergency measure, a special ab initio flight under the command of Flight Lieutenant H H Down was formed. He had to look after twenty young officers, two of whom were direct entry for permanent commissions from one of the universities, while the rest were short service commissions. In addition to Bill Down, Flying Officers Silvester, French, Bibby and myself, plus sergeant pilots Simpson and Betts, became the flying instructors. Flight Lieutenant R H Holland was the ground instructor, and the whole outfit was organised as a miniature flying school. As a result I also found myself the instructor in navigation, doubtless the result of my dubious 61% pass at Calshot two years previously. How often do things return to bite us.

The course started in September and ended the following August, at which time the pupils qualified on service type aircraft, either Snipe or Bristol Fighter. Among this bunch was a character named Crackenthorp, who on one occasion, upon receiving a minor punishment for some misdemeanour, promptly handed in his resignation to the orderly sergeant, as he took the morning drill parade. We also had a problem with another young officer who appeared to believe that so long as he had cheques in his cheque book, he had cash in the bank! Life's learning curves bit him too.

Life was somewhat brightened in the mess that autumn, by the introduction of a new beverage and the inauguration of the Cork Club. Taking these items in proper order, the beverage – a white Italian vermouth called Giacomuzzi – was discovered by a civilian friend of mine, universally known as Uncle Fred. The gentleman, in addition to being a director of a family business in the city of London, was also a connoisseur of wines, and a frequent visitor to Bexhill. This vermouth when taken with just a modicum of gin, had a simply electrifying effect. Dull gloom being changed into an atmosphere of bonhomie and joie de vivre, by just one glass, in a remarkably short space of time. Two or three glasses could be absolutely depended upon to produce a riot, without any trace of aggressiveness. I personally never noticed any side-effects, so I imported a sample bottle or two into the mess, whereupon several cases were subsequently ordered. Unfortunately the following year Giacomuzzi went off the market and I was told later that the public health authorities had ordered an analysis, which revealed a constituent which should not have been there. I am uncertain whether I hold any responsibility for the introduction of the Cork Club, but as this racket – for racket it was – sprang into being immediately following the arrival of Giacomuzzi, maybe I cannot be regarded as entirely blameless.

In brief, the founder member, who eventually became known by the edifying title of the Arch Grand Bastard, had, before starting a branch, to find one collaborator to whom he explained the rules, the chief one being that only members are allowed to be present in the room during the initiation of a candidate, the rites being deemed highly secret. The initiation was simple. After being sworn to secrecy, the candidate was invited to sit at a table with the Arch Grand Bastard, and collaborator, whereupon three corks were produced and placed on the table, one in front of each sitter. The cupped hand of each sitter was then rested on the table in close proximity to his cork and on the command by the AGB – "One, two, three – corks," the last sitter to remove his cork from the table was obliged to stand the others a drink. Now this is where the catch came in. On the executive word 'corks', existing members, in this instance the AGB and the collaborator, stood fast, only the sucker grabbing his cork, thus being the last to pick one up!

Having fallen for this ruse and paid the penalty, he was now entitled to sit in and reap the benefit of further initiations. The Cork Club flourished for a considerable time and good fun was had by all. It must be borne in mind that the scheme soon absorbed all the regular members of the mess, both CFS and 3 Squadron, but there were always the new course arrivals, plus individuals passing through and in need of refresher courses. Oddly enough the foundation of this iniquitous institution coincided with a new Air Ministry order, forbidding treating in mess, mess guests excepted. Our mess president, John Russell, did his best to enforce this directive, but as he was invariably the first to break it, the periods of enforcement were, therefore, never very long.

On 19th October, the very first de Havilland Moth G-RBXT was flown from Stag Lane to Upavon and left with us until 6th November, when I returned it to the firm. We all flew this prototype, the object being to assess its potentiality as an elementary trainer. This first of an illustrious line, it must have had thousands of descendents all over the world, in fact there are still large numbers of Tiger Moths flying today.

We were all duly impressed, another feature being differential ailerons which eliminated a condition known as aileron drag. There were, however, one or two snags, the chief being the Cirrus engine, which was of the wet sump variety like the average motor car and, like the motor car, the oil would have been carried in the crank case. Therefore, on slow rolling or inverting the aeroplane, hot oil would pour out of the crank case breather, hit the pilot in the face and make an awful mess of everything. The later Gypsy engines were dry sump where the oil was carried in a tank and circulated through the engine's vitals by a system of pressure and scavenger pumps. This modification removed the mess from inverted flight.

In early November, arrangements were again in hand for the traditional firework display. Because of my pyromaniac reputation that had followed me from Iraq, the purchase of squibs and the general arrangements became my responsibility. The usual scheme involved a general rake round the mess for cash contributions, then holding back the actual purchase till the last minute in order to obtain a substantial discount from the firework vendors in Salisbury. No flies on us! As this was my second Upavon Guy Fawkes night do, and knowing all the officers' families were coming to the mess to watch, I reckoned that a surprise item in the form of an especially loud explosion at an unexpected moment, might liven things up quite a lot. Acting on this resolution, I paid a visit to the officer in charge of the demolition section of the Royal Engineers at Shrewton Camp. I had read that Lawrence of Arabia had managed quite well in his train wrecking exploits, with one or two 16 oz slabs of guncotton attached to a section of rail line, so decided on a similar process.

I found my RE man most co-operative and when I asked him about my requirements he said: "In this store there happens to be an open case containing sixteen slabs, you can take the lot if you like, provided you return the empty case when you bring the exploder back." This exceeded my wildest dreams and I returned to Upavon in great jubilation. I thought two would be great, what would sixteen be like?

After some thought, I placed all sixteen slabs on the rough, on the left of No.1 fairway of our golf course, about 120 yards downhill from the front of the mess and connected them by sixty yards of cable to the exploder. The evening of the 5th was fine and calm and the fireworks display in front of the mess was going nicely and being enjoyed by a large number of spectators on the mess steps. As the distance between the exploder and the charge was not very great I lay flat on the grass until a period of nothing noisy was going on, just a few roman candles 'poofing' off into the night sky, then pressed down the plunger. The charges went off with an enormous bang, which echoed and rumbled round Pewsey Vale and on towards Devizes. Any innocuous chat on the mess steps was instantly silenced and children buried faces into their mother's skirts.

Thankfully none of the spectators died of fright and as far as I can recall no windows were broken, however, the shock waves had an odd effect on Hamersley and Padre Brown's married quarters, two converted wooden huts of pre-1914 vintage. Owing to the flexibility of these structures, the walls performed a concertina act, throwing pots and pans, pictures and so forth, to the floor. We heard next day that the army garrison at Devizes, about ten miles away, heard and felt the explosion causing much speculation as to the cause. The blast left a considerable crater along the golf course but otherwise it was quite a successful evening's entertainment, with no casualties despite the fact that Gerry Pentland was observed on the edge of the roof over the entrance porch, lighting a cigarette from the flaming fuses of a bunch of crackers. Truly the Devil looks after his own.

The winter of 1925-26 was an intensely cold one, with one sharp spell of heavy snow and another of severe frost. During the snowy spell that grounded all our aircraft, Dirk Cloete [4], a new arrival, produced a pair of skis, with which we all had a fair amount of fun. John Boothman [5] was, however, a bit too adventurous and tackled the very deep declivity north of the mess and between numbers one and two greens of the golf course, the final gradient of which was of the order of one in two or even steeper. All would have been well had he not hit a hidden bunker at the bottom of the valley. It was a really nasty spill, which put him out of commission for a week or two with concussion and other minor injuries, but no broken bones.

Occurring also during this particular spell was another regrettable incident, following a lunch-time Giacomuzzi session. After the meal most of us engaged in a snow battle outside the mess, which eventually developed into a free for all. Silvester, a tall officer of outstanding deportment and a star pupil of the drill course at Uxbridge, was standing somewhat glassy eyed, watching the proceedings, when the commandant emerged from the mess, en-route to his office. Wilfred Freeman paused for a moment and viewed the fight with a somewhat disdainful eye. He then turned to Silvester and said in a tone of utter scorn: "Silvester, if you have any respect for your friends Greig and Beilby, you will pick them up and take them straight to bed," to which Silvester replied: "Yesh, Sir," and promptly fell flat on his face. Freeman's eyes rose to the heavens as he strode off towards his office without further comment.

The start of the frosty spell coincided with a very good guest night. One of the flight commanders in 3 Squadron, Jimmy Slater, had a distinguished war record and was the holder of the MC and DFC as a fighter pilot. He was a short, slight chap, of wonderful singing capacity, most of his songs being rather broad. A married man and consequently living-out, we did not normally see a great deal of him, so on these occasions he was especially popular as an after-dinner entertainer. As the evening progressed somebody suggested that as Jimmy was only a little chap, it would be fun to try to throw him up to the ceiling of the ante-room which was quite a considerable height. We accordingly manned a carpet and with a great clamour and after much tossing, eventually got our victim up to the objective. While defending himself from violent impact, he left one very grubby hand print on the spotless white distemper. The next afternoon, when giving a new officer instruction in aerobatics on a dual Snipe, the machine crashed. Both Jimmy and his pupil were killed [6]. Fatal crashes are usually looked upon philosophically, as an occupational hazard, but somehow this one came as a shock to all of us, following as it did the previous jolly evening. An air of depression hung over the mess and everyone, upon entering the ante-room, seemed automatically to glance up at the solitary and very grubby hand print on the ceiling. Personally I know full well, that many years later, I still glanced up at it when I entered that room. The funeral took place one afternoon a day or so later, the distance from the camp to Upavon cemetery being about two miles. The whole station was on parade despite the intense cold, the frost having reached its peak.

It is odd how so often, humorous situations develop on the most solemn occasions. During the march in slow time from the parade ground to the camp boundary, an elderly equipment officer, a short distance ahead of me, seemed to be having trouble with his balance mechanism and developed the staggers very badly. He recovered when we broke into quick time, then half way down the hill to the village, the intense cold caught up with a large number of airmen, who had to break ranks and dash to the side of the road to relieve nature. At the entrance to the village we came down to slow time again and the EO once more started to totter. It was all rather a nerve shattering experience with the somewhat ludicrous march terminating into a rather harrowing committal ceremony in the presence of Jimmy's widow and other relatives.

After it was all over, when we were once more in the mess having tea, someone remarked that there was excellent skating to be had on the frozen Kennet-Avon canal. Buscarlet, Beilby and I forthwith volunteered to drive down to Pewsey after tea and buy up all the available skates. We were also asked to purchase a supply of hot water bottles. We drove down in Arthur's Morris Cowley and after making the necessary purchases, repaired to the Royal Oak for something to warm us up before the drive back. We did not engage in a drinking session, though it was apparent that all was not well with our driver when we eventually emerged from the pub. Evidently he had given himself a preliminary boost before leaving the mess, partly to keep out the cold and partly to chase away dull care following the funeral.

Bus and I, with the greatest of tact, offered to drive the car back, but Arthur did not appreciate the gesture and became truculent. From the moment he let in the clutch we knew that the drive was going to be hectic. To state the situation in the mildest of terms and before the car left the village, we once again remonstrated and suggested that road conditions demanded due care and a very moderate speed. This to our regret only added fuel to the fire and once clear of Pewsey, the accelerator was pressed firmly to the floor by our enraged driver. The car weaved erratically back to base. The sparkling glitter of the headlight beams on the road, filled Bus and me with extreme foreboding and as we approached the sharp bend near Manningford, I knew we were for it. As the car took the bend all control went in a quick spin, terminating in a headlong collision with the offside bank.

The open-topped Morris turned over sharply onto its side catapulting the three of us onto the road, to the accompaniment of vast clattering from an assortment of skates and stone hot-water bottles, all of which fell on Buscarlet, who had been in the rear seat. I hit the tarmac on my left side and was pinned to the ground by the driver, who was now shrieking with laughter, the cause of his mirth being, for some extraordinary reason, that the engine was still running. Bus and I were both extensively bruised and shaken up by the impact, but Arthur had had the benefit of me as the unseen shock absorber, so came out unscathed. I eventually disentangled myself from the now hilarious driver and at once realised that the wrecked car constituted a serious obstruction in the middle of the road, so ran back to warn any approaching traffic, and was just in time to hold up my hands at an unfortunate motor cyclist. He immediately braked, waltzed gaily round and piled up just behind the Morris, fortunately without hurting himself or doing extensive damage to his machine. The poor chap at once got to his feet and apologised for his display. A few seconds later a large Daimler limousine in the charge of a liveried chauffeur and one occupant pulled up. The passenger was an army officer, Lieutenant Paine, en-route to Netheravon to learn to fly. I'm sure we impressed him!

There now being six reasonably sound people at the scene of the accident we all set about righting the Morris, and pushed it through a gate into a field to await collection next day. After saying farewell to the motor cyclist, we all piled into the Daimler and were driven back to the mess, where a terrific party was in progress. The natural aftermath of a reaction to a depressing day. We dismissed the Daimler and persuaded Lieutenant Paine, who was by no means unwilling, to stay the night and he was delivered to Netheravon on the morrow in reasonably sound condition.

In the early 1920s, the instructional system originally formulated by Smith-Barry quickly achieved world-wide acclaim, consequently potential flying instructors arrived at CFS from time to time, not only from the dominions, but from foreign air forces and civil flying schools as well. Early in 1926 we received warning that two Finnish Air Force officers, Captain Snellman and Lieutenant Pukkinen, would be part of No.19 course, and that Snellman would be with my lot. On the day of their arrival I and another instructor, Flying Officer George Trim RCAF, drove down to Pewsey station to meet them.

Hitherto all foreign pupils spoke English tolerably well. Here was a first class problem – these two had almost no knowledge of our language. How were we going to teach them the CFS patter over the Gosport tube? However, we largely overcame this by giving each one a copy of the patter, and telling them to get it translated into English. Fortunately they had a dictionary and a glossary of technical terms. When they had done this, we painstakingly went through the English version with them to rectify their pronunciation, so that now we could begin the practical demonstrations in the air. Snellman was quite a good pilot but I cannot recall ever having such a tough instructional assignment. However, progress was made and we finally got them through.

The month of April 1926 contained two noteworthy events, the arrival of a small number of Cirrus Moth light aircraft, built to AM order, and the first visit by a small detachment of CFS staff to a flying training school to test a cross-section of pupils and instructors. Our CFI and three instructors, one of them being me, went on this trip to No.2 FTS, Digby, and then on to RAF College, Cranwell. From then on regular visits were made to all flying schools in Britain, the object being to ensure that a proper standard of training was being maintained and to test instructors for re-categorisation.

Also about this time I dropped a very large brick. One morning after several days of continuous rain, I went up in my Avro to do a weather test and whilst in the circuit saw a large saloon car driving at exceedingly high speed through the camp, and in the direction of Andover. I thought to myself, I'll teach that blighter to bat along through our camp in such a manner. I dived down to the roadway, skimmed over the roof of the car and waggled my rudder at the driver. I repeated this operation several times until he slowed down between Everleigh and Ludgershall, taking a right-hand turn for Tidworth Camp. Not very long after landing my presence was requested at the commandant's office. When I entered I faced a very stern Wilfred Freeman.

"I have just had a serious complaint from the colonel of the Wiltshire Regiment, to the effect that a pilot of one of our aircraft flew in a highly dangerous manner over the top of his car about half an hour ago. As you were the only person airborne, what have you got to say for yourself?" As I had no hope of establishing an alibi, all I could do was to apologise and to mutter something about how unfair it was that senior army officers could exceed the speed limit on the main road thus giving quite unreasonable temptation to junior air force personnel to dive on them. Perhaps not the best of defences.

My punishment was stoppage of weekend leave for that month. However, before the following weekend, Wilfred sent for me again and I was ordered to go into Devizes and apologise personally to the colonel, adding a rider to the effect that acceptance of the apology would cancel the punishment I'd been given. Accordingly after work that afternoon, I changed into my best uniform and drove to the colonel's married quarters, arriving about 4.30. He was away for the day, but his wife very kindly invited me in for tea, so I apologised to her instead. She seemed to regard the whole incident as a great joke, was extremely charming and promised to square things with her husband. She was evidently true to her word, for the next afternoon I received an exceedingly pleasant note from the colonel, telling me to forget the whole affair. So, honour having been more than satisfied, off I went on leave that Friday.

The following month witnessed a temporary disruption of our normal routine by the advent of the great general strike of 1926. Emergency measures were brought into force into almost every walk of life throughout the country in order to maintain essential services. The task allotted to the CFS being the conveyance of mail across the Bristol Channel to South Wales.

A temporary airfield was established at Llandaff, near Cardiff, with my friend Beilby as OC ground party. All operations were successfully concluded and no aircraft landed in the Bristol Channel. However, at Upavon, two humorous incidents are worthy of mention. At the start of the emergency the convoy of transport was assembled ready for departure and Beilby, always with an eye on the main chance, was in the act of loading a bag of golf clubs and a tennis racket into his car, when the commandant walked past. Freeman stopped and watched this operation with interest, then remarked casually before strolling on: "Hello Beilby, off on your hols?"

The second was concerned with the communications. An instruction contained in the operational directive received from HQ, called for the continuous manning by both day and night of the telephone station in the adjutant's office. The officer detailed for this being known as the crisis officer. At that time Silvester was temporarily acting as adjutant and a small rota of officers to do duty as crisis officer was drawn up.

One morning the officer on duty, Flying Officer E A C Britten [7], was seated at the 'phone while Silvester was dealing with routine work. The telephone rang, Britten picked up the receiver and answered: "Crisis speaking". The caller hung up. A moment later this procedure was repeated and Britten appeared to be rather puzzled. A few minutes after a further and similar call, the CFI, my old friend Reggie Smart, stormed into the officer in a towering fury and blazed at Silvester: "Who the hell is the bloody fool in this office who answers, 'Christ is speaking,' every time I try to call you?"

One evening after the crisis of the strike was over, Arthur and I were returning from an evening out, and on arrival at Upavon we parked my HE and began the walk along the pathway to the mess. Some time previously an AM contractor had been engaged in rewiring the underground electric cables throughout the camp and for some reason had left an enormous empty wooden cable drum almost directly on this path. On a dark night one could easily collide with it with painful consequences. On edge, it stood seven feet tall and must have weighed several hundred-weights.

On this night it was brilliant moonlight but it still threatened our right of way, so we decided that by hook or by crook, we would remove it. With great skill and some considerable physical effort, we rolled the thing down the path, past the front of the mess and onto the edge of the first tee of the golf course. With one mighty heave our 'enemy' was on its way down a preliminary and comparatively gentle slope. We watched as it went bumpity-bump, and gathered speed towards a steeper slope – the scene of John Boothman's skiing mishap a few months earlier. It was lost to view as it sailed over this edge, and for a second or two there was complete silence, before a curious tearing and rending sound assailed our ears. We rushed down in the moonlight to find our monster spool reposing in the middle of the hard tennis court. It had completely wrecked the wire netting surround and had done considerable damage to the court's surface.

The following morning we did the proper thing, owned up and offered to bear the cost of making good the damage. The mess president, John Russell, accepted our offer and apologies, but imposed an additional penalty. The contractor was due to collect this empty drum quite soon, so we were ordered to hire a caterpillar tractor and tow the bobbin back up to the roadway. This we did without delay and left it on the side of the road, just at the point from where our launching had taken place.

Almost exactly one month later, Arthur and I, accompanied by Lance Browning, one of the flight commanders in 3 Squadron, had spent a convivial evening out and got back fairly late. Again moonlight bathed the area outside the mess, and again we came across the drum, still not collected, and appearing to be leering at us. I think we giggled rather childishly, as the same thought flashed home to each of us simultaneously. This thing just had to go. As there was no real malice in our hearts we resolved to launch the drum so that it would clear the tennis court by about 200 yards. Using the same launching point at the first tee, and taking careful aim, a really good shove sent the drum on its way.

Again we watched as it gathered speed, and as it again disappeared, there came an almighty crash like a thunderbolt. We tore down the valley to see what had happened this time. I regret to say that recently a magnificent structure had been built at the bottom of the valley, to house a miniature rifle range, a fact that we had completely overlooked. The drum had smashed through the main brick wall, leaving an enormous hole, and had done considerable damage to the butts as it shattered itself to pieces. There the bits lay amidst a pile of shattered bricks and wood. Considerably shaken we retraced out steps, fully realising that the cost of repair this time would be considerable and well beyond our combined resources.

Eventually we resolved to keep our traps shut, reckoning that those in authority would never suspect us of being such idiots as to drop the same clanger twice, and so it turned out. There was an investigation, but Arthur and I were not even questioned, so the mystery was never solved. Nobody got into trouble, and the long suffering tax payer footed the bill. All in all, a satisfactory ending to a sad story.

[1] Later Group Captain Norman C Saward. In WW1 he was shot down and taken prisoner in September 1917 flying a Camel.

[2] Australian Harold Alan Hamersley MC, a successful fighter pilot in France during WW1. He later became a test pilot for Avro, and held the altitude record at one time. A group captain in WW2, he died in December 1967.

[3] By 1939 Harold Hunter Down AFC, was a wing commander. He retired as an air commodore CBE in 1945.

[4] As the name might suggest, Dirk Cloete came from South Africa and had flown in the RFC/RAF in WW1, winning the MC in 1916. In 1917 he was at the School of Special Flying, Gosport, as an instructor, and then commanded a training school at Shoreham, for which he received the AFC in 1919. Flew with the SAAF in 1921-23 and in 1926 became CO of 9 Sqn RAF. Retired in 1927 and later became air advisor and director of Civil Aviation in Southern Rhodesia. Served again in WW2 and died in May 1970, aged eighty-one.

[5] John Nelson Boothman. RAF 1921 and in 1923 became an instructor at CFS. Iraq 1926-29 and then became OC of the RAF's High Speed Flight 1930-31 (AFC). As an air commodore in WW2 was awarded the DFC DFC(US) & CdG, and had risen to air chief marshal CB by 1947. Later Sir John KCB, retiring in May 1956 but died in December 1957.

[6] James Anderson Slater MC DFC was killed on 26th November 1925, along with Pilot Officer W J R Early, a day or so from his twenty-ninth birthday.

[7] By 1939 Edmund Britten DFC was a wing commander, having won his DFC in Waziristan in 1920. James Silvester also made wing commander by this date.

12

CRASHES

Throughout the 1920s and until just after half way through the 1930s, a great annual event used to be the RAF display or pageant, at Hendon. This generally was followed about a month later by a similar event, though on a reduced scale, at the RAF Staff College at Andover. In 1926 the latter show took place on 5th August, the CFS contribution to this entertainment being a display of individual aerobatics on two very dissimilar aeroplanes, a Snipe flown by John Boothman and the new de Havilland Moth, flown by myself – both machines performing simultaneously.

John Boothman was a superb aerobatic pilot and past master of inverted flight. This irked somewhat as the scope with the Moth, owing to its low power and unsuitability for inverted flight, due to the wet sump engine, was a trifle limiting. The small diameter loops, flick rolls and stall turns in the Moth would, in my opinion, show up rather unfavourably against the slow rolls and inverted turns of the Snipe. I therefore decided to compensate for this comparatively poor performance of the Moth, by ending my show with a really daring and exciting item. A falling-leaf manoeuvre from a height of 1,500 feet right down to the deck and then landing off the final leaf.

Falling leaf was an apt description, as the aeroplane appeared to flutter from side to side towards the ground with the engine only just ticking over. Technically it was nothing more than a quick succession of flick stalls, alternately to the right and left, simple to perform, but requiring accurate timing and coordination with stick and rudder movements, as the aeroplane was only partially under control during the descent. In fact, the period immediately following each flick entailed a momentary, but complete, loss of control.

I practised several times daily over one particular area of the north aerodrome at Upavon and got the timing absolutely perfect, regaining full control just in time for the final and sensational touchdown. The evening before the display I dined with the army, at a guest night with the machine-gun school at Netheravon. I mention this as it might possibly have had some bearing on what happened the following afternoon at Andover. However, I was brimful of confidence, particularly as I had never in nearly nine years of flying, crashed an aeroplane, or even badly bent an undercarriage. Force landed the odd time, but never actually 'crashed'.

The day of the pageant could not have been better, and the enclosure was filled to capacity with spectators. Right on time, John and I took off to do our show and at the end of our ten-minute slot, I started the falling leaf. It seemed to be going splendidly until the very last moment, when I realised to my horror that I had torn off one leaf too many, and was about to hit the ground with an almighty crunch. I tried to save the situation by fully opening the throttle, but alas too late, for it only added grist to the final impact. With the shattering of the propeller, the poor Moth seemed to dissolve in a cloud of dust and splinters. With the resumption of complete silence, I found myself still strapped in my seat, surrounded by debris, but completely unscathed. As a spectacle I could not have done the thing better, right bang in front of the centre of the enclosure. I was told later that women screamed and that as the wreckage subsided into a heap, a horrible volley of abuse emanated from the centre of the dust! [What Greig does not say specifically is that during that awful moment of silence came from the depths of the wreckage, distinctly heard by the crowd, one single, very clear and very rude word! Ed.]

Never have I felt such a fool. I imagined row upon row of bulging eyes, like a Bateman optician's cartoon, viewing my shame. I did not dare to step from the wreck until the ambulance arrived, and once rescued and aboard, I slumped down in the back of the vehicle, directing the driver to take me to the mess, not sick quarters, where I gulped down a large brandy, whilst mustering my courage to return to the enclosure and make my apologies to all concerned. This I eventually did, starting with the station commander, Wing Commander L S Pattinson [1], who was charm personified. "Don't you worry, old boy, we all make mistakes at times." I next saw Wilfred Freeman, quite sympathetic, but pained at the side having been let down. Reggie Smart also, was not too bad. Then I spotted old Topsy Holt, now an air commodore, who typically was rocking with laughter. "The funniest thing I have ever seen. If I can get you another Moth, will you go and do it again?" His cheerfulness did much to restore my morale.

I returned to Upavon with my tail between my legs and was not particularly gratified when on entering my navigation lecture room to see drawn on the blackboard, a horrible coloured chalk drawing of a wrecked aeroplane, and beneath it written the one solitary word – 'Teacher'. I was never allowed completely to live down my disgrace, particularly as Dick Fairey, the aeroplane designer, had managed to film the whole incident and made a regular practice in future of displaying it at dinner parties, then running it through the projector backwards, so that all the bits and pieces came back together, the resurrected Moth ascending back into the sky in a 'climbing leaf'. The accident, of course, was a gross error of judgement, due largely to overconfidence and possibly contributed to by the fact that I had been well dined the previous evening, thereby slowing up my reactions.

The 20th course which ended in July, and one ab initio course in August, marked the completion of an era in the history of CFS. Owing to radically changed Air Ministry policy, the unit was due to leave its ancestral home at Upavon in October and move to Wittering, near Stamford. This forthcoming change of location was regarded with equanimity by most of us, and with pleasant anticipation by some. In

one sense it was an adventure to break new ground, but I felt some regret at leaving our home-like mess and its very pleasant memories. Not
least being the Sunday returns on cold autumn and winter evenings
following weekend leaves, to a wonderful variety of viands both on the
hot plate and cold sideboard, supplying amply our physical needs before turning in. One particularly happy memory of these evening
meals, was dawdling at the table, cracking pounds of cob nuts and
drinking white port, in company with Len Cockey, a chap who had a
peculiar idiosyncrasy when offering alcoholic refreshment. He would
never say something like, what will you have, or other commonplace
phrase, it was always, "What about a tincture?"

One evening shortly before the break for summer hols, someone
suggested at bedtime that it would be good fun to have a nocturnal
timed car hill climb from outside the village and up the long hill to the
west. Although accepted with considerable enthusiasm, not many sup-
porters turned up and the event sadly ended in heated words and
much personal abuse. The plan was for each car to carry an observer
with a stop watch, to time the journey from the start to the mess steps.
In the end only four or five turned up, including Buscarlet in his 10 hp
Talbot, Dick Dauncy, in a Sunbeam, Bill Down in a new Morris Cowley,
with me in the HE. Bill Down was going to be late as he had some un-
finished work to do but would be along shortly.

Bill certainly was late and in the end Dauncy got fed up and started
his run, only to mishandle the car. I pulled up next to him to lend a
hand, and then Bus arrived, pulling up behind the Sunbeam. Dauncy
had jammed his near side wheel into a sloping grass verge and just as
we began to consider a way of getting him free, we realised that our
three cars on this dark road constituted something of a hazard. At that
moment, a late Bill Down was heard approaching from up the hill towards the start, racing full bore to make up the lost time. Far too late
he saw the rear end of my car. I was conscious of violent, screeching
tyres, then a frenzied scream from Bill of: "Greig, you bastard!" followed
by much thumping, banging and tearing of metal, as he tried to steer
his car through the obstructions. The only vehicle escaping unscathed
was Dauncy's, who was the cause of all the trouble. Everyone seemed
to be in a towering rage, particularly Bus, who was due to drive down
to Barnstaple in the morning, now an impossible prospect due to a

bent axle, broken spring and other damage. However, it all eventually simmered down and we returned sadder but wiser to the mess, where we sat down to worry over a story to tell our insurance people.

The next few months were to witness the arrival of three great aviators, as a welcome addition to the CFS staff. In order of their arrival, they were Dick Atcherley [2], Dick Waghorn [3], and George Stainforth [4], known respectively as 'Batchy', 'Waggon' and George. Of widely different personality in character, I was destined to rub shoulders with all three fairly considerably during the next few years. Batchy reported to CFS before we moved to Wittering, the other two after.

Of the three by far the most flamboyant was Batchy, whose exploits at one time earned him the title of 'Grock' of the air. In addition to his flying skill, he was also a past master of skullduggery and a practical joker par excellance. On a more serious note he was the possessor of a fertile imagination, an inventive brain, a ready wit and brisk repartee.

Reverting once more to the lighter vein of his vivid imagination, he was responsible for the production of the most extraordinary aeronautical jargon, three typical being: 'Oswaldtwistle landing', 'whortleberry' and 'flashes of gnats'. In more conventional terms, the first referred to a manoeuvre due to the pre-flap of an airbrake error by expert pilots to lose surplus height and forward speed immediately prior to touchdown, otherwise known as swish-tail. The second was what happened if, when the first was still in progress, the aircraft struck the ground. In a more personal reference to Batchy's exploits, what happened when he struck a low brick wall.

The flash of gnats really represented a frustrated ambition on the part of Batchy to emulate a swarm of flies flitting hither and thither whilst hovering over a cowpat. To do something similar with a formation of aeroplanes, was the height of his ambition. As it transpired, his final RAF appointment was as CinC Flying Training Command and I was staying with him just as he heard about his knighthood. His comment to another visitor was: "Well, I suppose I had better join a Knight Club." After retirement he became a director of Follands and boosted the sale of their Gnat aircraft, so back amongst the cowpats again.

Waggon and Batchy were great friends, who had been at Cranwell at the same time, the former being holder of the Sword of Honour for best all-round cadet and the latter, the Grove Memorial Prize for the best pilot of the course. Waggon I would describe as a strong character, with a highly developed sense of loyalty, very able, tough and a fine athlete. He never smoked and seldom had a drink, possibly a glass of port for a loyal toast on guest nights. This abstention was in no way due to any moral or religious scruples, he just did not like the stuff. In any case he could enjoy a noisy guest night on just lemonade, as indeed could Batchy, and he was endowed with a fine sense of humour and of the ridiculous. His untimely death as a result of an accident while flying as a test pilot at Farnborough in the early 1930s, was a great loss to the service and to his many friends and family.

George came under an entirely different category. About my age, he was ex-Sandhurst and left the army to take a short service commission in the RAF, eventually becoming a regular. On our first acquaintance he seemed more like a scientist or a boffin than a brilliant pilot. His far-away expression, usually in wrapt contemplation, gave entirely the wrong impression. He might possibly be in a continual tizzy on the ground, but in the air he was one of the most precise and accurate pilots I ever met. For a number of years he represented the RAF at Bisley, a simply deadly shot with rifle and pistol. In his late forties, and commanding a night fighter squadron in Egypt in WW2, he took off from Hurghada to give chase to a Ju88. Around about 700 feet, both engines of his Beaufighter failed. He and his navigator managed to bale out but their parachutes were not fully open by the time they struck the ground, and both died.

About six weeks before our move to Wittering, I got rid of my HE car and bought a little Gordon England Austin 7, which Pip Dauncy aptly named 'the Beetle'. It proved to be the most reliable four-wheeled conveyance I had so far possessed. One could drive it literally anywhere including into the mess, through the ante-room and out again. It remained my constant companion for over three years and at the time of final departing, was implicated in a fiendish but extremely clever practical joke made on me by David Atcherley, Batchy's twin brother.

On 6th October I ferried the last Avro from Upavon to Wittering, where we were now settling in, preparatory to receiving the 21st course. The airfield, a relic of the Kaiser's war, was situated alongside and to the west of the Great North Road, a mile or two south of Stamford. The hangars and technical buildings being of the same vintage were in contrast to the more modern domestic side, with brand new married quarters of the latest pattern. Our mess was very comfortable except for one fact, the central heating plant was incomplete and remained so for several weeks. To help keep one's circulation going in the cold ante-room, a few members headed by Silvester, Batchy and Pearson-Rogers [5], one of the new pupils, organised dancing lessons and endeavoured to teach those energetic examples of the terpsichorean art, the Charleston and Black Bottom.

Another activity of a semi-social nature inaugurated by Buscarlet, was the habit of periodically flying in formation during the mid-day break, then to have lunch at other training schools within easy reach, such as Cranwell, Digby and Spitalgate. This institution became known as the Lincolnshire Light Luncheon Club, and was run on a reciprocal basis. Its only rule was that visitors paid for their own lunch but not for any aperitifs beforehand.

At the end of October we received from de Havilland's on temporary loan, a Moth (G-EBOU), fitted with a small five-cylinder radial Armstrong-Siddeley Genet engine of about 65 hp. This was truly a delightful little machine possessing none of the disadvantages of the heavier Cirrus. All aerobatics in vogue at that time could be carried out with ease, including a new one – the Bunt. This manoeuvre was invented by Batchy when flying Snipes in 23 Squadron at Henlow a year previously. The title was also a product of his fertile imagination.

In execution one throttled the aeroplane back until just about to stall, then pushed the control column firmly forward, as far as it would go. The ensuing vertical dive would pass the vertical and when the machine was upside down after completing half the inverted loop, the pilot would half roll again to normal flight, but facing the opposite direction. G-EBOU proved to be a source of inspiration and we came to the conclusion that the Genet Moth was just the machine with which to put on a formation aerobatic show at the Hendon Air Display the following summer.

Batchy, Waggon and I put the proposal to Reggie Smart who fully agreed but no further action took place until the beginning of 1927. The end of 1926 saw the departure of Wilfred Freeman on promotion to a job at AM, his place being taken by Group Captain C S Burnett – old friend 'Screaming Lizzie' of Iraq days. The passage of time had mellowed our new commandant, his legendary fiery temperament being no longer in evidence. Nevertheless, he would occasionally blow his top whenever Batchy or Waggon were observed flying between the hangars! In time he came to recognise even these antics as normal behaviour for CFS.

My promotion to flight lieutenant came on New Year's Day 1927, and early the next month I started serious flying practice with Batchy and Waggon, using an assortment of single-seat fighters for the purpose, myself leading in a Siskin. To starboard came Batchy in a Gloster Gamecock, while Waggon stationed himself the other side in a Gloster Grebe. Although there were marked differences in the performance and handling qualities of the three aircraft, these difficulties were overcome by the proficiency of we three young men.

The possibility of CFS putting up an aerobatic show at the next Hendon display was a great incentive in these exercises, although nothing definite had so far been settled. I had a strong hunch that the Air Ministry would approve the Genet Moth owing to the very great public interest in light aircraft at the time, and the recent increase in private ownership of these small and economical aeroplanes.

In the selection and training of an aerobatic team, it is obviously desirable that the leader should be the man with the most experience, though not necessarily the most expert and polished pilot. It is, however, of paramount importance that those making up the balance should possess a very high standard in flying aptitude, and be able to fly in unison with the leader, even to the emulation of minor errors. The formation should always be tight, a quarter or half a wing-span being safer than aircraft spaced at wide intervals, where it is easier to lose sight of the other aircraft. It was always a joy flying with Batchy and Waggon, both tucked in so close that I could hear their engines without difficulty.

Our proposed Hendon formation was for five aircraft, so two more pilots needed to be found. George Stainforth was an obvious choice although he had yet to arrive at CFS. John Armour, a good aviator rather fancied his chances, but unfortunately when looping in formation he had a habit of inadvertently changing station from starboard to port when coming out, so consequently had no chance. As things eventually worked out, my good mate Arthur Beilby became the fifth-man choice.

It must have been about the end of February when the director of training, Air Vice-Marshal Hugh C T Dowding CMG [6], visited Wittering for the purpose of having a chat with pilots who had flown our one and only Gamecock. Apparently pilots on squadrons equipped with this type had been experiencing trouble in recovering from spins, so he was anxious to know whether any of us had had this trouble. We were unanimous in replying in the negative and insisting that the machine was, in all respects, nothing but a pleasure to fly. Unfortunately none of us observed one important fact, that our Gamecock was completely devoid of machine guns and other war-like impediments, a point that might well have been a vital factor in comparing its handling qualities with those aircraft in service squadrons. More anon.

Now being a flight commander as befitted my rank (!), I had occasionally to give preliminary flying tests to pupils prior to examination by the CFI, for categorisation as flying instructors. Towards the end of No.22 course, Flying Officer J Mollison reported to me for preliminary tests. I well remember writing when completing the remarks section of the relative pro-forma, to wit: 'This pilot thinks he is better than he really is'. I was not referring to his aptitude as a pilot, but to his unfortunate and somewhat supercilious manner of speech through the speaking tube, which might indicate unsuitability as an instructor. As the world later came to know, there was not much wrong with Jim Mollison's flying ability.[7]

Early in April the Air Ministry approved our Genet Moth proposals and I flew Group Captain Burnett up to Stag Lane on the 7th, in order to confer with F R A St. Barbe, of de Havilland, about details of equipment, final date of delivery, etc. Feeling well satisfied with the situation, we flew back home to find Wilfred Freeman had arrived from AM on a brief visit. On seeing me in the mess, he reported what to me then, was a shattering piece of information. "D'Arcy, it might interest you to know that a new flight lieutenant post has been added to the establishment of Fighting Area, to be known as area examining officer, and that you are to be the first officer to hold this appointment. You will be off to Uxbridge in a few days time." "But, Sir,' I said, 'what about my display formation team?" "Oh, don't worry," came Freeman's reassuring reply, "I'll fix it with the AOC for you to return to Wittering on temporary duty about two weeks before the pageant." I was not overwhelmed with confidence that this would actually happen, but the dice had been cast. Thus ended my first tour of duty with the Central Flying School.

On arrival at RAF Uxbridge one evening in mid-April 1927, I was still clueless and very apprehensive about my new job. I booked into the RAF Depot mess and was allocated a room in an old wooden building. That night I had practically no sleep owing to a severe attack of asthma. Consequently the following day I was really in no fit state to report to my new boss, Air Vice-Marshal Brooke-Popham [8]. However, it had to be done. Brookham as he was known in the service, quickly dispelled my fears, and within seconds of entering his office I felt completely at ease.

A tall man in his late forties, with a rather high-pitched voice, but a friendly formal manner, I was sure we would get on. Looking back, I do not think I ever met another very senior officer who personified kindness, tact, tolerance and human understanding. I always found him to be completely approachable and the absolute antithesis of the pompous self-important type, fortunately rare, who might, for example, deliberately keep one waiting an unnecessarily long time, while probably doing no more than completing his daily crossword puzzle.

Brookham outlined my duties roughly in the following manner:

"Well Greig, this job is very largely an experiment. You'll
be sharing an office with Rice, but when the weather is

*fine, I don't want to see you in it, you must be out with
the squadrons. You will have an unrestricted use of the
dual control Grebes and Siskins and I would like you
to fly with as many of the squadron pilots as you can
and assess their ability much as you have done at CFS.
Take part in their mess life and attend guest nights, as
I would like your candid opinion on the morale of individual squadrons, their weak points and any other
matters that should be brought to my notice. I also
want you to sit in on all courts of enquiry and fatal ac-
cidents, look into low flying and other complaints from
the general public.*

*"Another point. I am chairman of the Flying Sub-
Committee of the RAF Display and would like you to be
my secretary. However, as I have promised to release
you to the CFS for the actual display, Rice will take over
all your files when that time comes. Finally, whenever
you go off for the day, always leave a note on your desk
giving your whereabouts so that Taaffe, my personal assistant, can contact you if necessary."*

My office companion was Squadron Leader E B Rice, a South African,
and no relation to E A B Rice, my old 6 Squadron CO [9]. Our office
adjoined that of the SASO, Group Captain P L W Herbert, generally
known as 'Erb'. The HQ as a whole was situated on the ground floor
of Hillingdon House. The other floors were occupied by the Senior
Organisation HQ Air Defence of Great Britain, under its CinC, Sir John
Salmond and his SASO, Air Commodore F G Holt, my old friend Topsy.
Within forty-eight hours of my arrival, I managed to secure a room in
a modern stone building, and with this and a more settled frame of
mind, got rid of my asthma for the rest of my sojourn in this place.

In the mess, apart from the depot staff, there were a number of single officers who worked at ADGB and Fighting Area. Among these I
found a number of kindred spirits, whom I had known previously. The
CO at the RAF hospital was Harry Hewat [10] – a pleasant chap. He
made a practice of ticking me off for my habit of standing with my back
to the ante-room fire, thereby acting as a screen.

My new job started very unexpectedly, with a flourish. The first file to enter my 'In Tray', contained a report submitted by Pilot Officer Dauncy, the chap from Upavon, and whose driving caused that mishap on the hill race. He was now serving with 23 Squadron at Kenley, and his report concerned the subject of the spinning of Gamecocks. Apparently he had had considerable difficulty in recovering from a right-hand spin. The account was well put together and made sense, but in my opinion, then, it appeared very alarming and might well have been an exaggeration. My previous personal experience with the docile CFS Gamecock supported my suspicions.

It was therefore up to me to establish or not, whether Dauncy had been 'shooting a line'. To the spectators at the air displays of those days, the spinning nose dive was a thrilling aerobatic manoeuvre. In actual fact it is definitely not an aerobatic, but without plunging into highly technical rigmarole, a spin is a state of auto-rotation whilst descending vertically. The cause can be either accidental or deliberate. In the former instance it is generally because of loss of flying speed during a turn. When this happens near the ground, the result is invariably fatal. It will thus be readily appreciated that the teaching of deliberate spins and the means of recovery, is a vital part of every pilot's training. In a simple method of spinning deliberately, the pilot closes the throttle, at the same time pulling the control column back until the aeroplane stalls. Full rudder is then immediately applied and the machine will spin and will continue to do so, as long as the stick is held back. To recover, full opposite rudder is applied and the stick moved well forward. The aeroplane should then fall into a normal dive in which full control of flying speed is regained. Different types of aircraft have their own characteristics, some tending to resist incipient spins, others entering a spin only too readily. Likewise some recover easily, others do not.

On 20th April the CinC of ADGB was due to inspect Kenley, and 'Erb' had to be present at this function, so as Brookham's representative, he needed to be flown there. He asked me to take him, thus giving me the opportunity of testing Dauncy's Gamecock. Carrying parachutes had only been introduced during the past year or so, and although the squadrons were all now equipped, we had not yet started to carry them in our Communication Flight Bristols. Therefore, upon arrival at Kenley, I arranged to borrow Dauncy's parachute. In planning my test on Gamecock J7899, I aimed to do three spins to the left, followed by three to the right. The tail-plane adjustment would be set fully forward and neutral, then fully back for each series of spins.

For the benefit of the reader, tail-plane adjustment would mean a nose heavy aeroplane which would tend to resist spinning, the reverse being the case with the adjustment fully back. I climbed the Gamecock to a safe height – about 15,000 feet – carried out three fairly prolonged spins to the left and experienced no difficulty. On the first spin to the right, with the adjustment fully forward, I found recovery a little awkward, while recovery from the second at neutral was unpleasant, and after completing about six turns the attitude of the aeroplane changed. The nose rose towards the horizon and the rotation became very smooth. Forward stick movement and reverse rudder had no effect, so I eventually opened up the engine and after a couple more turns the spin stopped. So Dauncy had NOT been shooting a line. I did not do a third spin with the adjustment fully back.

Arriving back at Uxbridge I reported to Group Captain Maund [11], the chief technical officer of ADBC, and gave him an account of my flight. He immediately arranged for various alterations to be carried out on the Gamecock and I agreed to return to Kenley for further tests. On the 27th I flew J7899 again and found no improvement so the machine was once more returned to the rigging experts for further alterations. After lunch in the Kenley Mess, I decided that it might be a good idea to select another Gamecock at random, and carry out a comparative test. I selected one from the Battle Flight – J8039 – which meant that in addition to the normal equipment, it was carrying 1,000 rounds of live ammunition, the fact of which, from a loading point of view, had some bearing upon what eventually happened.

I followed the same procedure as on the previous flights and after about a dozen turns to the right on the first test, with the tail adjustment fully forward, the spin became very flat and refused to respond to any of my recovery efforts. I resorted to regular sawing motions with both engine throttle and control column but to no avail. After about twenty-eight complete revolutions and the loss of about 6,000 feet or so, I concluded that the spin was quite stable and with my approach to the deck becoming distinctly uncomfortable, decided to part company with the Gamecock. I did not know, however, how difficult it might be to heave myself out of the cockpit, due to the centrifugal force of the spin, so thought it essential to get out in good time. It took some effort to climb out of the seat, although it probably didn't take that long, and my body had only just emerged from the cockpit, when the aircraft stopped spinning and bucked over onto its back, catapulting me into space in the process.

By the time I had found the rip-cord I was travelling head-down with no sensation of falling but a howling gale going by. On giving the rip-cord handle a violent tug, it came away so easily that it flew right out of my hand and for one unpleasant moment I thought it had not been properly connected. However, the canopy opened with a crack and I was jerked round into an upright position. My borrowed harness was not as tight as it should have been, so gave me a nasty jolt in the ribs. Hanging in the air and drifting earthwards, I was struck by the remarkable silence, apart from the sound of air rushing out of the apex of the canopy. I could hear dogs barking, cars hooting and the whistle of locomotives, about 3,000 feet below. Almost immediately I spotted the Gamecock descending below me in a very wild and flat inverted spiral. Would it crash into Whyteleafe gas works, Caterham barracks, a row of houses, or what? I saw it circling all these places and many more, but luckily a strong westerly wind took it into a ploughed field just east of Warlingham. With the sound of the crash like a bursting bomb, flames shot into the air as the fuel tank exploded.

The drift of the wind took me well past Warlingham and steadily in the direction of Biggin Hill and I began to wonder if I would ever reach the ground. This thought was quickly dispelled when terra firma seemed to be coming up to meet me – far too quickly in my opinion – during the final few hundred feet. On passing over the tops of some trees, I pulled up on the lines and with much crackling, landed in the middle of a large bush. On disentangling myself and the shroud lines from the foliage, I noticed that I was practically alongside a narrow country lane and on the other side was a fairly large country house, which I shortly discovered was Fairchilds, Chelsham. After gathering the parachute into a clumsy bundle, I crossed the road and entered the spacious grounds of this dwelling, walked up to an open French window and deposited my bundle on the threshold before the astonished gaze of two white-haired ladies, until that moment enjoying a cup of tea.

I apologised for the intrusion, explaining briefly what had occurred and asked if I might use their telephone. With great presence of mind one of them dashed from the room, returning almost immediately with a decanter of whisky and a syphon of soda. They were both very charming and we just had time for a chat and a couple of whiskies, before a car from Kenley arrived. I thanked them for their hospitality and enquired their names, and on being told Daniels, I replied on the spur of the moment: "Not by any chance related to the local JP of that name, and chairman of the Oxted Court?" "Why, that's our dear brother, so you know him?" one replied. I made some rather evasive response and got into the car.

On the way back I had a look at what was left of the Gamecock and on arrival at Kenley reported to Ray Collishaw, my old friend of Iraq days and CO of 23 Squadron, and apologised for not returning one of his aircraft.

The next day I received a very nice note from the JP in which he expressed the hope that I was none the worse for my experience. He obviously did not realise that we had already met, on what for me had been very painful circumstances. The previous December I had been driving my Austin 7 down to Bexhill from Wittering when just north of Godstone, I was caught in a speed trap. The police officer in charge of the operation informed me that my speed, over a given distance, had been noted as 43½ mph. When returning to Wittering on the Sunday evening, forty-eight hours later, I was again approaching Godstone and had made up my mind to keep to a steady 20 mph between the village and Caterham, in case the trap was still in operation. To my consternation I found that not only was it still in operation, but it had been moved to the south of the village and I was caught again. The same police sergeant informed me that my speed time was 38 mph, so still way above the legal limit.

In due course I appeared before the bench at Oxted, with Mr Daniels in the chair. I was fined £6 for the first offence and £4 for the second. Ten pounds from an air force officer's pay about a week before Christmas was a bitter blow, one that caused me to reflect upon the apparent inconsistency of British justice. In this instance I had in no way been driving dangerously, no pedestrians or other traffic being visible, but still ten quid for breaking an absurd speed limit on the open road. If the reader will recall, I was only fined thirty shillings three years previously, and that involved knocking over a policeman!

On the day following the Gamecock incident, I was interviewed by Sir John Salmond. After hearing my report he asked me to continue the spinning investigations. With tongue in cheek I signified my willingness to do so, but was considerably relieved when within the next twenty-four hours, I was released from the responsibility. B E Baker [12] and his gang of test pilots at Farnborough took on this task.

Pip Dauncy, who had been directly responsible for this departure from my normal routine, left Kenley shortly afterwards to become a test pilot at the A&AEE at Martlesham Heath. Unfortunately he was killed the following year whilst so employed. By his death, the RAF lost a very promising officer and extremely able pilot [13].

[1] Lawrence Arthur Pattinson DSO MC DFC, WW1 soldier and airman. MC in 1915 and then squadron commander 1916. DFC in 1918 leading a squadron in the Independent Air Force, then he commanded No.41 Wing (DSO). A full service career saw him rise to Air Marshal Sir Lawrence, KBE, CB. Died in March 1958.

[2] Batchy and his twin brother David were both well-known RAF officers, who both reached air rank. Both would be involved in the Schneider Trophy races. David was lost in a Meteor over the Mediterranean in 1952, but Batchy went on to retire in 1959 as Air Marshal Sir Richard, KBE CB AFC & Bar and died in April 1970.

[3] Flight Lieutenant H R D Waghorn was fatally injured flying a Hawker Horsley on 5th May 1931 at Farnborough. He and his passenger baled out following a problem and while the latter survived, Waghorn was badly injured and died two days later.

[4] George Hedley Stainforth AFC had been regular army following Sandhurst but moved to the RAF in 1923. He and Batchy Atcherley won the King's Cup

Air Race in 1929, and then he flew with the Schneider Trophy team. In 1931 he held the British high speed record (407 mph) and was then with the Experimental Section at RAE, Farnborough. He was killed in action in 1942 commanding a night-fighter squadron in the Middle East (Wg Cdr).

[5] By 1937, Henry William Pearson-Rogers was a squadron leader and graduate of the RAF Staff College. He retired as a group captain, CBE, in 1948.

[6] Later Air Chief Marshal Sir Hugh Dowding GCB GCVO CMG, CinC Fighter Command 1936-40 and defender of Britain in the Battle of Britain. Became Lord Dowding and died in 1970.

[7] James Allan Mollison, a Scot, joined the RAF in 1923 and served in Waziristan and India before becoming a qualified instructor. Leaving the service he became an instructor with the Australian Aero Club and later a pilot with Australian National Airways. Made several record-breaking flights in the early 1930s. Married to Amy Johnson. Flew with the ATA in WW2; died in October 1959 aged 55.

[8] Eventually Air Chief Marshal Sir H Robert M Brooke-Popham GCVO KCB CMG DSO AFC Ld'H. Sandhurst 1898, army, learnt to fly in 1911, RFC 1912, France 1914-18. AOC Fighting Area 1926-28, later AOCinC ADGB 1933. Retired 1942. Died October 1953.

[9] By 1938 Group Captain Edward Brownsdon Rice was commanding No.4 School of Technical Training at St Athan, Glamorgan.

[10] By 1939, Group Captain H A Hewat MB Ch.B, principal medical officer to British Forces in Iraq.

[11] Later Air Vice-Marshal Arthur C Maund CB CBE DSO. CdG. Army and RAF WW1, then served in South Russia in 1919. In 1939 he was AOC(Admin) to British Forces in Iraq. Died in December 1942 due to heart trouble.

[12] Later Air Marshal Sir Brian Baker KBE CB DSO MC AFC. A successful WW1 Bristol Fighter ace, in 1918 he commanded a Home Defence Squadron at Biggin Hill. After a varied career in the service he retired in 1950 and died in October 1979.

[13] Flying Officer Harold Campbell Gambler Dauncy, KIFA 23rd January 1928.

13

HEADQUARTERS FIGHTING AREA

During my earlier sojourn at Kenley, three years or so previously, I had developed a considerable affection for this station, although there had been a few changes in the intervening years. A brand new mess had taken the place of our old one on the hill for one thing, which now accommodated the Air Ministry works and buildings department. The chaps there also displayed a good variety of skullduggery.

There were incidents that today might seem incredible and which could not now be tolerated in the traffic-congested atmosphere over southern England. For example, there was a case of Pilot Officer Holden who, to relieve the tedium of orderly officer duty on Christmas Day 1926, took up the dual Grebe and looped it round Tower Bridge. This enterprising young man was unfortunately killed in a collision whilst formation flying some months later [1].

Of the various incidents that happened during my four years at Fighting Area, one was particularly noteworthy. I cannot recall the exact date, but one morning most of the daily papers carried an alarming front page headline: 'Mystery Plane, without lights, flies down Fleet Street at midnight.' Or words to that effect. The offending aeroplane had done just that and at roof-top height, thus creating a stir amongst the press officials, hard at work on the morning issue. A number of wild statements regarding the machine's origin and purpose appeared in print, but only one solid fact emerged. It was a small, fast and rather noisy aircraft, so suspicion immediately fell on fighter squadrons. However, a quick check on the fighter airfields revealed that all aircraft flying the previous night had all landed half an hour before the Fleet Street event, and further investigations elsewhere also proved fruitless. This state of affairs did not satisfy Brookham, who asked me to keep on the alert for clues. Checks on the time and logbooks during the various visits revealed nothing, but I had a hunch that I would eventually identify the pilot. I felt there must have been collusion or a cover up, those in the know keeping their traps firmly shut. I therefore decided to bide my time, and several weeks later I happened to attend a Kenley guest night.

Among the pilots in 23 Squadron, there was a chap named Tavendale, a graduate of Reading University and one of the first to be granted a commission under the university entrance scheme. Tavendale, moreover, a couple of years earlier had spent a few weeks as a civilian, living in our mess at Upavon. This had been with the blessing of AM, to see whether he liked the look of the RAF, so consequently I knew him fairly well.

As the evening wore on my attention for some reason or other became focussed on Tavendale, and I decided to await a suitable opportunity for doing some discreet sounding. This eventually occurred in the early hours, when we were the sole occupants of a settee, with both of us full of good cheer and with glass still in hand – and in a typical back-slapping mood. I finally steered the conversation round to the Fleet Street do, my crowning comment being: "By George, I really do admire the chap who had the guts to beat up the press boys. Just the sort of thing you would do, old Tabernacle." A rather sheepish smile spread over his countenance as he replied: "As a matter of fact, and confidentially, old boy, it was me." "However did you get away with it?" I asked, "Why weren't you rumbled?" "Well," he continued, in conspiratorial tone, "the OC night flying committed a bit of a boob in mustering the aircraft, thought everyone was on the ground, so got all the flares in whilst I was still cruising around. When I returned, the field was in darkness, so I landed by my wing-tip flares."

So the mystery of the phantom plane was solved and my ego considerably boosted in the process. However, in view of the somewhat underhanded method of interrogation, tantamount to a breach of hospitality, I stayed in line with the Kenley boys, kept my mouth shut and took no further action, other than having a fatherly chat with Tavendale the next morning. He kept on the straight and narrow and committed no further misdemeanours. Regrettably many months later he flew into the North Downs on a flight back to Kenley in bad weather and was killed instantly.

Among the other characters in the junior ranks at Kenley, were two who outshone all the others as super aviators – H A 'Grandpa' Horniman [2] and Bruin Purvis. The former was a flying officer approaching thirty-five years of age, hence the nickname. Purvis was only a youngster, having graduated from Cranwell the previous year. Both were past-masters at aerobatics and gave superb individual displays at Hendon; Horniman in 1927, Purvis in 1928. Purvis eventually qualified as a test pilot at Farnborough. I did not meet him again until 1943 when I became CO of the Aeroplane and Armament Experimental Establishment (A&AEE) at Boscombe Down, where he was group captain and chief test pilot while being in charge of performance testing. In 1946 he left the service to become chief civilian test pilot at Boscombe Down. He was still flying aged sixty but blacked out at 4,000 feet flying with a friend in a private aircraft, and went into a coma. His friend landed safely and later a brain tumour was removed but he never fully recovered.

Most of my time during the period following my spinning show and my temporary return to CFS in mid-June, was devoted to secretarial duties in connection with the forthcoming display at Hendon, or visiting airfields with Brookham. Display files began to pile up on my desk and I found this aspect of my work a bit tedious. It was at this time I began to be aware of Brookham's idiosyncrasies. In passing a file to a subordinate for comment or action, he would invariably end every minute or instruction on an interrogative note, such as – 'Do you agree?' For the life of me I could not see a very junior flight lieutenant disagreeing with his AVM. However, he did this with everyone, regardless of rank. A friendly habit and very typical of the man.

I often spent time at the de Havilland aerodrome at Stag Lane, watching the building of the Genet Moths. They were a happy family, and Geoffrey de Havilland, the head of the firm, was a calm and very kindly man. In fact my association with them gave rise to an urge to leave the RAF and join them. However, I decided that to relinquish future claim to a service pension would be too much of a gamble.

Hubert Broad [3], the chief test pilot at Stag Lane, at this time was working on some interesting projects. The first of a long line of Gipsy engines, to replace the Cirrus, was now in production, one being fitted to a tiny racing monoplane called the Tiger Moth – not to be confused with the famous biplane of the same name that came later. The firm had also produced a prototype of a very fine general biplane fitted with a Napier Lion engine, called the Hound, intended to be ordered in quantity for the RAF. It established a number of world records for speed and rate of climb, which outshone all others in open competition. Despite this the government awarded the contract to another firm, whose product was definitely inferior in every way to this one. Apparently political or other considerations took precedence of sheer merit in this instance.

Until our service Genet Moths were ready, the firm gave me carte blanche with G-EBOU, the prototype which I flew frequently to Wittering for our formation pilots to practice aerobatics. I was also invited to race this machine at two flying club meetings, the first being the Hampshire Flying Club's pageant at Hamble on the weekend of 14-15th May, and the second at Bournemouth on the 4-6th June. On the occasion of the first of these events, I took my old friend Arthur Beilby with me, leaving Stag Lane on Saturday the 14th. As the Hamble pageant was not due to start till the following afternoon, I decided to fly down to Bexhill and before leaving, some of the de Havilland brass gave us an excellent lunch at the Bald Faced Stag, at Edgware, so we took off in G-EBOU in very good form.

As we were passing over Croydon aerodrome and approaching Kenley, to my utter amazement and alarm, Beilby shouted back: "I'm going to wing-walk." To the best of my knowledge, he had never done this before, and moreover, the Genet Moth, being a light machine of small wingspan, was singularly unsuited for this form of activity. The lunchtime drinking must have affected him. I yelled for him to sit down but quite undaunted he lowered the plywood flap at the side of his cockpit and began to clamber out, stretching a long right leg in the direction of the front spar of the wing. As I had already anticipated that the emergence of this leg would upset the airflow over the tail, the machine at once gave every sign of going out of control. Violent yawing and pitching resulted, as his foot missed the spar, and went through the fabric instead. Luckily this gave him a considerable shock and he clambered back into his seat in an ungainly manner, with all the speed he could muster, remaining silent and immoveable for the rest of the journey. We landed in a suitable field between Bexhill and Cooden, and after folding the wings, had the Moth towed into a local garage for the night. After a good evening out, plus some serious talking to Arthur, we flew on to Hamble next morning.

These early flying meetings were great fun. To limit the numbers on the triangular or quadrilateral courses of only three miles or so, the races were handicapped and had to be run off in heats. Even then one had to keep one's eyes skinned, particularly at the corners. I regret to say I was never placed, possibly my handicap was unfair, or the engine lost power, or even my flying was sub-standard! However, I didn't mind, though I must admit it irked somewhat to be seen off by Lady Bailey. No doubt her Avian was faster than my Moth.

Winifred Spooner was another woman pilot at these meetings, also the sixty-two-year-old Duchess of Bedford, who at that time had not yet qualified as a pilot, but flew at every meeting as a passenger. The emergence of Amy Johnson, Dorothy Spicer, Pauline Gower and Jean Batten, from their cocoons, had not yet come about. The most consistent winner at most of these meetings was Squadron Leader C A Ray, the test pilot for Boulton & Paul. He flew a rather clumsy-looking machine called a P9, powered, I believe, by an old 90 hp RAF or 80 hp Renault engine. There was nothing spectacular about his flying, all his corners being taken in what seemed to be very wide sweeping turns with about 45° banks. His consistency was, however, quite remarkable.

The Bournemouth meeting in June brought home to me very vividly how dangerous this form of racing could be around a very small course. The race course at Moordown served as the airfield, there being no aerodrome there at the time. We were taking part in the first race on 6th June, a medium power handicap. In the middle of one turn I was suddenly conscious of extraneous noises, and on looking up, saw the landing wheels of another competitor – a machine flown by Dudley Watts, a young pilot and private owner – only a matter of two or three feet from the centre section of my Moth. I was pretty quick about pushing my stick forward and getting out of the way. A matter of moments later, at another corner, two aircraft collided, a Westland Widgeon [G-EPBW], flown by L P Openshaw [4], Westland's test pilot, and a Blue Bird, flown by Squadron Leader W H Longton [5] of the RAF. I was a short distance behind but did not witness the actual impact.

The crumpled wreckage of both aircraft spun down directly in front of me, bursting into flames on impact with the ground. Both men were killed. 'Scruffy' Longton, a very able pilot, was a regular performer at the RAF display. I had noticed in previous races that he made a practice of climbing in all his turns and diving down again on completion, a habit that might well have been a contributing factor to the accident. This unlucky meeting was marred by yet another fatal accident. Major H Hemmings, flying Alan Butler's DH37, appeared to stall before slipping into the turn in front of the race course grandstand and crashed on the railings. The crash cost Hemmings the loss of an eye, his passenger being fatally injured.

The Genet Moths for the RAF display were finally ready by 18th June, and I flew one to Wittering to start a period of intensive rehearsing. Before leaving Uxbridge I passed over an enormous bundle of files to Ed Rice, who took them with all the goodwill in the world! A nice friendly chap with a good sense of humour. Sad to relate fate was not very kind to him, for he died in the hands of the Japanese in WW2. [Air HQ, 224 Group; PoW 16 Feb 1942, held at Bangka, Sumatra, Singapore and Taiwan. Died 5th Sept 1943, buried Hong Kong. Ed.]

The time allowed for our aerobatics at Hendon being limited to fifteen minutes and bearing in mind the low rate of climb and speed of our Moths, the first essential was to work out a suitable sequence based on our experience with the prototype, G-EBOU. This machine was most controllable and very responsive, recovery from spin invariably taking place within half a turn, with appropriate stick and rudder movements. However, the fuel system would not permit continuous inverted flight, so upside-down flying had to be done in a glide. As the system never air-locked on G-EBOU, the engine never failed to start immediately after half rolling from an inverted position back to level flight. The flight conference was held in the mess and after some discussion and drawing up plans on mess note paper, the following sequence was decided upon.

Take off and climb to 2,000 feet.
A loop, followed by –
A bunt.
A burst of Prince of Wales feathers.
Followed by a spin; the formation was then to regain about 500 feet of altitude before –
   Half rolling into position for an inverted glide across the
   length of the aerodrome.
   Finally a loop at very low altitude followed by a flypast in
   front of the enclosures and –
   Land in formation.

The aircraft would be disposed as follows: Batchy Atcherley, Arthur Beilby on my right, Dick Waghorn and George Stainforth on my left. Our very first formation practise on the 19th revealed two snags. When spinning for the first time it was found that owing to varying idling speeds of individual engines, the five aircraft did not stall simultaneously, consequently, despite opening up the spacing of the formation prior to spinning, the stalling time lag resulted in the interval between aircraft being irregular and in some instances, dangerously compact. In fact I almost had the impression that Waghorn's machine was so close, that our wings were almost knitting like the cogs of a wheel.

We had no R/T intercom at all, so all movements were initiated in response to hand signals and wing waggling. The start of the spin was made when directly facing a definite land mark, each pilot counting the pre-arranged number of turns prior to recovery action, to resume

normal flight directly facing the same landmark. Luckily we all kept
our heads, stuck to the agreed drill and recovered facing the right direction. It was nevertheless, a rather uncomfortable experience.

Snag number two occurred when half rolling from the inverted glide
to level flight. All engines failed, for some moments, to answer to the
throttle owing to air-locking, a condition never experienced with the
prototype. This resulted in unavoidable loss of height and uneven
spacing of the formation. Our problem was immediately placed in the
hands of our engine expert, Tubby Whitmore, and our senior NCO
Flight Sergeant Stocker. The spinning difficulty was overcome by setting the slow running in each engine, so that it practically ceased firing
on closing the throttle, and Stocker decided that the only way to remedy it was by applying air pressure to the petrol tanks, which normally
depended on gravity feed. This we did quite simply by fitting a device
like a miniature ship's ventilator to the top of the tank with a bell
mouth facing directly into the slip stream.

Stocker's idea worked perfectly and we had no more technical difficulties. In all respects, including technical acumen, we could not have
had a better bunch of chaps. As the reader might gather, Tubby was a
short and very stout man, with a fat man's wheezy and rather subdued
voice. He had been in the flying business since the very early days, an
ex-engine room artificer commissioned in the Royal Navy, who served
with the RNAS throughout WW1. He possessed a grand sense of humour, his sallies being brief and to the point. In January 1917 he was
off on a cruise aboard HM Seaplane Carrier *Ben-My-Chree* in the
Mediterranean. The ship was hit and set on fire by a Turkish shore battery, and for his part in the action, Tubby was awarded the Distinguished Service Cross. The story goes that some little time later he
ran across a friend who, on seeing the distinctive ribbon of the new
medal for the first time, was responsible for starting the following conversation:

> "Hello, Tubby, wherever did you get that medal?"
> "Didn't you know, I was the hero of the Ben-My-
> Chree."
> "What, were you first over the side?"
> "Bloody nearly!"

Stocker, a slight and very energetic man, who always seemed to do things at the double, was eventually commissioned and in due course retired as a wing commander engineer. A cheerful, hard working and very resourceful chap.

Our technical difficulties were now over and we set to, in real earnest, on our intense period of rehearsal, which went ahead without further hitch, except that on 23rd June, when completing our first period of formation practise, and on the final leg of the approach, something rather odd happened. The formation was about to cross the Great North Road, when I suddenly felt that a giant had grabbed hold of my Moth, pulling it up into the air. So instead of looking ahead to the point of touchdown, I found myself gazing in alarm at the hard tarmac surface of the road immediately below. However, this deflection was but momentary, a sharp pull on the stick restored the status quo and we landed in fair order. As we taxied in, I noticed that Batchy had taken off again and was engaged in some crazy flying. Being Batchy, there was nothing unusual about this, except that there was what appeared to be quite a long streamer of torn fabric and loose timber, trailing from his port wing tip. On switching off at the hangar apron, I then looked at the tail of my machine and found that the starboard elevator had been twisted a half circle.

I had a friendly chat with Batchy when he eventually taxied in and suggested that although I fully realised that he was a keen, efficient and enterprising young officer, anxious to obtain accelerated promotion, he might at least have the decency to refrain from trying to bump off his flight commander. I do not know whether this incident had any effect on Tubby Whitmore's black list, alleged to have been kept by this worthy for the purpose of keeping in proper order of precedence the names of those keen types who, in his opinion, were destined for an early appointment at the pearly gates. For a short time Batchy headed this list.

To cut a long story short, our event at Hendon went off well and we got an excellent write-up in the aeronautical press. We put on a repeat performance a few days later at the Birmingham Air Pageant, after which I finally left Wittering to resume my proper task at Uxbridge.

Three of the Genet Moths performed again at Hendon the following year, their petrol systems having been properly modified for protracted inverted flight. A highlight of the 1927 event was of far reaching importance to British aviation and the RAF, with the formation of the RAF's High Speed Flight at the Marine Aircraft Experimental Establishment at Felixstowe and the participation of a team of three aircraft in the International Schneider Trophy contest for seaplanes at Venice in the early autumn of the same year, resulting in a victory for Britain. Flight Lieutenant S N Webster [6], flying the Supermarine S.5, reached an average speed of 281.65 mph.

Rumour of the government's proposed support for this event had circulated to CFS during the previous year and there was some speculation as to whether pilots of this unit would be taking part. However, as this was a contest for seaplanes, previous service in the RNAS was considered to be an essential pre-requisite to qualify for selection. I hasten to mention these events at this juncture as the rules governing the selection of pilots might be revised as a result of experience gained with the 1927 flight. As it happens, in the following year I became personally involved.

Meantime, the rest of July and August were fairly uneventful and I could usually get out and about among the squadrons. At the beginning of September, I started a month's leave, and on the 20th, received a telegram from Mr St. Barbe of de Havillands, asking if I would like to deliver a Moth to Copenhagen for them, as they were short of pilots. Needless to say I was delighted but as it needed to be undertaken in the next forty-eight hours I had a problem. For one thing I had no passport, and I would also need AM permission. The former could be overcome by a trip to London and the Foreign Office, but the latter was much more difficult.

I was staying in Bexhill and thought my best avenue was to enlist the aid of my AOC, so rang Brookham. He appreciated the situation and told me not to worry, but to go ahead and make the arrangements. Within a couple of hours I received the 'all clear', so raced off to London, got the passport, then went to Stanfords in Charing Cross Road for the necessary maps. Before leaving Bexhill, I had arranged for my friend Claude to come with me for the ride and on the morning of the 22nd we arrived at Stag Lane, ready for the off. Being a serving officer there would be no question of remuneration, St Barbe merely making good any out of pocket expenses and paying my return fare to London.

We expected to hand over the Moth at Copenhagen and then catch the boat to Harwich the same evening. Consequently our kit consisted of traditional pyjamas and a tooth brush and I travelled in rather an ancient and shabby suit of plus fours. The weather on the day of departure was most unpleasant, with a moderate gale blowing from the south west, with low cloud and driving rain. However, having promised to deliver G-EBSI by the following day, we took off after an early lunch at Stag Lane, intending to spend that night at Rotterdam. After contour chasing under extremely low stratus for one hour, we arrived at Lympne to clear customs and top up with petrol.

My passenger was having an uncomfortable journey, as he was a large man and had to squeeze himself into the front cockpit, which already held a spare wheel, a propeller, plus sundry packages of other spare parts. The weather at the coast was appreciably worse and we required men at the wing tips before taxying out. Before leaving the watch office, I asked the chap there for a magnetic bearing to Cap Gris Nez. "Piece of cake, old boy. Just fly down the pier at Folkestone, take the compass reading and carry on with that heading." I took this to mean the pier with the dance hall at the end, and not the harbour pier.

Off we went, flew along the pier and crabbed our way across the Channel, just above a very uninviting sea. Owing to a strong cross beam wind, we expected the crossing to take about half an hour. Forty minutes later there was still no sign of land and I was beginning to get a little worried in case I had compensated too much and was heading down the Channel. In fact, this proved to be the case and after another five minutes or so, the cliffs at Wimereux loomed directly ahead and we turned down wind to fly along the coast. I continued to hope that my passenger would not be air sick, not that I worried about his personal comfort, but the risk of his partly digested lunch hitting me in the face was disturbing. The airfield at Ostende looked inviting, so down we went to stretch our legs and wait awhile for the weather to improve.

Whilst taking on more petrol an official in uniform arrived, addressing us in French. We showed him our passports, and then the aeroplane logbook. All we got in return was a scornful glance followed my much gesticulating and a lot of talk that I could not understand. The chap seemed to get more and more exasperated and the pouring rain did not help matters. Eventually, he raised his eyes in despair, shrugged his shoulders and walked off. By this time the weather had improved so we took off for Rotterdam. On arrival we found the Dutch authorities spoke excellent English and were not worried that our travel documents were incomplete. By dusk the weather had cleared and after finding an hotel, we toured the city's night spots.

In marked contrast with the weather thus far, Friday dawned calm and cloudless. After breakfast and settling our accounts we took off in brilliant sunshine for Hamburg. An uneventful flight across Holland and Germany brought us to this city for lunch. On arriving at the airfield, we taxied to the only hangar which appeared to contain aircraft, three small Klemm monoplanes, and we were greeted by three German members of the new club, one of whom, Hans Vordihoff by name, spoke excellent English. He seemed to like the opportunity of entertaining a British aviator and after giving instructions about refuelling, swept aside our enquiries about Customs, and marched us off to their clubhouse, where he gave us lunch, washed down with more than an ample sufficiency of excellent wine. Our host was interested to hear that I had flown night bombers during the war, informing me that he had done likewise on Gotha bombers on London.

We took off again in excellent spirits for the last leg of our journey, flew over the ancient port of Lübeck and down along the Baltic coast, arriving over Copenhagen an hour and forty-five minutes later. As we circled Kastrup airport we noticed quite a gathering of people around the one hangar and it struck me that they were probably awaiting the arrival of some important personage, and that we had better taxi discreetly out of their way.

As we had arrived on time, I presumed that someone or other would take over the Moth without delay and that we might, with any luck, catch the night boat to Harwich. We landed and began to taxi towards the perimeter, taking care to avoid the awaiting throng. However, an official signalled us towards the hangar and the crowd surged in our direction. Conspicuous within this party was a very massive, bearded man, who walked with a pronounced limp, accompanied by a small boy of about ten years old, who appeared to be an Eskimo. As I switched off, three of the party came forward and introduced themselves in excellent English – Bengt Rom, Christianson, and a Lieutenant Steinbeck. After brief introductions, I handed over the logbook and other papers and stated that we were anxious to catch the next boat home and could we have transport and make reservations as soon as possible. It was then that I regretted my inadequate briefing at Stag Lane, for the chief spokesman, in terms of utter astonishment and consternation, said: "That is unthinkable. Don't you realise that for us, this is an event of national importance. Not only is this Moth the first private aeroplane ever to be owned by a Dane, but it has been purchased by our great national hero, Peter Freuchen, the famous arctic explorer. We have reservations for you at the Hotel d'Angleterre, in Copenhagen, and assume you will stay with us for several days."

Recovering from this shock and feeling very embarrassed, I was introduced to Peter Freuchen and his son, the little Eskimo boy, Mequsaq. He was the most impressive figure of a man, his limp being due to the loss of one foot through frost bite. As a young man he first went to the arctic during the first decade of the century, where he established a training station at an Eskimo settlement in north-west Greenland, giving it the name Thule. A great friend of Knut Rasmussen, he became the world's greatest authority on the Eskimo people. His explorations covered the whole area from Greenland to Alaska, including Hudson Bay territory, and Baffinland. He later travelled extensively in Siberia. His Eskimo wife, Naurana, died in the early 1920s, leaving him with a son and daughter, Pipaluk. His training station at Thule later became a part of an American airbase.

Lieutenant Steinbeck then took me in hand, explaining there was to be an official reception at the airport the following day, for the ceremonial hand-over of the Moth, so would I fly it to the local military airfield forthwith, so that riggers could make any adjustments necessary, paint out the British civil markings, and put on its new Danish identification letters.

It was only a short flight of less than ten minutes and then he drove me into the city. Driving past the harbour, I noticed a twin-engined Rohrbach flying-boat tied up to a buoy, a large affair that looked as though it had been mainly built of corrugated iron. At the hotel we had a spacious bedroom with private bath, and after tidying up we went downstairs to find a number of the welcoming committee, including Freuchen, waiting to take us out for the evening. We did not realise it, but we were destined for the next four days to grope our way through a fog of food and drink, Danish hospitality being really wonderful.

The evening proved a blur of calls at small inns, drinking and snacking on sea food, a drink tasting of aniseed being particularly distinctive, until finally we arrived at the main restaurant, finding more food and drink, then rounding this off with a tour of various night clubs. I particularly remember some shrimps on heavily buttered black bread, which, while most appetising, was particularly thirst promoting. I have no idea what time we got to bed.

Saturday dawned bright and sunny and despite hangovers, we were ready by 11 am to be collected and driven to Kastrup for the official luncheon and hand over. The Moth was already there, complete with new markings and the name of a weekly magazine, of which Peter Freuchen was editor, painted in large Gothic lettering underneath its wings. After the ceremony, we adjourned to the rest room for lunch, which lasted for three hours. Good food and a seemingly everlasting round of toasts, most of which I could not understand, ended with a long speech. By this time I was feeling very bloated and fuddled, then suddenly realised that this speech was concerning de Havillands and as it ended, everyone raised a glass and turned towards me. I became aware that a response was awaited. Even when fully compos mentis, I am no speaker so was feeling pretty demoralised at the thought. I managed to stagger to my feet and delivered a profound if somewhat incoherent oration, the gist of which was that the Danes were jolly good chaps, de Havilland marvellous fellows, that we had had a great lunch and Copenhagen was a wonderful place. I felt convinced nobody understood a word I had spoken but sat down to tumultuous applause.

Claude and I were now in dire need of a snooze, after this continuous onslaught of Viking hospitality, but it was not to be. Bengt Rom and Christianson, who since our arrival had acted as our ADCs, announced that we were off to the opera. It seemed as if we might get a chance of an hour or two slumber, and a respite from eating and drinking, if we could settle down in the dark of an opera house, so we accepted. However, upon taking our seats we noticed with slight apprehension that a quite substantial shelf ran along the back of the seats in front, and not many minutes passed before a bottle of Johnnie Walker, four glasses and a syphon of soda, were conveniently to hand. It was a challenge we could not decline and the bottle was empty long before the performance ended. Back at the hotel we invited our two friends to lunch the next day, which they accepted, and left. Our problem, of course, was that our plan for a very short stay meant we had not brought much money with us.

It was still quite early and as we strolled through the bar, intending to head for our bedrooms, the barman requested my attention, and said that the German pilot of the Rohrbach flying-boat was a guest at the hotel and was most anxious to make my acquaintance. He was absent at that moment but was expected back shortly. So we sat down and ordered a nightcap and soon afterwards the man arrived. The barman's description of 'famous German airman' was quite right. His name was Ernst Udet [5], one of the most famous German fighter pilots of WW1. To my cost I had no idea he was also a great chap for a party and could, with ease, drink most people under the table. However, his knowledge of English about equalled mine of German, so the barman, a cosmopolitan type, came to our rescue and proved a very efficient interpreter. In reply to my enquiry about the flying-boat, Udet told me that he intended to attempt an east to west crossing of the Atlantic, but it had been plagued with endless mechanical problems. In fact, the flight never did take place.

On the question of the 1914-18 war, he was most interesting. I was intrigued to hear that he had escaped by parachute on one occasion [29th June 1918, from a Fokker DVII. Ed.] when his machine had been disabled in combat. The only parachute used by the Allies in WW1 was that static line type issued to balloon observers. Udet was inclined to put some emphasis on the fact that the German flying corps did not bear any ill-will towards the British flyers and always made a point of entertaining, when possible, captured airmen in their mess before being sent off to prison camps. This feeling of goodwill, however, was not extended to the French. Our session was still in full flow when the barman informed us it was time to close the bar. Quite undaunted, we suggested to him that he should continue interpreting for us during a round of Copenhagen's night spots, to which he agreed. The four of us started at the Tivoli Gardens, ending up much later in a night club.

By this time I had got my second wind, so round followed round, Udet sitting with a benign expression on his face, the drinks seeming to have little effect on him, while I was beginning to feel befuddled and rather peculiar. Suddenly I was aware of a phenomenon I had hitherto never experienced. There were two Udets, two Claudes and two barmen, while all the bottles on the bar were likewise duplicated. My homing instinct kicked in and I decided to make a getaway whilst I could still stand up. How I got to the hotel I cannot recall and it was four years before I met Udet again.

By morning I felt dreadful, more so when I remembered the lunch date. I roused Claude and took a hot bath. On reaching the lounge I arranged with the head waiter for a table for four and asked him to call me when my guests arrived. When he did so, he had a puzzled expression on his face, and so did I when he said I did not have two guests, but thirteen! This alarming piece of news shook us to the core and we concluded that our invitation had somehow been interpreted as to include the whole party that had entertained us on the night of our arrival. In view of our limited finances I quickly consulted the menu and ordered everyone the set lunch. Then our guests were ushered in.

Despite our apprehension the party went off quite well. During the meal, Bengt Rom informed us that the following day, Monday, was the eve of the king's birthday and that we were being taken out on a special celebration party, followed by a further event on the Tuesday. As he was aware that we did not want to prolong our visit too long, he had reserved two seats on the KLM flight leaving Kastrup for Croydon, at 9 am on the Wednesday, via Amsterdam.

The next day went off well and that evening all our guests turned out again to take us around. With the exception of Steinbeck, who was wearing his No.1 uniform, all were clad in evening dress, and nobody seemed put out that we were still in our original civilian garb, and we must have looked very conspicuous, but nothing was said. However, we went the usual rounds and what I did find a little startling was that whenever we arrived at any hotel or restaurant, the band stopped and immediately began to play our national anthem, and everyone rose to their feet.

Our last full day went off without any problems other than over-indulging once more on food and drink. We did rise rather too late to attend the equivalent of their trooping the colour but I am sure we were forgiven. The memory of the last evening is vague. I did lose Claude when everyone seemed to split into small groups but eventually I got back to my room at 4 am, showered and collapsed on the bed. Next morning I found Claude's room empty but he turned up at 7.15 am, red-eyed, blotto, and giggling insanely. I had already gathered his things, so we got onto the bus sent to collect us and then drove to the airfield. As we approached the aircraft, his giggly mood evaporated and he became very silent. I sensed trouble ahead, especially if the flight happened to be turbulent.

We boarded a Fokker F7 [H-NADX], a high-wing monoplane with a single Bristol Jupiter engine. To my great relief the captain invited me to occupy the second seat with him up front, especially when on taking off we found the air was quite bumpy. Glancing back into the main cabin, I observed Claude with his face inside a paper bag. The flight to Hamburg took two hours, twenty-five minutes, Claude's head remaining in the bag for the whole trip. When we landed we went to the restaurant, Claude looking thoroughly dejected. I prescribed a port and brandy. Anyone who served in the Middle East between the wars will know the meaning of an 'Egyptian breakfast'; two cups of tea, one down and one up – in other words drink one down then bring it, and anything else, back up again. That's what happened to Claude's port and brandy.

A further flight of three hours, thirty-five minutes, took us to Amsterdam where we transferred to NADF for the final hop to Croydon. It took us eight and a half hours, with Claude retching the whole way. The conveyance from Croydon dropped us at the RAF Club and I managed to guide Claude to an armchair in the lounge, where he became unconscious. Harry Hewat, the PMO from Uxbridge, was there, and when he saw Claude, asked what I had done to him. I explained briefly, and Harry suggested we had found a new malady – Copenhaganitis. We managed the drive down to Bexhill the same evening but the following day I was laid low with a temperature and sore throat. Later we heard that Lieutenant Steinbeck crashed Freuchen's new Moth on their first trip together.

Whilst in Copenhagen, the British team had won the Schneider Tro-

phy contest at Venice, but on returning to England, the High Speed
Flight was disbanded. However, Major Mario de Bernardi then gained
the world air speed record for Italy, with a speed of 298.94 mph in November. This did not satisfy the Italian, and by March 1928 he had increased this to 318.64.

Meantime, a small nucleus of the High Speed Flight was retained at
Felixstowe under the command of my old pal from Iraq days, Sammy
Kinkead. He had flown the Gloster IVB in the contest at Venice but
had force-landed with a cracked prop-shaft on his fifth lap. It was now
up to him to wrest the air speed record from the Italians.

I carried on with my normal duties in Fighting Area, keeping out of the
office as much as I could and never failing to keep Brookham posted
as to my whereabouts. However, even the finest organisation is liable
to an occasional breakdown and on one fine morning I decided to
spend the day at Duxford. Before leaving I dutifully left a note saying:
'Gone to Duxford', and went. However, on my arrival at the Com.
Flight, Northolt, I was informed that Duxford was fogbound. Being reluctant to return to my desk, I decided on the spur of the moment to
visit Upavon, but forgetting that Brookham was also due there later
that morning. Shortly before lunch I happened to be standing with
my back to the fire in the staff ante-room, enjoying a pink gin, when
very much to my surprise and consternation, in walked Brookham.
"Hello, Greig, I am glad to see you are having an enjoyable day at Duxford," was his only comment.

In March 1928, tragedy struck the RAF a bitter blow. Sammy Kinkead
was killed whilst making an attempt at the speed record. A week or
two later a list of volunteers was called for, so that a replacement pilot
could be selected. As a result of experience gained by the HSF in 1927,
the original decision to employ only pilots with previous seaplane experience was shelved, as it had been found that the handling qualities
of the Gloster and Supermarine racers, were practically identical with
those of the modern fighter and bore no relationship to the service
seaplane anyway. I put my name down and early in April it came out

of the hat, so I was told to report to the MAEE, at Felixstowe on 1st May to take over the high speed experimental section.

My fist task however, was to hand over all my stuff to the long suffering Ed Rice. A few days later, Reggie Lydford arrived at Hillingdon House to take over my job. I regret to admit I left an unblemished record in Fighting Area, on a low note, one which brought home forcibly the wisdom of that old adage – Pride Cometh Before a Fall. On 27th April, RAF Tangmere was due for its annual AOC's inspection and in accordance with the usual practice, inspecting staff would fly down in formation, Taaffe and Brookham in the leading machine, 'Erb' and myself in the other. Three days previously I had flown 'Erb' to Up-avon and back in one of our Bristols. The weather on the 27th was perfect and I was feeling on top of my form with my new job pending. An 'ace' like me could do no wrong was my feeling, as I flew again Bristol Fighter H1685 to Tangmere.

In the days prior to the advent of the high-speed monoplane, the tricycle undercarriage and rigid air traffic control, much individuality was displayed by pilots in their method of approaching to land. In my own case I was fond of coming down for the last 500 feet or so, in a steep side-slipping turn to the left. I judged my approach so that the easing off of the bank and final check resulted in a touchdown on the left wheel and tail skid together, the machine still being slightly inclined to the left. In fact, I was really quite adept at this method of landing and on this occasion I was determined to show Tangmere just how clever I was.

Arriving over the airfield, the parade was already drawn up in review order on the tarmac, the aircraft of 1 and 43 Squadrons being in one continuous line. Individual machines, with a rigger and fitter at each wing tip and the pilot in front of the propeller, all stood at attention. The rest of the station personnel were in a line of flights etc, in front of these aircraft. Taaffe and the AOC had just touched down as I started my very dashing side-slip turn, the aim being to complete the manoeuvre where it could be viewed to its best advantage, dead in line with the centre of the parade. My judgement at the arrival point was exact, but I am afraid there was just something a little adrift with the method of execution. Was I just a little too slow? Did the Bristol stall? Did I pay the penalty of sublime overconfidence? The answer to all three questions is yes.

At the vital moment in making contact with the ground, the depressed wing refused to answer to the controls. The port wing tip and wheel met terra firma simultaneously and with a tearing crumpling sound, slithered along a few yards, The machine, having completed its run, ended up perched firmly on its nose, tail in the air. Deceleration had been fairly rapid but 'Erb' and I sustained no injuries and climbed out onto the ground in front of the assembled company, and joined the AOC. Unlike Andover there was no convenient ambulance for me to crawl into so as to hide my shame. I felt that every man jack, officer, NCO and erk, were just about splitting their sides with suppressed mirth.

A brighter moment came after the inspection when the CO of 43, my old mate Cyril Lowe, said he knew how I must be feeling and why not take his Gamecock [J7918] up and throw it around for a bit. I accepted his invitation and spent the next half hour rocketing around the sky. I felt much better, and with another Bristol having been sent down for me, I flew home. 'Erb' for some reason, elected to return to Uxbridge by car. Brookham never referred to the crash at the time, but never let me forget it, always managing a sly jibe whenever the occasion arose.

My time had at last come to leave Fighting Area after an interesting and enjoyable year. In accordance with the current service custom, I was given my confidential report to read and initial. Brookham had been extremely kind to me, but the old man had made one shrewd observation in the section headed: 'Is this officer recommended for the Staff College?' He had written: 'Yes, if he can pass the qualifying examination.' This indeed, was a home truth, as in my heart of hearts, I realised that I had neither the capacity nor the inclination to cope with this exam. However, I did subsequently make two attempts at it. [7]

[1] Pilot Officer Arthur Leslie Holden, died 16th May 1927. His partner in crime in the duel Grebe had been Pilot Officer Griffiths. They were both in mess kit and after the tower, had beaten-up a crane situated at the time on the roof of Swann & Edgars. Later, due to poor weather, they had to land in order to ask directions for Kenley.

[2] Group Captain Robert Henry Horniman CBE. RNAS in WW1; instructor at Cranwell and in the early 1930s was experimental pilot at RAE. In WW2

worked as MAP overseer at Hawkers.

[3] Hubert Stanford Broad had been a RNAS fighter pilot in WW1, then with Smith-Barry's SSF Gosport, where he was credited with learning the art of 'side-slipping' an aircraft. After much association with flying and air races, he was with the 1925 Schneider team, and won several important trophies in the late 1920s. In WW2 he was chief production test pilot for Hawkers. Made MBE and also holding the AFC, he died in July 1975.

[4] Laurence P Openshaw had been a flight sub-lieutenant in the RN when he took his flying certificate in March 1915.

[5] Squadron Leader Walter Henry Longton DFC** AFC, had been a pre-WW1 motor cyclist. On becoming a pilot he was retained as a test pilot (AFC) but in 1918 finally got to France, and was one of the very few fighter pilots to be awarded three DFCs. At the time of his death he was with No.1 FTS at Netheravon. He was thirty-four.

[6] Sidney Norman Webster had just got in at the tail-end of WW1 with the RAF, and then saw service in India and Egypt. Retired as air vice-marshal CB AFC & Bar, in August 1950. Died in April 1984.

[7] Readers will recall that Greig did not feel disposed to mention the award of the DFC back in 1921 so it will come as no surprise that he did not mention the award of the Air Force Cross in 1928. The award was Gazetted on 19th May 1928, and the citation reads:

This officer served as a Flying Instructor at the Central Flying School for over three years, and by his extreme thoroughness, untiring energy and keenness, set a high standard to all.

Flight Lieutenant Greig has since been employed as Area Examining Officer in the Fighting Area and has performed excellent work in that capacity. On one occasion he displayed remarkable courage and skill in carrying out a test in connection with the investigation of the report that a particular type of aeroplane had a tendency not to come out of right hand spins. On the instructions of the Air Officer Commanding he took an aeroplane in which this tendency was very marked, put it into a spin, and found that he was unable to check the spin after about twelve turns. He spun from 12,000 to 6,000 feet, and then, realising that the aeroplane was completely out of control, managed with difficulty to leave the machine and descend by parachute – the machine being completely wrecked after spinning into the ground. It was, moreover, only by direct orders that Flight Lieutenant Greig was stopped from carrying out further similar tests.

14

THE HIGH SPEED FLIGHT EXPERIMENTAL SECTION

Ever since the early days of the RFC and RAF, the service more than held it own with the other two services in regard to quaint or colourful nick-names, and the Marine Aircraft Experimental Establishment upheld this fine tradition. 'Pregnant' Percy once referred to a distinguished RFC officer and included amongst others were, a 'black nark' and a 'slack-arsed charlie'. The former was a senior admin. officer flight lieutenant, the latter a flying-boat pilot of the same rank. What was even more odd, however, was the fact that we had officers in the station accounts section named Squadron Leader K R Money and Pilot Officer N Wallett.

I arrived at Felixstowe on the evening of 1st May 1928 and reported to the adjutant first thing the next morning. After filling in the usual arrival form, I was told to report back for interview with the station commander at 10.30 am. On leaving his office I made my way with a feeling of pleasant anticipation, to the hangar that housed the high speed aircraft. This building appeared to be closed but as I approached a side door opened and a flying officer without wings emerged. He gave me a cheerful greeting: "Ah, you must be the new flight com-mander? I really don't know what you have come here for, because there is nothing to fly. All three Glosters are back at the factory for modification, the two remaining Supermarines are at Calshot, but we are promised a Flycatcher, which is still in pieces in the ARS. Otherwise, all we've got at the moment is a hangar full of junk."

On recovering from the immediate shock of this discouraging an-nouncement, I shook hands with Tom Moon [1], the flight's engineer, and followed him into the hangar. I had had a passing acquaintance with Tom in the summer of 1922, during a month-long leave in Egypt, and it was exactly as he described it, a mass of junk. The remains of a Gloster I Bamel and a Gloster III, odd floats and wings, famous racers of yesteryear, bits and pieces and innumerable drums of experimental fuel, heavily impregnated with tetraethyl lead. The whole place was festooned with every conceivable component but not one complete aircraft.

Tom conducted me to my office and then expanded further on his introductory remarks. The three Glosters, the IV, IVA and the IVB, were racing biplanes designed by H P Folland for the 1927 Schneider Trophy contest at Venice. They were of superlative design, powered by the 12-cylinder Napier Lion engine, which had three banks of four cylinders, disposed in the shape of an inverted broad arrow. In order to reduce the total front area to an absolute minimum and to ensure maximum stream-lining, the top of the wings were swept downwards to the plywood monocoque fuselage, the wing roots forming a contin-uation of the faring to the rear of the two side blocks of the engine. The vertical block fairing was continued along the fuselage embracing the cockpit canopy and continuing down to the tail fin. This arrange-ment ensured maximum aerodynamic proficiency, but had one serious disadvantage – the wing roots obstructing the pilot's forward view when landing and taking off. The modification now being embodied by the makers entailed raising the top wing and fitting a centre section plane. All this would, of course, impair the performance quite consid-erably and as these machines were to be used for training only, this did not matter over much.

The two Supermarine S.5s were a different kettle of fish, mono-planes with a higher landing and take-off speed. The calm water area available between Felixstowe, Harwich, Dovercourt and the open sea, was considered inadequate, hence their retention at Calshot, together with a small maintenance party detached from MAEE. The general idea was that I should get my hand in on the Glosters at Felixstowe, then, when I had acquired sufficient confidence and experience, fly down to Calshot to gain further experience with the S.5, before attempting any speed records. My immediate reaction to this was, why the devil fly in two places, why not have the three Glosters and a permanent detachment of personnel at Calshot? Much simpler, surely.

At 10.30 am, and feeling a bit despondent, I reported again to SHQ for my interview with the station commander, Wing Commander G R Bromet [2]. Geoffrey Bromet, an aviator of pre-1914 vintage, was an extremely nice man, and my initial interview with him did much to ameliorate what I took to be an irritating situation. Nothing to fly after all the flap of getting away from Uxbridge. He concluded the meeting roughly in this manner: "As you have had no previous seaplane experience, I have instructed Wardle, the OC of the Seaplane Flight, to take you in hand, show you the ropes and let you gain experience on as many types as we have available. I'll ring him to say you're on your way over."

On leaving his office I wended my way to the Seaplane Flight hangar, an immense affair containing a vast and extremely ugly assortment of aircraft. Shipborne craft of that era were generally squat, fat, un-proportioned things, referred to generally by my friend Batchy, as 'Bloody Bananas!' The flight offices were glass house affairs, along the south wall and I eventually found the door giving access to the flight commander, Flight Lieutenant A R Wardle [3]. On turning the door handle I was a little surprised at receiving a not inconsiderable static shock from the metal. However, I managed to retain my composure and entered the office without so much as batting an eye lid. Wardle was sitting at a large office table and there were a number of other rather serious-looking officers seated around the room, with every available chair occupied. Being a newcomer I thought that perhaps one of them might offer me a seat, but there was no sign of movement. Surly lot of sods, I thought to myself. The corner of Wardle's table seemed to be clear and inviting, so without further ado, I plonked myself down on it. There was an immediate stabbing pain into my backside and I leapt to my feet with a yelp. The entire assembly simply hooted with joy and I at once realised I was amongst friends. Examination of the table corner revealed a simply fiendish contrivance. In just the right position a small hole had been bored through the woodwork and inserted therein was a large darning needle which in turn was connected by wire and a system of bell crank levers, to a concealed toggle, just by 'Warble's' chair, so he could activate it. These were obvious chaps after my own heart and I felt that my flagging morale was once more on the upgrade.

Warble Wardle could not give me my introduction to the sea-going aircraft right away, as the one and only dual control seaplane was unserviceable. However, six days later he took me up for an hour in a Fairey IIID [N9731], a cumbersome affair with flat bottom floats and very heavy on the controls. I did a few landings and take-offs, was instructed how to approach buoys and slipways, in the vagaries of wind and tide, the importance of landing along and not into a swell if a heavy sea was running, and so on. He then left me to try my own devices and to learn the rest of the sea-faring craft by the time-honoured method of trial and error.

Three days later my Flycatcher [S1060] emerged from ARS, so at last I had something to fly as and when I pleased. The Flycatcher was a single-seat fighter designed primarily for operations with the fleet, the undercarriage being adaptable for either wheels or floats. It could therefore operate from either land or water or from the deck of an aircraft carrier. Compared with other contemporary fighters it was rather cumbersome and heavy on the controls. My first flight in this machine on the 10th, brought home to me the limitations of seaborne aircraft of small size. The sea was roughish when I flew it on the 18th, and on my take-off, the green water split the wooden propeller.

One morning towards the end of my first month at Felixstowe, I was summoned to the CO's office where Bromet told me that he had been asked by AM to submit a list of pilots suitable for training on high speed aircraft, in order that a selection might be made in good time for the formation of the 1929 team to compete in the next Schneider Trophy contest. He said my experience at CFS and Fighting Area, qualified me to make the selection. Later the same day I gave him a list of twenty names, headed by Batchy Atcherley, Dick Waghorn and George Stainforth. John Boothman was in Singapore but keen to be in the team, and eventually he did so for the 1931 contest. Of the others on the list I can still call to mind the following: Grandma Horniman, Harry 'Bruin' Purvis, Chris Staniland, Philip Barwell, Geoffrey Tuttle and Allen Wheeler [4].

Regarding my earlier adverse comment on the section being split between Felixstowe and Calshot, a further condition had become apparent right from my very first day; Felixstowe seemed to bring on my asthma, whereas at Calshot I never had a sign of a wheeze. However, I carried on flying all sorts of seaplanes at Felixstowe until July, when the first of the Gloster racers started arriving back from the manufacturers. Also at this time I was allocated a Gamecock II [J8804], as a 'hack' which was kept at Martlesham Heath. This proved a great boon to fly whenever the weather was unsuitable at Felixstowe, or I simply wanted something really pleasant to throw around the sky.

Also at this time occurred an event which from my point of view is worth recording. One day at lunch time, Wardle tackled me in the mess and told me that they had in their flight, an aircraft that none of them could really do much with. A large general purpose Fleet Air Arm thing called 'The Pike' [Parnell Pike, N202. Ed.]. The trouble with this, although it handled in the air quite reasonably well, and was no trouble at all in getting off the water, was that it was practically impossible to land with any great satisfaction. On an approach, they told me, the machine did not check when pulling back the stick but merely flew onto the surface with an awful bump. Wardle wondered, with my great experience, whether I might possibly find the answer for them. I therefore agreed to have a shot at flying – and landing – this machine after lunch.

The Pike was an ugly machine. A square-cut affair with absolutely square wing tips, a zig-zag inter-plane strutting system, a very deep fuselage and the pilot's seat was right up on the top centre section in front of the wings and immediately behind the engine. However, I climbed in, with SAC Davies as passenger, started up and took off. No trouble in the air although a bit heavy on the controls. Once I had become more familiar with it, I came in for my first approach, which I considered quite normal, eased it back – with no check noticed – and then found, with the stick right back, that the machine did indeed fly on and on, then hit the water with a resounding thump.

Off I went again for a second try, coming in this time on a flatter approach with lots of engine, but the same thing happened. At this juncture I noticed that everybody in the Seaplane Flight had turned out onto the jetty, watching my performance. On my third approach, with a similar crunching smack on the water, it seemed as if the machine wanted to become a submarine. On the fourth and final attempt, the resounding bang was followed by a terrific crack and the port wing tip and float dug into the sea, the machine assuming an alarming angle in the water. I quickly scrambled out of the cockpit and into the upper wing, and to restore stability I sat on the opposite wing tip until a rescue launch arrived, took me in tow and delivered Davies and me to the slipway. Here the machine was attached to a trolley and pulled up onto the tarmac. What Davies thought of all this I never found out.

On examination it was found that the starboard rear undercarriage strut had collapsed. Everybody in the Seaplane Flight seemed to be fairly jubilant, for they had already put in an adverse report of the beast and in reality were just waiting for someone to come along and break it in order to confirm their opinions, and get it struck off. Well, at least I had achieved something useful for the seaplane boys!

The Gloster IV, the first of that particular series, was the first machine to arrive back from the makers. In fact the IV, IVA and IVB all looked identical but to the discerning eye, it was obvious that the latter two had much reduced total wing area, with the object of giving higher speeds, resulting too in higher take-off and landing speeds. The machine had a distinctive tail, the fin and rudder was rather fish-like with half the fin above the fuselage and other half below, both connected by a long, narrow chord rudder. However, it was plain that the IV had been modified, the bottom fin had been removed, and a very large top fin and top rudder substituted. No reason was given for this but later events proved that there was a cause. The three Glosters and the two Supermarines were all fitted with engines of the same type, a Napier Lion, that in its original form developed 450 hp, while in its racing form and high compression and rpm, had been boosted to 900 hp.

As soon as the Gloster IV [N224] had been erected and the engine ground tested, I took her out on the first suitable day for taxying trials. A characteristic of all racing seaplanes was that they were all wet on take-off, during the period prior to hydroplaning. Owing to the high loading and floats digging fairly deeply into the water when the aircraft was at rest, opening the throttle produced a bow-wave which got sucked up, swirled round the fuselage, into the pilot's face, down his neck and over everything else. As soon as the aeroplane was hydroplaning it became perfectly dry. After one or two more trips out on the water, I decided that I was ready to take it into the air. It was then that I came in for a bit of a shock for unknown to me, the boffins on the station, including Nick Comper [5], who was a practical aviator himself and a good designer of light aircraft, decided it would be a very good thing, as I had never flown aircraft with a very high wing loading before, if I were to take up some standard seaplane that had been heavily loaded with lead ballast.

They decided that the Fairey IIIF was a suitable machine for this purpose and I was duly informed by the station commander that I was to fly this before taking up the Gloster. Needless to say I was extremely annoyed, for one thing there would be no possible resemblance between an overloaded Fairey, either on the water or in the air, to the Gloster, so I rather blew my top, whereupon they withdrew the suggestion. However, they did come back with something more sensible. Sidney Webster was now a test pilot at Martlesham, so he was asked to come over and test fly the Gloster to make sure the modifications did not have any adverse affects on its handling qualities. I had no argument with this at all, and agreed it would be a good thing to do. In due course Webster turned up, flew the machine, landed and then pronounced it perfectly fit to fly.

At this juncture it might be as well to make some comment on the conditions under which these very fast aircraft were flown. Owing to their high wing loading, their landing and take-off speeds were very high indeed, certainly high for those days. Consequently one had to be very careful both in regard to weather and water conditions, the ideal being a day with light breezes, say ten miles an hour, a level sea and with a pronounced ripple to give a level ride. This also assisted in a quick clearance from the dirty period of take-off to smooth and dry hydroplaning on the step of the floats, ending with a trouble-free un-stick. A pronounced ripple also gave a good definition to the surface and aided one's judgement of height during the approach and landing. These conditions generally prevailed up to a wind speed of about 15 mph. Above this speed, white horses appeared and the sea became a bit rough.

I recall George Stainforth attempting a take-off under adverse con-ditions and damaging the undercarriage of one of the S.5s. About the most dangerous condition is a swell, which should be avoided at all costs. The flat calm gives the sea a mirror-like quality, consequently in landing, it is practically impossible to judge one's height unless there are objects of flotsam floating about on the surface. On take-off too, float adhesion can be very pronounced and it's difficult to start hy-droplaning. A glass-calm sea is considered to be a contributory factor in Sammy Kinkead's death, when in addition to these adverse water conditions, there was also a thick haze.

It will be readily understood that requiring ideal conditions places a severe limitation on the amount of flying that could be done with high speed aircraft. To quote from personal experience, during the period 25th July 1928 to 7th September 1929, I completed thirty-four flights in Glosters and Supermarines, logging a total of only eleven hours, twenty-three minutes flying time, the complete total of my flying experience on racing seaplanes.

I made my first Gloster IV flight on 25th July, an altogether delightful and comparatively uneventful experience, which lasted thirteen min-utes. Having thus broken the ice, as it were, it would not be out of place now to make some comment on the handling of these machines. The take-off on all racing types went through three stages, the initial one being met on opening the throttle, when the bow wave from the floats is sucked up by the propeller and delivered in a soaking spray over the fuselage and pilot. One could see practically nothing until stage two – hydroplaning – was reached, when one grabbed a piece of chamois leather and wiped one's goggles and windscreen. Stage two generally went smooth and uneventful, until stage three – becoming unstuck – was reached. Technique from then on was, climb, level out, manoeuvre, etc., simple and pleasant and quite similar to conventional single-seat fighters.

During hydroplaning however, a lateral oscillation sometimes developed a sort of a patter from one float to the other at a fairly high frequency. This never caused any concern however. But if the machine developed fore and aft pitching motions, known as porpoising, during any stage of take-off, there was only one sure remedy – close the throttle, slow down and taxi back for another attempt. Any other form of remedial action or an attempt to carry on, was only courting disaster, for in these circumstances the amplitude of the pitching invariably increased until the machine was eventually thrown into the air without flying speed. If this happened, a crash was almost a certainty. In the 1931 High Speed Flight, Lieutenant Brinton, one of the naval pilots attached to the HSF, was killed through committing just this one mistake [6].

In general handling, at top speed and level flight, our racing seaplanes compared fairly well with the fighter aircraft of a decade later – the early Hurricanes and Spitfires. However, we operated at one great disadvantage, we had neither landing flaps nor variable pitch propellers, a development that was still to come. Although during our time, research was taking place with a variable pitch prop, called the Hale Shaw Beecham, at the Gloster works at Cheltenham. The trailing edge flap, as most people know, gives increased lift to the wing and also provides a braking drag during the final part of the approach and landing, thus reducing the landing run.

Landing these racing seaplanes was quite straightforward, but required patience and a light touch. Owing to the lack of flaps, and the high wing loading, approach speed was fast and the gliding angle very flat. I used to reckon that one could use up to two miles of landing space, depending on wind and water. It was absolutely essential to make a tail down landing and touch water right on the heels of the floats. This entailed a long and careful hold off to ensure that all flying speed was lost before touching down. To touch down on the step of the floats was asking for trouble, as the aircraft would at once bounce into the air again, with the consequent risk of stalling.

I managed to carry out two further flights with the Gloster IV, before the IVA [N222] was ready at the end of August. I took it up on the morning of 31st August, although once I became airborne I felt as though the aeroplane was starting to get out of control, as it developed a terrific snaking action and was directionally unstable. I went round a very large circuit, very flat, sawing with the rudder the whole time, but the moment I corrected the swing in one direction the machine swung in the other – a most unpleasant experience. The swing was also apparent on the initial part of the approach, but I had little or no trouble with the actual landing, the snaking damping out as I flattened out. Once back I reported the aircraft as unsafe in its present condition and both the IVA and IVB went back to Glosters, to have the tails modified in line with the basic IV. Once this was done there was no further trouble.

Maintenance carried out on the Napier engines was exacting in the extreme, owing to the fact that they were experimental and highly boosted. For example, sparking plugs were changed after every flight, regardless of the duration, and as these plugs cost £2 each, that in itself was quite an expensive operation in those days; there were twenty-four plugs to each engine. Also, each engine was removed for a complete strip down and inspection after every five hours of flying, although this was later extended to ten.

About mid-September, I moved down to Calshot to become acquainted with the S.5. Also at this time a new pilot arrived, Chris Staniland, a chap I had known when I was in Fighting Area, a very good fellow indeed, who quickly adapted himself to web-footed business and soon went off solo in the Flycatcher. However, he was unlucky, for he hadn't been with us for more than a couple of weeks when AM discovered that his short service commission was due to terminate the following March, so he was withdrawn and posted back to his squadron at Northolt. When he left the service, Chris became quite famous as a racer of Riley cars at Brooklands, and also joined the Fairey Aircraft Company, eventually becoming their chief test pilot. Regrettably, during WW2 he was killed whilst on an experimental flight. Almost immediately after Chris departed, Batchy Atcherley and George Stainforth arrived at Calshot, and both went solo very quickly on my hack machine. There were no Glosters down there, so they couldn't be initiated to high speed flying until I moved back to Felixstowe.

No story involving the RAF at Calshot could possibly be complete without some reference being made to a chap who I considered to be its
most famous character – Mr Swain, the officer's mess steward. Mr
Swain, originally a chief petty officer in the navy, came to Calshot in
1925 and was almost immediately installed as steward. A little below
average height, very stout, with a benign, rather rosy complexion, he
ran that mess with a rod of iron. At the end of WW2 he remained in
his job and I think he was still in harness when he died. A most capable
man, very efficient, but he was an absolute tyrant in many respects. I
rather think that Atcherley, Waghorn, Stainforth and myself became a
bit of a thorn in his side, as he did not altogether appreciate high-spirited young men and their various pranks about HIS mess. I think everybody, senior officers included, were frightened of old Mr Swain. I heard
it told that on one occasion a very senior officer in the mess, shouted
across to him: "Swain, come here just a moment." Mr Swain carried
on with what he was doing and paid not the slightest notice whatsoever. The officer repeated himself, addressing him then as MR Swain.
Swain then set down his knife and fork, or whatever he'd been fiddling
with, came across and gave the officer his undivided attention. I
crossed swords with him personally on one occasion.

Towards the end of September I had some friends, including a
brother on leave from the Far East, visiting me for a weekend and I
thought it would be rather pleasant to entertain them on one of my
high speed launches. My rescue craft consisted of a WW1 coastal motor
boat, very, very fast indeed, with a top speed of around 45 knots, but
as it had no reverse gear, it really wasn't much use, and two 375 hp
Thornycroft-powered motor launches. They had galleys and a number
of bunks for sleeping, but no bedding, so I approached Mr Swain, and
asked him if I might borrow some from the mess. "Sorry, Sir," replied
Mr Swain, "all these things are on my personal charge, and all allotted
to individual bedrooms. They are all clean and furthermore, there are
none to spare at the present time."

I was rather taken aback by this and so waited till he was out of the
way, before having a snoop round on my own. I knew there was one
block of living quarters practically unoccupied, so after lunch, went
from room to room and helped myself to sheets and blankets I found
all neatly stacked in the various wardrobes. I took them down to the

jetty and thence to one of the launches, feeling rather pleased with myself for having foiled the august Swain. That evening, after tea, I was sitting in the ante-room, when in walked an enraged Mr Swain. In a terrible fury he addressed me in no uncertain terms in front of every-one present, telling me that I had behaved in a disgraceful manner, helping myself to items on his personal charge and would I please re-turn them immediately. So I did – but not till the following Monday morning, after my guests had departed. Needless to say the atmos-phere between us was rather strained from then on.

However, I decided in the end that this state of affairs could not go on indefinitely, so I had to plan some way of making peace with the old boy. All through our time at Calshot, we were rather plagued by representatives of the press, who were always hanging around for a story, and I for one got rather fed up with them. I did not appreciate, being a young man, that possibly they might also be fed up with the interminable wait for weather and only able to pick up snatches of news to send off to their editors. When we did occasionally fly, there were announcements on our progress from time to time, on the BBC, the same evenings. As it happened, nobody possessed a radio in the mess, so we could never listen in. But then I discovered that Mr Swain had a very good radio in his quarters, so one evening I tackled him. "Mr Swain, I hear you are the only person who is the proud possessor of a radio. There are various bulletins concerning myself and my team on the air, and I would consider it a very great favour if I could come along to your room one evening when I know something was about to be broadcast, and listen in." Well, this broke the ice and the tension com-pletely and with a gracious smile he said: "Do come along this evening, Sir, and have a chat and listen to the radio." In due course I arrived at his door and spent quite a considerable time chatting with him and lis-tening to the radio. As I was about to dash off to change for dinner, the old boy said: "Any time you want to listen to the news, Sir, just come along to my room. You will be most welcome."

Talking of the press, there were many personalities amongst them, some of whom caused me no bother at all. I remember a couple of them, the first being a chap named Harry Harper, who had been re-porting on flying ever since it started in this country [7]. The other was a charming character, rather eccentric looking, Major F A de Vere

Robertson VD MA [8]. I liked him very much. You could pick him out a mile away as he had a curious style of dress, Norfolk jacket and breeches, Inverness cape, deer-stalker hat and the possessor of a large moustache. He might well have been a character from a Conan Doyle thriller. He was a simply charming chap, and wrote for the *Manchester Guardian* and *Flight*, among others.

As a further digression, I would like to record the story about an incident which occurred during 1927, shortly before the '27 team left for Venice and the Schneider Trophy effort. A few days prior to their departure, they received an official visit from the AOC Coastal Area, Air Vice-Marshal Dan Scarlett. He had come over by pinnace from Lee-on-Solent and as it was a very official occasion he was dressed in civilian clothes. Old Dan had the reputation of being not particularly fussy sartorially. He was dressed, I am told, in rather a shabby old lounge suit and was wearing a bowler hat with a decidedly greenish tinge about it. After inspecting the flight and the equipment, he was escorted down to the jetty and a signal was flashed to the pinnace to pull in alongside, to pick the old boy up. He said his goodbyes and was standing on the edge of the jetty, his back to the water, and still chatting away, when the boat arrived alongside. Unfortunately the cox'n must have arrived just a shade too quick and shot by the collecting spot. The poor old AVM didn't notice, bowed politely to everyone, turned and stepped straight into the sea. There was a terrible pause for a moment, the only sight being his bowler floating on the water, before his spluttering form bobbed to the surface. Duly rescued he was taken ashore and provided with a new set of clothes. It must have been quite an ordeal, for everybody there must have been splitting their sides with suppressed mirth. The old chap was not a bit put out and in his borrowed garments, sailed back home to Lee-on-Solent none the worse for his dunking.

Between 1st October and 3rd November I managed to get in five flights in the S.5s [N220 & N219], the longest being of twenty-four minutes duration, the shortest, seven minutes. The object of these flights was to find a propeller of suitable pitch with which to attempt the air speed record. I remember the finest pitched propeller I tried out got me off the water at a most terrific pace – we absolutely leapt into the air – but no top speed at all, even though the engine was screaming at about 4,000 rpm. On 3rd November we decided that it was no good carrying on with further trials, and settled on the final propeller we tried out. In between we made two or three visits, one by spending the day at Supermarine at Southampton. We met R J Mitchell [9], who was working on the machine for the next contest, and he showed me the mock-up and got me to sit in the seat to explain the layout of the instruments, and so on. He then asked me my opinion as to the view from the cockpit, and other pertinent questions.

I also paid a visit to Napier's at Acton, west London, and one to Rolls-Royce at Derby. Finally I visited AM at the request of Major Buchanan [10], who was at that time, I believe, deputy director of technical development. He wanted to discuss some points with me and after our chat, I was interviewed by the Air Member for Research, Air Marshal Sir John Higgins [11]. Higgins was known throughout the service by the odd name of 'Bum and Eye Glass', a nickname which had pursued him right from his early days, I think because he always wore a monocle.

After finishing with Sir John, I went along to see Wing Commander Sydney Smith [12], who was to be in charge of all the ground organisation for the Schneider Trophy contest the following year. While there he said I should go along and meet 'Orly', and upon asking who this was, he replied that this was Squadron Leader Orlebar [13], who was going to take the flight from me at the end of the year, to form the 1929 HSF. As can be imagined, I found this bit of information quite a shock, for I had just started getting used to being my own master for the last few months. I really felt a bit put out. However, I went along to Orlebar's office – the mere fact that he worked in the Air Ministry rather put me off – but I found him absolutely charming and I asked him about his history. I gathered he had been a test pilot at Martlesham Heath, had quite a bit of experience, and later discovered he had also become a graduate of the staff college. He was known for his great flair for administration, great charm of manner, and had all the social graces – in other words, he had all I lacked. On parting he said he would try and get down to Calshot in time for my record-breaking attempt and wished me the best of luck.

I had old Moon with me as we drove back to Calshot and I felt rather glum about the situation, but the following year I realised what a boon it was having Orly in charge. I could never have coped with the various situations that cropped up in 1929, such as MPs coming down to visit, numerous high officials and VIPs from all over the place – Orly took all that in his stride. Left on my own I am sure I would have made a hash of it all.

[1] Technical officer to the HSF, Thomas Henry Moon was a squadron leader by the start of WW2, and a qualified engineer.

[2] Later Air Vice-Marshal Sir Geoffrey, KBE CB DSO Ld'H. RN and RNAS in WW1, he also served with distinction in WW2 with Coastal Command, retiring in 1945. Lieut-Governor of Isle of Man, 1945-52. Died in November 1983.

[3] Later Air Commodore Alfred R Wardle CBE AFC, retired in December 1952. WW1 soldier and airman, Air Ministry WW2 and AOC Ceylon 1947-49. Retired in December 1952, died in July 1989.

[4] F/Lt Christopher Stainbank Staniland RAFO. RAF 1924-29, then with Simmonds Aircraft Ltd, till CFI at Fairey Aviation; Group Captain Philip R Barwell DFC would be accidently shot down by Spitfires when commanding RAF Biggin Hill in 1941; Later Air Marshal Sir Geoffrey W Tuttle KBE CB DFC, and future head of BAC; Allen H Wheeler CBE BA retired as an air commodore in 1955.

[5] Flight Lieutenant Nicholas Comper AFRAeS RAF(Rtd), had taken his 'ticket' in May 1916 and had served in the RFC/RAF in WW1. Founded several aircraft clubs and companies, as well as designing several machines. In 1925 he had won the International Scratch Speed Race for light aeroplanes at Lympne. By the mid-1930s he owned Comper Aircraft Co. Ltd.

[6] Lieutenant R L 'Jerry' Brinton FAA, killed 18 August 1931 in S.6B No.N247.

[7] Harry Harper had been writing about flying since 1907, mainly for the *Daily Mail*. At this time he was around fifty years of age, and he had seen Blériot land in England back in 1908. He attended most of the early race meetings, and also wrote a number of books on early flying.

[8] Robertson had been in the Indian army and invalided out in 1915, so joined the RFC at age 38, serving as a technical officer, attached to the propaganda section at AM. He was also a freelance journalist post-WW1 and wrote several books on aviation.

[9] Reginald J Mitchell, the famous designer for Supermarine Aviation whose work on the Schneider Trophy racers eventually paved the way for the Spitfire fighter, a machine that, along with the Hawker Hurricane, saved Britain in 1940. He died in June 1937.

[10] John Scoular Buchanan CBE FRAeS AMIME, assistant and then deputy director of technical development at the Air Ministry.

[11] Air Marshal Sir John F A Higgins KCB DSO AFC Ld'H. A former artillery officer, he joined the RFC in 1912 and by 1918 was a major-general. Commanded forces in Iraq 1924-26 and then became a Member of the Air Council for Supply and Research. After retiring in 1930, he became a director with Armstrong-Whitworth Aircraft Ltd. Died in June 1948.

[12] Later Air Commodore Sydney William Smith CBE DL. Army in 1913, RFC 1914, then Egypt and Iraq 1919-24. Director of Organisation at AM till 1928. Served in Bomber Command early in WW2, then OC NE Command, Air Training Corps, having retired in September 1941. Died in December 1971.

[13] Augustus Henry Orlebar had been wounded at Gallipoli, before becoming a fighter pilot in 1916, flying Spads, Camels and Snipes. From 1919 to 1925 he worked and flew with the A&AEE, receiving the AFC for his work. In 1934 he became SASO, Aden, and at the start of WW2 commanded RAF Northolt. Sadly he contracted cancer of the jaw and died in August 1943 as an AVM.

15

THE AIR SPEED RECORD & THE 1929 SCHNEIDER TROPHY CONTEST

On the morning of 4th November 1928, the atmosphere and the surface of the water seemed good, so I decided to have a shot at the record flight. One had to do four runs over the three-kilometre course, which ran between Calshot Spit and Fawley Pier. There were two timing teams there, two scientists from Farnborough who had the latest thing in electronic timing gear and also the official Royal Aero Club timers, two old chaps, who since the year dot, had been timing races at Brooklands by the time-honoured method of looking along a stick and pressing the button of a stop-watch. The regulations governing the three km record laid down that the aircraft had to be in level flight a certain distance before passing the starting line of the measured course, but at all other times during the flight, it would be in order for the pilot to get up to a height of about 1,000 metres – 4,200 feet or so. I therefore took very long runs at the course, starting with a northern run somewhere in the neighbourhood of Ryde, and the south run from somewhere near Romsey. I flew at the maximum permitted height each time before losing height in a shallow dive, thus gaining a little surplus speed before entering the level flight area. It was then a case of going flat out in a straight line, the engine screaming at full pelt.

The four runs in N220 were completed satisfactorily, with four-masted ships and liners going whizzing by, and I eventually came down and landed. Shortly after landing, Harold Perrin [1], the secretary of the Royal Aero Club, came up to me and said: "Bad luck, Greig, Bernardi's record is, as you know, 318.64 mph, and you have averaged 319.57 – but not enough for the record. To obtain the record, it is required that you are a clear five miles an hour faster over an existing record. However, you have got the British Seaplane Class 'C' Record, so the flight hasn't been a failure."

Needless to say I was rather disappointed and had a secret hope that possibly I might be allowed a further attempt, although at the back of my mind I thought we got the absolute maximum out of the S.5, and another attempt might well be a waste of time. The authorities at AM shared this view and I was not given another shot. One point of interest was this, the two timing devices, and the difference between them, only amounted to a fraction of a second. However, philosophical as always, I contented myself with the fact that on this November day I had achieved a record of sorts.

As can be imagined, Batchy and George were now champing at the bit to fly Glosters, so we wasted no time in returning to Felixstowe. During our time at Calshot we had all behaved fairly well, no serious practical joking, other than squibs etc., in the morning canteen break times. However, next year at Calshot our practical joking was to take on a new dimension and very much more subtle methods employed in annoying our other companions on the station. At the end of the month, Squadron Leader Waugh, flying a huge Southampton I [N9899] of 201 Squadron, took WingCo Smith, Batchy and me on a flight along the proposed course for the 1929 Schneider race.

It was early December before we got settled back at Felixstowe. With the advent of winter, the chances of flying the Gloster machines were few and far between. Nevertheless, we managed to get George and Batchy through their handling trials on the sea and runs up to take-off speeds without much difficulty. I repeated all the instructions I had received from my predecessors about flying limitations placed on high speed aircraft, such as no undue strain and no aerobatics, etc., and both of them seemed to take all this quite seriously. However, eventually a day dawned when conditions were about as good as one could expect at this time of year, with the sea just a nice ripple, a light breeze, but fairly a pronounced haze. I thought the haze might deter Batchy from doing anything rash, so orders were given to bring out the Gloster IV after lunch. When we all returned to the slipway, the extraordinary thing was that there was an atmosphere of tenseness and expectation about the place. There were groups of mechanics lining the jetty and tops of the slipway, as well as people milling about who had nothing at all to do with our flight.

Eventually we got Batchy off. He made a perfect take-off and disappeared into the mist and when he reappeared he was up fairly high, around 2,500 feet, or perhaps a little more, but everything seemed to be well. Then, what everybody expected, happened. After a shallow run slightly downhill, Batchy carried out a superbly executed slow roll to the left, followed by one to the right. He then changed course, back over in the direction of Felixstowe town and did a straight loop, followed by a loop with a half roll off the top. Naturally all spectators were highly amused and showing obvious signs of this amusement, whereas I was in a blazing fury, all my orders having been contravened. I am not sure if I was so much annoyed by the contravention of orders, or that I had not had the savvy to do the same things myself. By the time Batchy was back on the slipway again, I had simmered down somewhat and just gave him the mildest of rebukes.

After topping up the Gloster, George got into the seat to run up the engine. By now I had calmed down and in fact said to George that provided it wasn't broadcast to all and sundry he could emulate Batchy if he so wished. Well, George repeated Batchy's performance, but with the addition of a spin, which I didn't altogether like, but on the other hand, when the machine landed successfully and we towed it onto the slipway, everything was in perfect order, so we all went up to the mess for tea. As it turned out, the weather deteriorated from then on and that virtually ended our flying for the year, with the exception of a couple of trips in the Gamecock II at Martlesham.

At the end of the year I handed over to Orlebar and at about the same time Dick Waghorn joined the unit, having just returned from winter sports in Switzerland. He was an expert skier and represented the RAF in various events. Almost the first action on Orlebar's part was to appoint me as 'teacher' to the rest of the flight. However, very early in January the weather clamped down completely, with extremely intense frost that even produced ice in Norwich harbour, which made for very good skating. All flying was at a virtual standstill until the end of January, so I did not have an opportunity to fly any of the Glosters until the first day of February. By this time both Orly and Waggon had done their familiarization work on standard seaplanes.

It was now that the RAF medical service started taking an intense interest in us, chief among them being Group Captain Flack, an eminent psychologist. He was much concerned by what the affects of high speed flying would have on us, particularly in regard to blackouts, and he visited us for a conference on the matter. He told us that he was designing a device at Northolt, that would induce blackouts and invited us down when it had been perfected. One of his recommendations to help was that we start to chew gum. Little did he know but this was destined to cause a certain amount of discomfort to many people in the months to come. However, we obeyed and started to chew this spearmint stuff practically all day. In due course Orly and I visited Northolt to examine and try out Flack's device. On seeing the contraption we were absolutely flabbergasted. It was manually operated, a handle that looked like a very old handle and flywheel off an old-fashioned mangle, and operated by two very hot and bewildered airmen.

It was connected by suitable gearing to a long arm, at the end of which was a swivelling seat that could come out at right angles, or in practically any direction. Having come a long way to see this thing we felt obliged to try it, so I got in the seat and the airmen began to turn the handle. Very slowly the contraption started up until a sufficient speed had built up to swing the seat just a little both ways. While not all that comfortable, the two poor airmen were soon sweating like pigs and close to complete exhaustion. To cut a long story short, the device was completely useless and it was another twelve years before I saw a properly manufactured and properly designed machine to manufacture centrifugal force experiments on humans, and that was in Canada. It was not, however, manually operated, but was propelled by a 300 hp electric motor.

Before returning to Felixstowe, I took a trip into London to visit a very famous practical joke shop, Davenports of Holborn. I made various purchases and then my eye alighted on a starting pistol. It was a beautiful model of a small Browning automatic, which fired a .22 percussion cap and if used properly to start races, had a magazine of six charges that all went off with a resounding crack. I thought this was a good gadget to have around the mess to scare people out of their wits, so bought it. It certainly could be startling if fired immediately behind some unsuspecting victim.

I did some flying in the early weeks of 1929, mostly in an Avro Avocet floatplane [N210], but only one abortive flight in a Gloster on 4th February. My second flight of the year with our Gloster Racers, was on 18th March, a fine day with a clear sky and unlimited visibility. Flying around I was having a most enjoyable time for several minutes before heading back. It was then the thought struck me that all this time we had limited ourselves to landing and taking off in the same expanse of water between Felixstowe and Harwich harbour. It so happened that I was looking down on the Stour estuary, a wide expanse of water at high tide that extended quite a considerable distance inland. So I thought, that's a jolly good piece of water, so down I went and made the first landing in high speed aircraft [N224] on the River Stour. In 1931 it came in for considerable use and I believe also, the Supermarine S.5s were flown up to land there. However, that was all past my time. At the end of this same month, the River Orwell had also been brought into use. It was not quite as good as the Stour but quite passable, and of course the water, unlike the sea, was almost always smooth.

Some time in April we all moved down to Calshot, aircraft, equipment, the whole darn lot. The transfer was completed without any difficulty, although the aircraft had to be transported by road on trailers, but the hack aircraft were flown down. For me this final period at Calshot got off to a very bad start. I was jacking up my car one day with a long-handled garage jack when the ratchet slipped. The handle flew into the air and bashed me across the right eye, giving me a very severe black eye and severing a small artery, plus giving me something of a concussion. Whilst suffering from this mishap, I developed an attack of boils, which would not respond to treatment and I had to put up with them the whole summer. At times I felt quite ill and had to take to my bed with a slight temperature. I got so depressed I told Orlebar that he should not count on me flying one of the aircraft in the contest but he argued until we came to a compromise. Waggon and Batchy would have first choice while I was to take whatever was left. It didn't mean an awful lot at the time because we had no news of the new aircraft or when they were likely to turn up, So for a while I was out of action, and devoted some time to thinking out horrible pranks to play on the station, in the mess, with visitors, and so on. What do they say about idle hands?

My co-conspirator in all this was Batchy Atcherley, because we were the only two in the mess not living out. I was racking my brains when my thoughts turned to that starting pistol, the firing of it behind someone's back, by this time, having turned rather flat. A further moment of inspiration brought to my mind old Group Captain Flack's chewing gum so I thought this would go very well if it could be fired from the pistol. The problem of course, was that the pistol in its present form discharged out of a hole in the side of the barrel, the magazine being underneath. I therefore took the pistol straightway to the workshops, borrowed some tools, put the barrel in a vice, taped the normal discharge hole, drilled a screw thread in it and screwed in a plug. When this was done I drilled out the barrel as with a normal gun, and thus the thing was ready for a trial.

Returning to the flight office, where other members were seated around reading papers, I told them that I was about to carry out ballistic trials. Chewing a piece of gum into something pliable, I rolled it between the two palms of my hands, so as to form it into the requisite size. Putting this into the barrel I got Batchy to hold up two copies of *The Times*. Taking careful aim from about one to two yards away, I fired the gun, and to our great delight the pellet went completely through them with no bother at all.

As we had the office to ourselves we decided upon more practical trials and drew lots as to who should be the first human target. Waghorn proved to be the unlucky victim, so I reloaded the pistol, told Waggon to bend over and proceeded to take careful aim from a short distance and pulled the trigger. The effect on poor old Dick was simply electric. He leapt into the air with a howl of pain and then burst into shrieks of laughter and spent the next few minutes running round the room rubbing his bottom. When he had returned to normal we got him to drop his trousers so that we could examine any possible injury. This he did and upon inspection we found a splendid trade mark, a blood blister on his posterior about the size of a shilling [today a 10p piece size, Ed.], perhaps a little larger. As he seemed to suffer no further discomfort, we decided that the time was ripe to carry out extended trials in the mess.

That evening, Batchy and I visited the billiard room, and walked round, watching carefully about. There were only a couple of tables so it didn't take long for us to size up the occupants. Once chosen, I got myself strategically placed behind a player who was about to tackle a rather difficult shot, which entailed leaning well out across the green baize and one knee resting on the table's edge. As he slowly drew back the cue, ready for the strike, I pulled out the gun and fired. The effect again was simply electric. The guy miscued, the ball went goodness knows where, and he jumped down from the table looking very startled and in a certain amount of pain and discomfort. Everyone else in the room, of course, began to fall about laughing.

It soon became apparent that we had to be fairly selective in the choice of victims and not indulge in indiscriminate play. If the victim happened to be wearing a good pair of trousers, it could be a little incommoding, if not downright annoying, because the pellet of chewing gum, which was always spherical and very soft, had a nasty habit of embedding itself in the fabric and became a little difficult to remove. Therefore our attacks had to be few and far between. With visitors, of course, we felt obliged to go for it without hesitation, especially if they were of some importance.

This reminds me of the one all-but regrettable incident. One lunchtime, Batchy and I were in the mess, and in the ante-room was

Commander Harold Perrin, our friend of the aero club. Harold was a shortish man, very thick set, robust figure, snow white hair despite his youngish age, clean shaven and with a fairly florid complexion. He always made a point of being immaculately turned out, and on fine days would generally wear beautifully creased white flannel trousers, with a double-breasted blue blazer, and a yachting cap on his head. On the occasion in question, we found him talking to someone in the ante-room, and on the spur of the moment I told Batchy to walk casually past Harold and then put his hand in his pocket to pull out a handkerchief. As he did this he was briefed to make sure he dropped a coin or something on the floor. This Batchy proceeded to do, with some skill I might add, and old Harold politely bent over to retrieve the item. I made the most of this opportunity, whipped out the gun and fired a pellet. Well, poor old Harold. To his credit he did not yell out, but merely straightened up with remarkable agility, and stood and gazed at us with a look of withering scorn, although not entirely without suppressed pain. We felt we had rather overdone it this time and apologised to the old chap, but he took it all in very good part, so that was all right.

Having dealt at some length with the question of the chewing gum pistol, this brings one's attention to rather more important matters, one about some of the personalities on the station. Some of these seem to have been forgotten or overlooked by people who have written on the subject of the Schneider Trophy. From my point of view, one chap of very considerable importance to us, was the senior station meterorologist, Mr Jackson. Like the average trawler man or deep-sea fisherman, he had a natural faculty for gauging the weather, quite apart from the skilled stuff done with anemometers, balloons, etc. He was rather the type who if you asked what sort of day it was going to be, he'd pop out the room, sniff the air, look up at the sky, wet one of his fingers, hold it up to gauge the strength and direction of the wind, and give you his forecast.

It so happened that the course for the contest had been decided upon, and we knew what the new type of aircraft were promised but still with no date as to their arrival. Another thing we did not know was the exact date the contest was to be held. We decided in any event to ask Jackson to look-up past summer records to see when good weather might be expected. Without too much hesitation he said that in his experience the best days are 6th and 7th September. Such was our faith in the man, that we decided that these would be the contest dates.

Teams had started arriving in southern England during August and by the start of September all was about ready. As hosts, we planned things for the contest, and on the 6th the navigability trials were to be held and the speed contest proper on the 7th. Subsequent events proved Mr Jackson to be 100% correct, his prognostications could not have been more accurate. Both days proved to be absolutely perfect in every possible respect.

The Italians arrived on 29th August, complete with their own medical officer, their own chef, and so on, plus all their ground crew and equipment. Not long after they arrived, within a day or two, the head man of the Italian air force arrived, General Balbo [2]. I always regarded Old Balbo as an outstanding character. A good looking man with a Captain Kettle beard, he had a very cheerful manner and a strong leaning towards very fast sporting cars, having brought with him a very fine sports Alpha Romeo. The Italian officers, when they became members of our mess, always struck me as being a little nervous. I don't know if they had heard something, but they always seemed to regard Batchy and I with some suspicion. Can't think why. Anyway, not to disappoint them, one day we found a dead porpoise on the beach, and it just happened to end up in turn, into one or two of the Italian pilot's beds.

The French were unable to put up a team but the Americans had one super aircraft to enter, to be flown by Al Williams, but owing to engine problems they never made it. However, the Italians had brought several aircraft with them, with two brand new Macchi 67s, which might be regarded as the equivalent to our S.6, and a Macchi 52, the one with which de Bernardi had secured the world speed record two years earlier. They brought some others but they were only display aircraft and did not fly. Like us they too had early engine troubles and for a while it looked as if they would have to pull out but finally all was well.

Fortunately our new aircraft arrived in August. It was not long before the first was checked over and Orlebar was seated in the cockpit to taxi around, get the feel and take off. All went well except the actual take-off. Orly adopted the usual technique the same as applicable to single-seat fighters, with the stick fairly neutral with very little back pressure on it. He disappeared in the usual flurry of spray, evidently got it up onto the step but failed to become airborne, so returned to the slipway. The aircraft was refuelled and a rather despondent Orly asked me if I'd like to have a shot, being unable to understand why he had failed.

I went out to the take-off area, put the nose into a south-westerly direction and opened the throttle. Well, I repeated Orly's performance, getting it up onto the step all right, but never was there a sign of it becoming airborne. I stuck with it but after about two and a half miles, perhaps more, the engine boiled and I had to shut down. When I got back, the machine was given another look over. Next morning Orly tried again, this time putting more backward pressure on the stick and finally he got it into the air. Orly reported the machine OK, with the exception of a little bit of shudder somewhere or other, but nothing that couldn't be put right.

The next matter to be settled was who was to fly the new aircraft, as I was still not fully fit. I was very reluctant to have anything to do with the two new S.6 machines because Batchy and Waggon were absolutely dead keen on them. Orlebar was not going to fly in the contest, so it was decided that all things being equal and providing I was reasonably fit, plus the machine being up to scratch, I would fly one of the new Gloster VIs when they arrived. When the first one did arrive [N250], Orly flew it, reporting that although a beautiful machine to handle, it was also a good looking one. However, the engine did keep cutting out very badly and wouldn't stand running at full throttle. Orly immediately handed it over to me for a second opinion. It was certainly a wonderful machine to handle, both on the water and in the air, despite its high take-off and landing speeds, something in the order of 110 mph.

I decided to take it down the three km course on 2nd September, flying at fairly low level but as I did so it started to cut out, banging and vibrating etc, so I pulled back the stick and shot upwards for a few hundred feet because the engine suddenly boiled violently and a jet of hot water came through the grill in the side of the cockpit and sprayed across my left shin. I could not get my leg out of the way so it was extremely painful. I tried everything possible, closed the throttle, used my forward momentum to climb up to about 500 feet or so, during which time the boiling thankfully ceased. I opened up again at low to medium revs, the engine ran perfectly so I came in to land. We still had work to do.

It would be highly presumptuous for me to write at length on the subject of the new aircraft, as much has already been written by writers more competent than myself, from a technical point of view particularly. However, a brief reference would not be out of place. The two new aircraft that were to compete were to be the S.6, designed by Reginald Mitchell, and the Gloster VI, designed by Henry Folland [3]. The S.6 was bigger and heavier than the earlier S.5 and powered by a large Rolls-Royce racing engine, designed, I believe, to give 1,500 hp, but subsequently proved to give much more, culminating at around 2,400 hp. The Gloster VI was a much smaller machine, powered by a new racing Napier engine, that was to produce 1,350 hp.

The Rolls-Royce engine was a twelve-cylinder job, set in two banks of six in the form of the letter V. The Napier conformed to the original Napier, three banks of four cylinders. Both engines had teething troubles, particularly the Rolls, but training went on much as usual. I was flying out over the Solent one day [20th August, N224. Ed.], practising turns at quite a high altitude – 2-3,000 feet – when suddenly there was a very loud 'ping' – loud enough to be quite startling. I looked over both sides, and saw a bracing wire dangling in the breeze, fortunately a landing wire and not a flying wire. In the old days of braced biplanes and for that matter the S.5, one set of stream-lined high tensile steel wires supported the weight of the aircraft, the structure generally whilst in flight, and the other set bore the weight of the wings when the aircraft was actually on the water or on land. In this instance a landing wire had failed, consequently there was no risk of the aeroplane falling to pieces in the air. However, I made a careful landing, so that nothing further would 'ping'.

When up for the specific purpose of practising turns we always carried an accelerometer on board, this being a device for measuring and recording the amount of 'g'. There were also two devices in use for measuring the actual diameter of our turns, one being a camera obscurer in the castle at Calshot, the other a series of conspicuous calibrations on the roadway along Calshot Spit. After much experimentation it was found that the very tight turn was not entirely satisfactory. (a) It was uncomfortable, and (b) there was considerable loss of speed due to centrifugal force and an additional drag. Four and a half 'g' was found to be eminently satisfactory.

Another personality who entered the scene at this time was Major Colin Cooper, who I believe was the chairman of International Stores. Anyway, he was obviously an immensely wealthy man, had a beautiful yacht which was anchored quite close in on Southampton Water, and also had one or two very good speed boats. Major Cooper had been in the RFC during WW1, so consequently there was a common bond between us. He was a very generous man, entertained fairly lavishly and always had a fast motor boat at our disposal with which to pop up to Southampton. At the time of the contest he handed over his yacht to the AOC Coastal Area, Air Marshal Lamb, to act as a flag ship. Off duty he took us out on numerous occasions, one of which was a trip to the Empire Theatre.

At the end of that show he took us backstage and into the dressing room of Gertrude Lawrence, where we also met Tallulah Bankhead. The two actresses were very much taken up with their own affairs and not overly interested in this sudden male invasion. Then on the way back to Calshot, we pulled alongside Selfridge's yacht and went aboard. By this time it was getting late for us. On deck we found a lot of people sitting about the place, including Lady Seagrave, and while we felt it unsociable to leave too quickly, we soon had to get to our beds ready for the next day.

Most mornings Batchy and I would rise early enough to go for a run in the New Forest, which was most refreshing and kept us fit. Once I recall we were tripping through the bracken, doing some exercises that we had picked up at Uxbridge – looking a bit like a couple of fairies – when we suddenly danced past an old tramp, sleeping rough. As we approached he came to, his mouth gaped open, and must have thought he had visitors from another planet. The only other form of exercise we took was to drive down in the evening to Beaulieu and swim in the river, tide permitting. The water there was nice and warm and one could stay in and splash about for quite a while. Another attraction with this was that we could get good refreshment at the nearby Montague Arms Hotel.

By this time the flight was equipped with pontoons that were simply first rate, as the aircraft could be wound up onto the pontoon and kept out of the water. Furthermore, they could be towed out into the Solent to a take-off position, without taxying long distances with spray bursting all over the pilot.

It was now that visitors started to descend on us in vast numbers. MPs, various technical institution people, Boy Scouts – all sorts. You name it, we had it! Batchy and I thought it would be a good idea to have a little exhibition of various components of our high speed aircraft for the benefit of our visitors. With the assistance of our technicians, we set up some trestle tables in the hangar, upon which we placed interesting components, flying and landing wires, bits of cowling, the odd carburettor – lots of similar bits and pieces. When we'd done we did not feel totally satisfied so we built a little sort of box-like shelter out of spare aircraft wings, etc, placing it almost adjacent to the display tables. In this we set up a starting impulse magneto, a device used for starting the seaplanes, which could be turned by hand to produce a succession of fairly powerful electric sparks. We connected the magneto to all the devices on the tables and eventually had an airman trained to take charge of it. He had a peep-hole and was instructed to wind the handle whenever we were showing strangers around, and if we pointed to an item, and suggested that the visitor might pick it up and try it for weight (as all the components were super-light), he would crank the handle vigorously. This arrangement worked splendidly and at all times of the day one could go into our old hangar and see some unfortunate individual dancing about, suffering temporarily from a severe electric shock. Childish, but fun!

Concurrently with members of the House of Parliament visits, we had a visit from the Air Council, headed by the chief of the air staff, Old Boom Trenchard [4]. The Air Ministry officer in charge of our ground arrangements, Wingco Sydney Smith, had as his secretary, Aircraftsman Shaw, one time Lawrence of Arabia. We didn't know at the time, but Aircraftsman Shaw was Sir Hugh Trenchard's pet aversion and on the occasion of this visit, the old boy was talking to Batchy and me, when he suddenly spotted Shaw engaged in earnest conversation with Lady Astor. A black look at once suffused his countenance, and Trenchard nodded in their direction and said: "I wish you fellows would keep an eye on that chap, I don't like this sort of thing happening."

From a technical point of view the high-brow visitors were comparatively easy to contend with, for they'd swallow anything we told them, while looking immensely interested and knowing, but the worst lot was the school boy. Various schools from all over the place came down in parties and I was often lumbered with the job of showing them around. The problem was they were knowledgeable little creatures, so one couldn't pull the wool over their eyes or anything like that. I remember on one occasion, going into the question of how the aeroplane was controlled, one little fellow, who was investigating very much on his own, suddenly called my attention to what appeared to be a short bracing wire at the rear end of one of the Gloster IVs and said: "Now what's that for?" For a moment I hadn't the foggiest idea, but didn't dare try to bluff it out, so deftly sent for our technical flight sergeant standing nearby, and got him to explain it to the little lad. It doesn't pay to look stupid in front of school boys.

The contest was now only days away. Orly held a conference to decide the final arrangements, as to who was to fly individual aircraft. I was still very much below par with these wretched boils, but not on the sick list, added to which, on the occasion of my second run up Southampton Water on the Gloster VI, the boiling engine had raised an enormous blister on my left shin. This thing had now started to look decidedly angry and I had to report to sick quarters to have it dressed. As far as I was concerned the Gloster VI was out, for technical reasons, so being unable to fly one of the other machines because Batchy and Waggon had prior claims, and both being very keen on the S.6, not to mention both chaps being absolutely on the top of their form, that seemed to be that. So I would fly the S.5 [N219], and at least I had the satisfaction of knowing that it would at least complete the course flying at full throttle. After all, it had flown in the 1927 race, so I hoped it knew the form.

There was also some little doubt with the two new Glosters, so the instructions given to Batchy and Waggon, with regard to their respective aircraft, was this. Waggon was to fly his machine [N247] slightly throttled back to keep the coolant temperature down to 96° centigrade, which was just below boiling point. Batchy was given permission to fly [N248] flat out, but to throttle back on the first sign of boiling. With all this settled, we were ready for the navigability trials.

Throughout the years since the first contest back at Monaco in 1913, the rules for the navigability trials had remained more or less the same, each aircraft having to complete successfully, three take-offs and three landings, one of each being with a full load. Between the first and second take-offs, the seaplane had to be taxied at speed in excess of twelve knots for a distance of at least half a mile, then each aircraft had to be moored out for seven hours, presumably to see whether it had sprung any leaks and would stay afloat. All the 1929 competing aircraft successfully completed these trials.

September 7th dawned bright and clear, with a promise of a very hot day to come. The speed test was to take place round a quadrilateral course, the start and finish being Ryde Pier, with the turning pylons placed off Bembridge, Hayling Island, Southsea Pier and finally off Cowes. Each aircraft had to complete seven laps of this course, each leg being a distance of fifty kilometres, thus making a total of 350 km overall. A little device was placed in each cockpit to help the pilot keep count of the number of laps he'd flown. It consisted of a piece of three-ply, with seven finger-width holes drilled through it, and covered with tissue paper. The idea was that as each pilot completed a circuit, passing Ryde Pier, he would poke a finger through the hole. As soon as the seven holes had been poked through, he knew that the total distance had been covered. Yes, we were well up on technology in 1929.

As a final precaution against oil leaks, two instruments were blanked off, the oil pressure gauge on the dash-board and the boost gauge. The cockpit was also fitted with a device to ensure ample ventilation, as the machines would probably get very hot indeed before the contest was finished. All was now ready, so we adjourned for lunch on the Spit. Waggon, Batchy and I did not return to the mess for lunch as we were rather tensed up. As we had practically no appetite and could not face the thought of any food, we just hung about at the end of the Spit, resting ourselves as much as we could, while trying to relax.

Starting order for all aircraft had been previously arranged. Waghorn would go first, followed at regular intervals by the other aircraft. All our watches had been synchronised, so that we approached Ryde Pier as the signal gun was fired. As the weather was intensely hot, I decided to dispense with my very tight fitting flying helmet and instead I soaked two wads of cotton wool in caster oil and placed them in my ears, so as to eliminate undue deafness. One must realise that flying at full throttle behind a 900 hp engine only a few feet ahead of you, would be absolutely deafening. Finally the machines began to take off. I eventually left the water without much trouble, except that the cotton wad in my left ear was instantly sucked out by the slipstream. I hung about in the proximity of Cowes until I reckoned that the gun was about to go off for my turn, and down I went towards Ryde Pier. It was to be my longest flight yet in racing seaplanes. From take-off to touchdown I would altogether be about an hour in the air.

In a very short period of time, from opening the throttle fully, I was very, very conscious indeed of a rapidly increasing temperature. The fuselage of the S.5 was very narrow and one fitted inside it just like a glove, so down each side ran the oil coolers, which turned the inside of the cockpit into something approaching an extremely hot Turkish bath. I began to sweat profusely and a glance at my oil outlet temperature gauge revealed that it indicated something around 136° centigrade. The engine lubricant was pure castor oil that had two virtues: (1) it did not lose its lubricating qualities at high temperature, and (2) it would not boil readily. The same could not be said for mineral oils.

I did not suffer from blackouts at any of the corner turns, even the steep ones but after a while I started to feel as though I was being suffocated. The inside of the cockpit became seriously hot and very thick with the fumes from the engine, the noise from which did nothing for my equilibrium. On the straight run from Cowes to Ryde, I felt that I really had to do something about it, so I throttled back momentarily and pulled up to possibly 5-600 feet in order to try to get a breath of fresh air, then opened out and carried on. It was the only time I had to do this and I completed the race satisfactorily, although it didn't seem satisfactory to me, because I thought pulling up for that breath of air would knock a great deal off my last lap speed. Timing records were to show that this was not the case, as apparently my speed had varied only a mile and a half an hour on either side of my average speed of 282.11 mph.

I landed well away from all shipping and when I came to rest on the water, I climbed up and sat astride the fuselage. Not more than a minute passed, when I noticed a boat approaching at considerable speed. I wondered who it could be because it was very much in the 'out of bounds' area for that day. It pulled alongside my port float, and it was then I recognised Earl Howe, the famous racing motorist. He at once held up a large basket of the most beautiful peaches and better still, a glass with a bottle of iced champagne. Never was a cool bubbly drink more welcome than on that occasion, and I managed to cope with the peach as well. After a second glass he waved farewell and went off to dispense hospitality to other chaps as they landed.

Of the other contestants, Dick Waghorn flew the fastest race, except for the fact that he had forgotten the number of laps he had flown and didn't trust his finger-punch device, so tried to do an extra lap, just to be sure. In the process he ran out of petrol and had to land where he could, fortunately well away from surface craft. He won the contest with an average speed of 328.63 mph. Batchy on the other hand had a bit of bad luck. Either during take-off or just after, he lost his goggles, so had to keep his head fairly well tucked inside the cockpit, so consequently cut one corner too fine and was disqualified. However, he did break the 100 km record. [5]

Of the Italians' two Macchi 67 aircraft, both were unlucky and had to force land, with steam blowing out everywhere. Both of them were in great trouble, one pilot even got quite a scalding. Tommaso Dal Molin, however, in the old Macchi 52, flew a faultless race, his lap average just beating mine by two miles an hour [284.20]. As a result of losing the wad from my left ear, I was absolutely stone deaf on that side and about 95% on the other, and found this a considerable source of embarrassment for some days.

That evening we all attended a banquet on board the Royal Aero Club's official ship, the liner *Orford*, moored out at Spit Head. I quite enjoyed the dinner but needless to say I couldn't hear a word of any of the speeches, nor any talk from the people sitting on either side of me, so just had to sit and suffer. This festivity was followed by a number of others, one or two of which I managed to attend, with a certain amount of difficulty, owing to my uncomfortable leg, which showed no sign of really rallying round and getting better.

I'm not quite sure of the day, but I think it was the following Monday, two days after the contest, that we all lunched at the Ritz Hotel in Piccadilly, as guests of the Air Council. This was very enjoyable, except for my deafness, which at least was starting to wear off. In the evening we accepted an invitation to see the race on the silver screen, at the Tivoli Theatre in the Strand. We were given seats of honour in the middle of the first row of the dress circle and I quite enjoyed seeing the contest run again from start to finish. At the end, a searchlight – or limelight – came on from the back of the stage and was focussed directly where we members of the two teams were sitting. The entire audience got to their feet and made a terrific noise – I believe!

Although we appreciated this adulation we, I at any rate, found it was vaguely embarrassing. Upon leaving the theatre we found that it had got around that we were here and the whole area, right across the Strand, was completely choked by an enormous crowd of people, all wanting to shake hands with us, and with the Italians as well. We were dressed in plain clothes but the Italians were still in full uniform, and I recall the Italian doctor of the team became terribly worried in case any of his men were dragged away by undesirable women.

When I finally got back to Calshot, I retired to bed as I had started to run a bit of a temperature and had to rest my leg. It was whilst in this state, that I heard George Stainforth, in the Gloster VI, which was now running satisfactorily, had broken the three-kilometre record, although this was again beaten shortly after by Orlebar in the S.6. I found this vaguely depressing, 90% of which was because of me feeling so seedy, plus a bit of self pity. Luckily it soon passed off.

So the 1929 High Speed Flight had now finished its task, and we were all due for posting elsewhere after a good spell of leave. I heard that I was going to No.9 Bomber Squadron at RAF Manston in October, but early in 1930 I was due for duty overseas, my destination being No.216 Bomber/Transport Squadron in the Middle East. I will now, therefore, bring this narrative to a close, as I consider the decade now ending had not only been the most interesting but also the most enjoyable in my service career.

Perhaps just one more story. While with 9 Squadron, we had a large guest night to say farewell to a number of the mess, and thought it demanded by special attention in the practical joke line. A quick trip to my joke shop in Holborn and I was all set, purchasing a supply of percussion caps mounted on sticks for inserting into cigars or cigarettes, plus a selection of delicious looking chocolate sweets that had inside them a lump of green soap.

At the dinner, because I was president of the week, I found myself on the top table next to the station commander, Group Captain R C M Pink [6]. Shortly before the dinner I visited the mess, mustered some silver dishes in which to put the chocolates, these being distributed around the tables, and then doctored a number of cigarettes in the large silver cigarette box that would be offered around over coffee.

A spirit of good cheer prevailed throughout the meal and after the loyal toast, I gave permission to smoke. The box began its rounds and it was not long before a succession of sharp cracks occurred, accompanied by a great deal of laughter. Then, what appeared to be a super bang, followed by more roars of laughter, from the whole assembly, but almost immediately this changed to a complete and deadly silence. I knew at once something awful had happened. I glanced slowly around and there was poor old Pink, slowly turning almost purple with rage, in his hand the remains of an exploded cigarette.

He at once called for the orderly officer and mess steward, ordering them to find the culprit of this bit of skullduggery, but of course neither of them knew anything. Pink was then saying that the culprit, when found, was to be immediately placed under close arrest, so I thought I had better own up. This I did in the most apologetic manner and looking very sheepish. Luckily he had begun to simmer down after his initial shock. He then addressed me in words which everyone could hear, and they were couched, not in a tone of anger, but rather a mild rebuke, stress being placed on the fact that I was old enough to know much better.

The noise had just simmered down when I suddenly remembered the sweets. It would be awful if the group captain now bit on one, so I quickly ordered a waiter to collect them all up. However, I was not in time to stop Colonel Greenfield, the station education officer, taking one. There was just time to observe the old boy with rather a puzzled and disgusted expression on his face, starting to foam slightly at the mouth, as I made myself scarce.

I still had a long way to go in my service career, but as time went by life was to become considerably more serious, maybe I shall write more later. However, farewell to the 'Gay Twenties', which for me had produced in good measure, some success, a few frustrations but a good deal of fun.

[1] Harold Ernest Perrin, who at this time was in his early fifties, had been secretary of the Royal Aero Club since 1903.

[2] General Italo Balbo was the Italian air minister. A pilot in his own right, his name became synonymous with large formations of aircraft following his trans-Atlantic flight in 1933 at the head of a big formation of seaplanes.

[3] Henry Philip Folland MBE FRAeS had been assistant designer for the RAF, Farnborough in WW1 and had been responsible for such aircraft as the FE2b, SE5 and later the Nighthawk. His Bamel had won the Aerial Derby for 1921, 1922 and 1923. With the Gloster Company he had also designed the Grebe and Gamecock amongst others, now being that company's chief engineer and designer.

[4] Marshal of the RAF Sir Hugh, later Lord, Trenchard GCB DSO DCL LL.D Ld'H. Former soldier, then airman, commanded the RFC in France 1916-17, and the Independent Air Force in 1918. Chief of the Air Staff 1919-29. In 1931 became commissioner of the Metropolitan Police Force.

[5] In 1927, F/Lt S N Webster had won the Schneider Trophy race, and now F/O H R D Waghorn had won the 1929 contest. The rules of the contest said that the country winning the coveted trophy three times in a row, would keep it for all time. In 1931, thanks to the intervention, and money, from Lady Houston, the team that year again won, the winning pilot being F/Lt J N Boothman. The trophy is now kept at the Royal Aero Club in London's Pall Mall.

[6] Air Commodore Richard C M Pink CBE had distinguished himself as CO of No.2 Indian Wing in the spring of 1925, operating against rebel tribes in Waziristan. Died of cancer in March 1932.

AFTERWARDS

by

Norman Franks

Although Air Commodore Greig finished, what became, the first part of his story, at some future date he obviously decided to continue with his life story, probably sometime in the 1970s. There had been 326 typed pages of the first part, and to this he added a further 178 that took the tale to somewhere after WW2. Greig had already decided that part one was by far the most interesting and that is how we perceived it, so this chapter is merely a précis of his life from 1930.

After leaving the High Speed Flight, he was posted to 9 Squadron at RAF Manston, equipped with the Vickers Virginia bomber, a large twin-engined biplane, on 28th October. What he does not mention is his marriage on his thirtieth birthday, to Lorna Dean. The ceremony occurred in Bexhill, and according to reports in local newspapers, it was quite an event, with the streets around St Barnabas Church in Sea Road being packed with well-wishers. The church could take around 1,000 people but it was estimated to have had some 1.300 inside on this day. His best man was Arthur Beilby. By this time Greig was quite the local hero, and at the reception at the Carlton Hotel, he and his bride were treated like present-day celebrities. There was even a model of his Supermarine S.5 hanging from the ceiling.

In March he and his new wife went overseas, to Heliopolis, to join

216 Squadron, where he found his new CO to be Wing Commander E A B Rice, who had been his boss in 6 Squadron in Iraq. 216 were flying equally huge Vickers Victoria bombers. He served with 216 Squadron for two years and had a few adventures, such as the time he had to take some army officers on a sight-seeing tour of the Palestine battlefields in June, but had to make a forced landing in the desert with engine trouble. Then in mid-July he was ferrying personnel of 47 Squadron from their leave in Cairo, to Khartoum, a trip of some 1,200 miles. He completed this task although a sand storm forced him to land until it had passed.

In 1931 it became 216 Squadron's turn to make the annual flag-waving flight down to Cape Town, which commenced on 12th January. The squadron made calls at numerous places on the way south. After a four-day stay at Cape Town the journey back was equally long, with more flag-waving en route. The whole trip took 58 days, and entailed 171 hours and 55 minutes actual flying time.

In October the squadron was involved in assisting British forces on Cyprus following a rebellion that began with the burning down of Government House. The task was to transport British troops from Egypt to the island, via Ramlen, Palestine, with every available aircraft being used. Once on the island they stayed for some eight days, and although they took no active part in the anti-rebellion actions, they did fly several low-level flights, to demonstrate to the rebels that the British were there in strength.

Greig moved from 216 to the Aircraft Depot at Aboukir in January 1932, where he became station adjutant, although the prospect filled him with horror, and he loathed it. The job wasn't helped by the return of his asthma. However, although desk-bound he often managed to slip away and test-fly newly assembled aircraft that were awaiting collection. Sometime at the end of June there was another rebellion, this time in Iraq, and Greig managed to wangle his way back to Heliopolis to help transport troops. In the event he did no troop-carrying sorties, but flew all over the place taking spare parts etc, to wherever broken down aircraft needed them.

In due course he was back at Aboukir and still hating his job, and suffering with his asthma once more. However, in the autumn of 1933 he was on the move once again, this time as adjutant at Amman, in the Judean Hills, where the climate better suited his medical distress. In fact it had vanished within eight hours of his arrival. The station commander had been someone he knew in 30 Squadron in Iraq, Group Captain F L Robinson. Another old friend was Len Cockey, now commanding 14 Squadron. His duties again kept his feet on the ground but occasionally he managed to get airborne for some sight-seeing, over amazing landscapes and spectacular ruins from the ancient world. In early 1934 there was a social call from Sir Miles Lampson, the High Commissioner for Egypt, and Greig was assigned to collect him from an airfield just north of Jerusalem, then take him on a tour through southern Jordan, the Dead Sea valley, etc.

His tour in the Middle East was coming to an end but in April he asked permission to lead a formation of 14 Squadron aircraft over to Iraq, as he was anxious to see the old haunts that he used to fly over fourteen years earlier. He found the country very much changed, mainly due to the development of the oil fields On 10th May the Greigs began the journey back to England. They were now four – daughter June and son Jamie having been born during this time.

After home leave, his next posting came through on 19th August – to go to the Royal Aircraft Establishment at Farnborough. He was put in charge of the Aerodynamic Flight, the other two test pilots in this flight being Pat Fraser and Clouston, a New Zealander who later achieved fame in long distance flights [1]. Although Greig had no scientific training, Frazer, a South African, had most of the answers when it came to it. Greig's forte, of course, was in his ability to fly any type of aeroplane with a good degree of accuracy. He also found two old friends in the engine-testing flight, Batchy Atcherley and George Stainforth, so the old gang was together again.

At Farnborough Greig managed to fly a great many different types of aircraft and also had his first introduction to retractable undercarriages, flaps and variable pitch propellers. However, that November he was promoted to squadron leader and as there was no place on the establishment for this rank, he had to go.

So, in March 1936, following a short Instructor's Refresher Course at CFS, he reported to a brand new flying school – No.9 FTS – at Thornaby-on-Tees, commanded by Group Captain Elliott-Smith [2], being appointed Chief Flying Instructor in charge of the intermediate training squadron. Just over a year later, he was posted back to CFS, this time as chief instructor, and his new commandant there was none other than Group Captain James Robb.

At nearby Andover, Batchy was doing the staff course and Greig immediately drove over to meet him, only to find that he had gone out for the evening. Greig made his way to Batchy's room to make certain, and was surprised to find it in immaculate order. This was too good an opportunity to miss, so he re-distributed all Batchy's stuff, including shuffling many files of paper that had been piled neat and tidy ready for the next day in the classroom. He then left a note that read: 'You'll never guess who's been here?'

A few days later Robb told Greig that there was about to be an annual inspection by Area HQ, but as he had to go up to AM, Greig would have to take the parade. While whiling away the evening, who should arrive at Upavon, but Batchy. They had a drink and a pleasant chat before Batchy said he must leave in order to be ready for school. Greig, with some trepidation, returned to his room and was pleasantly surprised to find it as much as he'd left it, with the exception that 'someone' had cut all the bristles from his toothbrush and slashed his toothpaste tube in half. Feeling mighty relieved to have got off so lightly, he turned in.

The next morning his batman arrived and just as Greig was coming to, the man asked what he had done to his socks. Fully awake at once, Greig saw the man was holding up a new pair of socks that had been cut completely in half. Alarm bells rang. A swift check on his wardrobe and his heart sank. Every single button had been cut from all his uniforms, every button had been cut from all his shirts, and even off his greatcoat. In a drawer he found a handkerchief with a needle and thread through it, and a note saying: 'You'll never guess what these are for?'

His batman was still trying to get enough buttons on a shirt and uniform by the time Greig needed to be taking the parade but fortunately the next senior officer had the good sense to take over. When Robb returned and heard about it, he was highly amused, while Greig also came in for a good deal of leg-pulling in the mess.

Greig's marriage to Lorna ended around this time, but he became fully occupied with his job, which he found pleasant and challenging, as he also had to tour the other flying schools. In addition the new monoplane fighters were starting to come on stream, so it was an interesting period. In November 1938 Greig was promoted to wing commander, which he regretted, as it meant leaving CFS. However, his new job was as commanding officer of 75 Bomber Squadron, at RAF Honington, where the station commander was another old friend, Group Captain Bill Sowrey [3]. He had known Sowrey longer than anyone else in the Service for he had been CO of the training squadron at Newmarket where Greig had learnt to fly.

There were two squadrons at Honington, both equipped with HP Harrow aircraft, 75 and 215. Greig found this an entirely different set of circumstances, far different than he had been used to. In July the squadron began to re-equip with Wellington bombers, and moved to Stradishall and thereafter began the usual training routine towards getting operational. When WW2 was declared, 75 was just about operational and later in that month of September 1939, it moved down to Harwell.

On 4th October Greig flew a senior officer over to France in a Wellington, to Reims, the HQ of the Advanced Air Striking Force. The aircraft was armed to the teeth, according to Greig, with guns sticking out all over the place, but no hostile aircraft were encountered. 75 Squadron had a number of New Zealand personnel on strength, crews having come over to take Wellingtons back to their homeland, but once war had started, the New Zealand government suggested they keep both the aircraft and the crews, and from then on the squadron became known as 75 (New Zealand) Squadron. Training continued but by the end of the year a new challenge awaited D'Arcy Greig, in the shape of a posting to Canada. He had now remarried, to Betty Evans, known to everyone as 'Twink'.

Greig left Liverpool for Canada aboard the Empress of Australia, on 15th January 1940, along with nineteen other officers and around 250 other ranks. Among the officers was an old pal from Iraq days, Wing Commander David Bonham-Carter. The boat arrived at Halifax on the

24th, and Greig was sent to No.1 Training Command, RCAF, in Toronto. His family sailed for Canada on 4th May to join him.

The initial idea was that the Empire Air Training Scheme was to be put into motion but as this had been planned for a few months hence, Greig and some of the others were at a loose end. However, in April he was invited to visit the Department of Aviation Medicine at the Banting Institute in the University of Toronto. When the doctors there heard he had been a member of High Speed Flight, he was asked to help them in their work. The task was to develop means of countering the effects of oxygen needs at altitude and also the effects of centrifugal force on recovery from steep dives, air combat, etc. Greig immediately recalled those strange experiments conducted by Group Captain Flack at Northolt.

D'Arcy Greig was handed over to Dr W R 'Bill' Franks who was in charge of the centrifugal force work. He had developed an anti-gravity suit (known later as the Franks Hydrostatic Suit) but as yet had not found a suitable aircraft to test it. After much searching a Spitfire was found, it fact, the only one in Canada at that time [L1090]. When this arrived, Greig test-flew it and then began to test the suit, going up to around 16,000 feet and diving steeply and then making steep turns and pull-outs. In none of these did he have any symptoms of blacking out even when a 9-g pull-out was recorded, and nor did the Spitfire wrinkle any of its wing surfaces. Greig continued similar tests on and off, throughout the rest of the year.

In December the RCAF promoted Greig to group captain and posted him to No.4 Training Command in Regina, Saskatchewan. This began in the new year with a 1,800-mile motor car drive during the depths of a Canadian winter, while also edging into the USA at various points to use the highways. Once he arrived he reported to his new boss, Air Commodore Tom Cowley RCAF [4], and found he was to take over as senior air officer. For several months Greig, who was able to fly a Cessna Crane but usually a Lockheed 10, visited various units and then the school was moved to Calgary. In the October HRH The Duke of Kent paid a visit. Greig had earlier met the duke at Assiut in Egypt.

After some two years in Canada, Greig thought he would soon be recalled to England but in April 1942 he was sent to command No.31 Service Flying Training School at Kingston, Ontario. He discovered this unit was pretty large and most of its pupils were being trained for the

Fleet Air Arm, in consequence he found a number of Royal Navy people on the staff. The training aircraft were North American Harvards, plus a few Fairey Battles used for target-towing. One of the target-towing pilots was a young Jimmy Edwards, who became the famous comedian on radio and television. Later in the war Jimmy flew Dakotas and was on the Arnhem show in September 1944 winning the DFC.

Hearing that Greig was back on the eastern side of Canada, prompted the Banting Institute to request his presence again. He went along to see their new centrifugal apparatus. Asked to 'fly' in it he got himself togged up, including a number of electrodes stuck to his person, and took his seat in the contraption. It had a control column and it was fixed so that if the pilot relaxed his grip due to blacking out, the whole thing would slow down. As the thing got up to speed Greig began to feel somewhat uncomfortable until he finally passed out.

Getting him out of the seat, he came round but still felt decidedly unwell, so they took him to the mess and fed him brandy. Later he was told that the operator had accidentally jumped from the 3-g setting to one of 5-g – perhaps more. In an aircraft the g-force is usually momentary, but this had been sustained for quite a while. It took a couple of hours for him to recover sufficiently to return to Kingston and it was the last time he had any dealings with the apparatus.

September 1942 saw the end of Greig's time in Canada. After some delay at Halifax, he and his family eventually sailed off in convoy, aboard a banana boat, the SS *Covina*, packed full of bacon, along with several other RAF personnel, plus the actress Anna Neagle and her director husband, Herbert Wilcox. There was now an addition to the family, son David having been born in Canada. A daughter, Judy, would follow.

Once back in the UK, Greig went to Air Ministry and was told that being a senior officer it might be difficult finding him a job. Despite this, the officer asked what he was most experienced in, to which Greig replied, training and experimental work. Ringing for a file, the man, when turning over some pages, suddenly said that the Marine Experimental Establishment on the Firth of Clyde (but formally at Felixstowe) would

need a new CO at the start of 1943, so he could go there. In the meantime, why not take some leave. Which he did.

The place was at Rhu, on the outskirts of Helensburgh. Not very
large, it had only a few aircraft including a Spitfire on floats, two Walrus
amphibians, and a huge Sunderland flying-boat. The mess, however,
was excellent, for it had been the HQ for the Royal Northern Yacht
Club. However, his stay was short, for he then heard that the A&AEE
at Boscombe Down would soon be requiring a new CO, and so it transpired. It also came with promotion to air commodore.

Once ensconced, he found that the CO of the Performance Testing
Squadron was non-other than his old friend Bruin Purvis. His overall
boss was AVM Linnell [6] but before very long his place was taken by
his old flight commander in 6 Squadron, AVM Ralph Sorley. One of the
boffins at Boscombe Down was Barnes Wallis, of Wellington and bomb-
bouncing dams raid fame.

In February 1944 the RAF's first jet aircraft, the Gloster Whittle was
ready for general testing and Greig was among the party flown down
to Moreton Valence. None of those in the party had obviously flown a
jet before, but a few, including Greig, had a go and found it an interesting experience. The landing was the problem, for as the runway approached and the engine was shut down, there was no immediate
reduction in speed as in propeller-driven aircraft, where the prop
blades help in acting like an air brake. He had, therefore, to make a
couple more circuits before he managed to get the speed down sufficiently to use the wing flaps.

The next jet to arrive on the scene was the de Havilland 'Spider-
Crab', in about mid-April, fitted with a Halford engine. The name was
later changed to Vampire and it had a Goblin engine. Greig flew it for
some fifteen minutes on 22nd April and found it delightful.

It was at this time that the Ministry of Aircraft Production contacted
Greig with an eye to the future. While the war had still some way to
run, thoughts of how to shape post-war Britain were coming to the
fore. MAP suggested that Greig, along with one of his boffins, Mr E T
Jones OBE [7], should tour the country, examining different airfields
in order to select one for a permanent home for the A&AEE. Ernest
Jones had been a pilot in WW1, and was now the chief superintendent
at Boscombe Down. After some searching and then discussions, their

verdict was that Boscombe Down, with some development, would in fact be the best location.

In June 1944, Ralph Sorley visited Boscombe to suggest that some-one else should have a shot at taking over, and so another old friend, John Boothman, shortly arrived to take Greig's place. Greig now moved to No.3 Group Area of Bomber Command at RAF Feltwell. It was here that a personal tragedy occurred. His wife was cycling with young David in a seat behind his mother when an American soldier came round a corner in a truck, on the wrong side of the road. In try-ing to avoid it, David was thrown from the bike and suffered serious head injuries. Despite flying the youngster to Cambridge for specialist treatment for head trauma, he died on the operating table.

Greig remained at Feltwell until 1946, flying a variety of aircraft such as Ansons, a Spitfire XVI (SL718), Monarchs, Proctors, a Prentice and an Avro 19. Then he moved to HQ 91 Group at Abingdon that July. Sometime after the end of WW2, he received a letter from MoD sug-gesting that after a long and distinguished career, it might be time to retire. A farewell party at Abingdon, then some leave, filled the time until retirement came on 23rd November 1946.

For the next two years he became a civil servant and went out to Germany. At the end of this period, Greig came back to Sussex and one day spotted a light aeroplane club just outside St Leonards, just along the coast from Bexhill, next to Hastings. Without too much trou-ble he joined this club, and got a civilian pilot's licence. He even took Judy and Jamie up in an Auster aircraft. Sadly the club soon went bust.

Greig's second marriage ended, like his first, after a period of seven years, but he continued to live in Bexhill. With new stringent rules about private flying coming in, it was soon apparent that he would have to pass a much harder test in order to retain his licence. In 1951 he was given the name of Mr Pashley, at Shoreham, who would do the testing, a name that Greig seemed to remember, but couldn't place.

Arriving at Shoreham aerodrome, he sought out Pashley and within a short space of time they were airborne in an Auster. Pashley put Greig through the usual routine but came down and landed earlier than nor-mal. As Greig later discovered, Cecil Lawrence Pashley had learnt to fly in 1911 and held licence number 106, although he had been exper-imenting with gliders since 1908. Pre-war he had run a joy-riding and instructional outfit known as Pashley Brothers & Hale and his logbook showed over 17,000 flying hours. In WW1 he had been employed as a flying instructor. After that war he had been instructor and director of Southern Aircraft Ltd, and instructor to the Southern Aero Club. Pashley had ended the lesson early when he realised there was nothing wrong with Greig's flying ability, and he was pleased to renew his licence without further ado.

Greig remained in Bexhill for the remainder of his life. His third marriage occurred in the early 1970s, to Evelyn, but known to all as Eve. D'Arcy Greig quite naturally retained his interest in flight, flying and the RAF and continued to be well known in Bexhill – as he had always been. He had his own house built in Birchington Close, named Toadstool Hollow, although this is no longer standing. His love of speed could now only be had on the ground and he was a well-known figure riding around Bexhill on a large motor cycle. Not long after his retirement, Greig became the first president of the Bexhill branch of the Royal Air Force Association Club, and in order to help keep the branch going, also took on the role of chairman too for a period.

His logbook boasts a remarkable total of over 140 different aircraft types flown, plus one as passenger in Concorde, on the occasion of the Fiftieth Anniversary of the Schneider Trophy win (1981). Special celebrities were flown out over the Atlantic and back at 1,500 mph – his fastest speed ever.

Air Commodore Greig died in July 1986 and his funeral took place at Eastbourne Crematorium. His ashes were scattered over the Solent, along the 1929 Schneider Trophy race course, by his son Jamie. Jamie had intended to scatter the ashes at the time of the funeral, but what with one thing and another, they remained under his stairs for the following five years. Although he had been a Fleet Air Arm pilot during his national service, he no longer held a licence to fly, but eventually a friend offered to make the flight with him in a Cessna.

Jamie, being a practical man, put the ashes in a bottle, having first cut off the bottom, then resealed it but with a quick release mechanism. Once flying over the Solent, he held the bottle out of the window, uncorked the top, then putting the base into the slipstream, pulled the release. The idea was that the suction would eject the ashes in quick time, with the Cessna in a shallow dive.

Unfortunately D'Arcy was in no rush to depart and it took some time for the bottle to empty. All the while his pilot friend was asking if the ashes had gone, and Jamie could only say no, not yet. Jamie was also conscious that with the Cessna throttled back, in a shallow dive, and with a grey smoke-like trail of ashes streaming back, it would not be long before someone reported an aircraft in trouble over the sea! However, the bottle finally emptied and not wanting to retain it, Jamie, making sure there were no ferries nearby, let the bottle, that he had weighted with a lump of metal, fall towards the water. No sooner had he done so than he spotted a couple of chaps in a small fishing boat almost directly beneath them. Fortunately it missed. If his father had been looking down, he was sure to have been laughing at the joke.

[1] Later Air Commodore A E Clouston CB DSO DFC AFC & Bar. Made record-breaking flights to the Cape, Australia and New Zealand in a DH Comet racer in the 1930s. With Coastal Command 1943-44. Retired from the RAF in April 1960 and died in January 1984.

[2] Retired as Air Commodore Charles H Elliott-Smith AFC in 1944. Army and RAF in WW1. With SAAF 1941-42. Died in January 1994, aged 105 – and thought to be the oldest officer of air rank and possibly the oldest ever member of the RAF.

[3] Group Captain William Sowrey DFC AFC, another to receive the DFC for services in Iraq in the early 1920s. He had been a fighter pilot in WW1. His brother Freddie had gained fame for shooting down a Zeppelin in 1916. Freddie's son became an air-vice marshal CB CBE AFC.

[4] A T M Cowley had been in the RNAS in WW1 flying Short 184 seaplanes from Dover. On 6 May 1916 he had been forced down onto the North Sea, picked up by a German submarine and taken into captivity. After the war he became director of civil aviation for the dominions but had rejoined the RCAF at the outbreak of WW2.

[5] Flight Lieutenant James Keith O'Neill Edwards DFC MA, 271 Squadron. DFC gazetted 2 February 1945, for '...skill, courage and fortitude of a very high order'.

[6] Later Air Marshal Sir Francis John Linnell KBE CB. RNAS in WW1, then RAF. By May 1942 he was deputy AOC RAF Mediterranean & Middle East. Died in a road accident in November 1944, aged fifty-two.

[7] Ernest Turner Jones CB OBE M.Eng FIAS FRAeS would later become the president of the Royal Aeronautical Society, following a number of senior research and development positions.

AIRCRAFT FLOWN BY AIR COMMODORE D'ARCY GREIG DFC AFC AS WRITTEN IN HIS LOGBOOK.

Aircraft	Engine	Aircraft	Engine
DH6	90 hp RAF	BE2C	90 hp RAF
BE2e	90 hp RAF	FE2b	160 hp Beardmore
RE8	140 hp RAF	Bristol Fighter	RR Falcon
Avro 504K	Monosoupape	Avro 504K	AS Lynx
Avro Gosport	Avro	DH9A	400 hp Liberty
Sopwith Snipe	200 hp Bentley	Snipe two-seater	200 hp Bentley
Hawker Woodcock	Bristol Jupiter IV	Fairey Fawn	470 hp Napier Lion
Gloster Grebe	AS Jaguar IV	Bristol School Bus	Lucifer
DH Cirrus Moth	ADC Cirrus II	DH 80A Puss Moth	DH Gipsy III
Vickers Vimy	360 RR Falcon	Vickers Vimy	AS Jaguar
Vickers Vernon	RR Falcon	Gloster Gamecock	Bristol Jupiter VI
DH Genet Moth	AS Genet	Avro Rota (autogiro)	Civet
SE5A	Wolseley Viper	Vickers Victoria	Napier Lion XI
Vickers Valencia	Bristol Pegasus	S'marine S'hampton	Napier Lion V
Arm Sidd Siskin III	AS Jaguar IV	Arm Sidd Siskin IIIA	AS Jaguar IV
Hawker Horsley	RR Condor IIIA	Fairey IIID	Napier Lion IIB
Fairey Flycatcher	AS Jaguar IV	Avro Avian	DH Gipsy
Avian Seaplane	DH Gipsy	Widgeon	DH Gipsy
Westland Wallace	Bristol Pegasus	Gloster Gauntlet	Bristol Mercury
Vickers Vildebeest	Bristol Pegasus	Seal	Panther
Northrop Bomber	Wright Cyclone	Kay Giroplane	Niagara
Airspeed Courier	AS Lynx IVC	Scion	Niagara
Miles Hawk Trainer	DH Gipsy	B & P Partridge	Bristol Jupiter
Gloster Gamecock II	Bristol Jupiter	Pike	Napier
CLA 4	Cherub	Gloster IV	Napier Lion VIIB
Gloster IVA	Napier Lion	Gloster IVB	Napier
Supermarine S.5	Napier	Gloster VI	Napier
Vendace	RR Falcon	Avocet	Lynx
Cockle	Cherub	Vickers Virginia	Napier Lion XI
Arm Whit Atlas	AS Jaguar IVC	Westland Wapiti	Bristol Jupiter
Fairey IIIF	Napier	Fairey Gordon	AS Panther IIA
Hawker Demon	RR Kestrel V	Miles Hawk Major	DH Gipsy
Hawker Hart	RR Kestrel IB	ARC Flap Parasol	Lynx
Hawker Fury	RR Kestrel IIS	Miles Falcon	Gipsy VI
Airspeed Envoy	AS Cheetah IX	Vespa	Bristol Pegasus
Hawkon	DH Gipsy VI	Vickers Vincent	Pegasus IIM3
Avro Tutor	AS Lynx IVC	Hawker Audax	RR Kestrel
Avro Anson	AS Cheetah	Gloster Gladiator	Bristol Mercury IX
DH Tiger Moth	DH Gipsy Major	Miles Nighthawk	DH Gipsy VI
Miles Magister	DH Gipsy Major	Vickers Wellesley	Pegasus XX

Aircraft	Engine	Aircraft	Engine
Hawker Hind	RR Kestrel V	Bristol Blenheim I	Bristol Mercury
Drone	10 hp Carden	Fairey Battle I	RR Merlin
DH Don	DH Gipsy King I	Percival Vega Gull	DH Gipsy VI
Airspeed Oxford	AS Cheetah X	Cadet	Genet Major
Hawker Hurricane	RR Merlin	HP Harrow	Pegasus XX
Miles Kestrel	Kestrel XVII	Miles Whitney Straight	DH Gipsy M
BA Swallow	Pobjoy	Westland Lysander	Mercury XII
Hawker Hector	Napier Dagger	S'marine Spitfire I	RR Merlin
Vickers Wellington	Bristol Pegasus	HP Hampden	Bristol Pegasus
Chilton	Ford 10	Miles Mentor	DH Gipsy VI
Hawker Henley	RR Merlin	N. American Harvard	P & W Wasp
Miles M.A.T.	DH Gipsy M	Lockheed Hudson I	Wright Cyclone
Fleet 16	Civet	Fairchild 51	Wasp Junior
Fairchild 71	Wasp Junior	Fleet 60	Jacobs
Boeing D71	Wasp	DH Dragonfly	DH Gipsy
Vultee-Stinson 105	Continental	Harlow PC 5A	Warner Scarab
Beechcraft 16B	Jacobs	Lockheed 10B	Wright
Norseman	Wasp	Cessna Crane	Jacobs
Avro Anson II	Jacobs	Short Sunderland III	Bristol Pegasus
Supermarine Walrus	Bristol Pegasus	DH Mosquito	RR Merlin
Boeing B17 Fortress	Wright Cyclone	NA Mustang I	Allison
Bermuda	Wright Cyclone	Douglas Boston III	Wright Cyclone
Auster	Lycoming	Avro Lancaster III	RR Merlin 28
Vultee-Stinson Vigilant	Lycoming	Percival Proctor	DH Gipsy Queen II
S'marine Spitfire XIV	Griffin	S'marine Spitfire XVI	Merlin 266
Republic P47 T'bolt	P & W Wasp	S'marine Spitfire Vb	RR Merlin
Vultee-Stinson Reliant	Lycoming	Hawker Hurricane II	RR Merlin
M28	DH Gipsy Major	M4 half scale Stirling	Pobjoy
F9/40 Gloster Meteor	RR Derwent	M38	Cirrus
Traveller II	P & W Wasp	Spider Crab (Vampire)	Halford
Blackburn Firebrand III	Bristol Centaurus	Miles Martinet	Bristol Mercury
Miles Monarch	DH Gipsy Major	Avro 19	AS Cheetah XVI
DH53	Blackburn Tomtit		